ROBERT FULTON
ENGINEER AND ARTIST
HIS LIFE AND WORKS

BY

HENRY W. DICKINSON

ILLUSTRATED

BOOKS FOR LIBRARIES PRESS
FREEPORT, NEW YORK

First Published 1913
Reprinted 1971

INTERNATIONAL STANDARD BOOK NUMBER:
0-8369-5649-4

LIBRARY OF CONGRESS CATALOG CARD NUMBER:
73-148878

PRINTED IN THE UNITED STATES OF AMERICA

TO

MY FATHER AND MOTHER

PREFACE

SOME excuse ought perhaps to be offered for adding to the number of the biographies of Robert Fulton; I can only plead that, so far as I have observed, not one of them is altogether fair and impartial. Fulton's American biographers have credited him with greater achievements than the facts warrant, while English writers too often have dismissed him contemptuously as a charlatan, a filcher of other men's brains, or even as a traitor.

In order to judge between these conflicting views, I have endeavoured by research and by the collation of recently published materials, to get at the really important facts about Fulton and his inventions—facts which the lapse of time has helped to bring into their true perspective—and present them with sympathy, but without bias and without petty national feeling. Indeed the latter should never have existed, for Fulton was, if anything, cosmopolitan; born a British subject in a British colony, the seed-time of his life was spent in England, the fruition took place in France, and the harvest was reaped in his native America. That harvest was the introduction of navigation by steam on a commercial basis in the Western hemisphere. In the present year, when we are celebrating the centenary of its introduction into Europe, it may not be unprofitable to trace the steps which led to these far-reaching results.

Much of the material that has been made use of has been gleaned at first hand, and has not before seen the light. I am indebted to the Right Hon. the Earl Stanhope for copies of letters which passed between the 3rd Earl and Fulton; these letters are preserved among family documents at Chevening, Kent. George Tangye, Esq., of Birmingham, has given me every facility for copying the Fulton correspondence and drawings preserved among the Boulton & Watt MSS. in his possession.[1] Search at the Public Record Office has disclosed not a few interesting facts. Mr. Lane himself has drawn my attention to many sources of information.

Inquiries were prosecuted in France, and access to the original documents in the National Archives in Paris was obtained, with valuable results.

As might have been expected, Fulton's native country has afforded a wealth of information and original matter. Mrs. Alice Crary Sutcliffe, a great-granddaughter of the inventor, has placed me under a great debt of obligation by giving me permission to make extended use of her recent work, *Robert Fulton and the Clermont*, which, being based on family documents, is of the utmost value. Mr. Charles Henry Hart of Philadelphia has been good enough, *inter alia*, to help me in presenting adequately the artistic side of Fulton's career. Mrs. Frank Semple of Sewickley, Pa., by furnishing copies of early letters in her possession, has enabled light to be thrown on an obscure period of Fulton's life. I am indebted to Mr. John Henry Livingston of Clermont, to Mr. Edward B. Livingston, to Dr. Gilbert L. Parker of Philadelphia, and to Mr. Charles B. Todd for assistance. The U.S.A. Navy Department, the New York

[1] Presented by him to the city of Birmingham and shortly to be handed over into its keeping.

Historical Society, the New York Public Free Library, the Historical Society of Pennsylvania, the Smithsonian Institution, and the Jersey City Free Library have freely given me copies of documentary matter in their possession. I acknowledge with thanks the courtesies extended to me by the editors of the *Journal of American History*, the *Scientific American*, and *Cassier's Magazine*.

To the many friends, too numerous to be mentioned individually, who have given me help and advice, I offer grateful thanks.

Finally, I feel that Mr. Lane has done this work, whose shortcomings I am well aware are many, more than justice by presenting it to the public in such an attractive guise.

THE SCIENCE MUSEUM,
Dec. 1912.

CONTENTS

CHAPTER I

CHAPTER II

CHAPTER III

CHAPTER IV

CHAPTER V

CHAPTER VI

CHAPTER VII

CHAPTER VIII

CHAPTER IX

CHAPTER X

CHAPTER XI

LIST OF PLATES

ROBERT FULTON

ROBERT FULTON

CHAPTER I

ANCESTRY, BIRTH, AND BOYHOOD OF ROBERT FULTON

IT is always interesting to try and trace the influence that heredity has upon the development of the personality of an individual, and in Robert Fulton's case this inquiry is singularly suggestive.

To judge by the internal evidence afforded by the word itself, Fulton is a place-name of Anglo-Saxon origin. To understand the use of place-names as surnames, it should be remembered that when in the thirteenth century, owing to the spread of population, it became necessary to distinguish between persons of the same baptismal name, quite the commonest way was to add with a prefix the name of the place where that person owned or held land. As time went on the prefix was generally dropped. That the surname Fulton is of such local origin is almost a certainty. The earliest instance recorded is in 1272, when a certain Robert Fulton was charged with the duty of holding an assize, and probably the Robert de Fultone, Co. Cambs., who is mentioned in the Hundred Rolls 1273, was one and the same man. We are inclined to look upon this county as the place of origin of the surname, although the spot cannot now be identified, in spite of the contrary opinion of a well-known authority[1] who derives the Fulton family from some now vanished Scottish border village. Very

[1] M. A. Lower, *Patronymica Britannica*, 1860.

possibly he was led to this conclusion by the existence of a ruined peel or stronghold situated in the parish of Bedrule in Roxburghshire and known as Fulton Tower. Yet this building is not considered to date back farther than the fourteenth century.

Again we find a family of the name of Fulton holding lands at Muirkirk in the parish of Beith, Co. Ayrshire, in the thirteenth century. "Aleyn fitz Thomas de Fultone," "Nicol de Fultone," and "Henry de Foultone" "del counte de Lanark,"[1] which then embraced Ayrshire and Renfrewshire, are among the large number of vassals whose names appear on the Ragman Roll as having, at a Parliament held at Berwick-on-Tweed, on August 28, 1296, done homage to Edward I. when he invaded Scotland to substantiate his claim to the overlordship thereof. Here again the township or estate of Fulton, if it existed, cannot now be traced, so that it is an open question whether or not these Fultons were any relations of the Cambridgeshire family.

The surname has survived, and is fairly common at the present day, especially in Ayrshire, but not to the same extent as it is in Philadelphia and New York.

At the end of the sixteenth and beginning of the seventeenth centuries, the English Government inaugurated a new policy in dealing with subjugated territories in Ireland and that was to displace the native population by the introduction of English and Scots settlers, who were induced to immigrate by grants of lands. Among these settlers we find several of the name of Fulton, who joined in the plantation of Ulster. One family who trace their descent from the Ayrshire Fultons settled between 1611 and 1614 at Lisburn, Co. Down. Their issue are distinguishable there in the latter half of the seventeenth century as landowners, Royalists, and Episcopalians. One member of the family, William Fulton, migrated to

[1] Calendar of Documents relating to Scotland, i. 545, ii. 208–212.

[2] Burke's *Landed Gentry of Ireland*, 9th ed. 1904.

Kilkenny, and died in 1638, leaving issue apparently, as other Fultons are subsequently recorded there. The main stem of the family settled at Braidujle, near Lisburn, which has continued to the present day to be the family seat of the Irish Fultons. To some incident in the career of one Richard Fulton of Braidujle, captain of one of the companies of horse raised in support of William of Orange when, in 1688, he was called to the throne of Great Britain, is ascribed the family crest of a cubit arm grasping a broken javelin and the motto: "Vi et Virtute." It may be interesting to note that the ancient armorial achievement of the Fultons was: or, a lion rampant az., which appeared later with a bend gobony ar. and gu. sometimes erm. and gu.[1]

After a few generations Ulster, where the greatest number of these settlers were to be found, became, owing to the industry of its people, the most prosperous province of Ireland; while relying, of course, on agriculture, they had gradually built up flourishing industries in flax and wool. In 1699, however, the English Parliament, apprehensive lest Ireland should take away the trade of England in these and other commodities, placed heavy duties on imports from Ireland with the result that her industries were nearly all ruined. Great distress prevailed, and numbers of the people emigrated to the New England colonies to found new homes. Among these emigrants was the ancestor of the subject of this biographical sketch. The family tradition is that it was from County Kilkenny that he came, but unfortunately there is no evidence to establish his relationship either with the William Fulton of the city of Kilkenny, already mentioned, or in any other way with the Lisburn family, and through them with the Ayrshire Fultons. All that can be said is that it is a reasonable assumption.

Robert Fulton, senior, is first heard of in 1735 in the town of Lancaster, Pennsylvania; thenceforward records

[1] Burke, *loc. cit.*

show that he occupied various public offices and positions of trust in the town, such as Secretary of the Union Fire Office of Lancaster. As presumptive evidence of his Scottish origin, it may be noted that he was a rigid Presbyterian, and one of the founders of the first church of that persuasion in Lancaster. In 1759 he married Mary Smith, daughter of Joseph Smith, also a family of Irish extraction, of Oxford township, Penn., and brought his wife home to a dwelling-house that he had purchased on August 23rd of that year in what is now Penn Square, Lancaster. During their five and a half years' stay there, three daughters — Elizabeth, Isabella (Bell), and Mary (Polly)—were born to them. On February 8, 1765, Robert Fulton, senior, sold his house in Penn Square, and the same day purchased for the sum of £965 a farm of 364 acres on the Conowingo Creek in Little Britain township, whither in the spring of the year he took his family. The farmhouse was built of stone, two storeys in height, and at one end the roof sloped down to a low porch. Here it was that on November 14, 1765, their eldest son Robert was born. The farmhouse is still standing, although externally much altered in 1905 by the present owner, without, however, disturbing the old farm kitchen, parlour, and the room above where the boy was born.

In 1844, when the township of Little Britain was resurveyed, a section containing this property was cut off and appropriately named, in honour of this event, Fulton township.

The vicissitudes of the Fulton family, which we have just traced, have led quite naturally to the circulation of conflicting statements as to Robert Fulton's birth and parentage. Henry Bell, in a letter written in 1824, said that Fulton's father came from Ayrshire. Again, in 1876, he was claimed by a correspondent in the *Glasgow News* as a native-born Scot, his birthplace being given as Mill of Beith in Ayrshire.[1] Closer examination revealed the

[1] Lindsay, *History of Merchant Shipping*, iv. 587.

BIRTHPLACE OF ROBERT FULTON, LITTLE BRITAIN, PENNSYLVANIA

facts that a Robert Fulton was certainly born there on April 17, 1764; that he emigrated to America; and further, that he died in Antigua in the West Indies on November 19, 1819; it was admitted finally, however, that he was not the Robert Fulton whose life-story we are examining. There was also a Rev. Robert Fulton of the Braidujle branch of the family, a navy chaplain, who became vicar of St. John's and a landowner in Jamaica some time in the eighteenth century. These coincidences of name and date are sufficiently remarkable.

Robert Fulton came upon the world's stage at a time when new ideas in the political world were beginning to emerge, and when in the world of industry quite a number of capital inventions were being perfected; *e.g.* in 1765, the very year of Fulton's birth, James Watt took out his patent for the separate condenser which at one bound quadrupled the efficiency of the steam-engine. The people of our North American colonies did not, however, share in these advances; the manufactures which were struggling into being there were harassed by legal enactments imposed by the home Government, whose aim seems to have been to confine the colonists to agriculture and to the production of such raw materials as would serve the needs of manufacturers in England. Nor were these the only drawbacks, for the colonies were the outposts of civilisation; farther west was Kentucky, then the hunting ground of the red man, who was often roused by petty acts of oppression on the part of the white people to make terrible retribution.

Robert Fulton, senior, was not successful in farming, and on November 29, 1766, the year following his going to Little Britain, he and his wife mortgaged[1] the farm to Joseph Swift and two others, arranging for the repayments to be spread over five years. He took his family back to the town of Lancaster, where his second son, Abraham

[1] The mortgage is still in existence, and is in the possession of Mr. Joseph Swift, the present representative of the family.

Smith, was born, and where the boys passed their early years. The father was not long spared to direct the education of his sons, for he died in 1768, when the elder was only three years old, leaving his widow and five children scantily provided for, with the result that she was unable to keep up the repayments. The mortgages were foreclosed, and after one unsuccessful attempt on Feb. 5, 1772, the High Sheriff of Lancaster sold the Fulton plantation to William West and Joseph Swift for the sum of £805.[1] This depreciation in value, together with the arrears of interest, must have fallen very heavily on Mary Fulton, so that it is not difficult to imagine the straitened circumstances of the family at this period.

Joseph Swift subsequently acquired William West's share in the property, and it is an interesting fact that the house and the greater part of the estate have remained in possession of five generations of owners of the same name in unbroken succession till the present day.

Mary Fulton appears to have been a woman of superior attainments, and she taught the boy till he had attained his eighth year, when he went to the school of one Caleb Johnson, a Quaker and a Tory, who had the somewhat narrow-minded scholastic ideas and methods of those days. Fulton did not distinguish himself at school—he was a boy of an original turn of mind, and such a one rarely fits in with a recognised curriculum. He displayed a taste for painting, however, but its practice was not deemed by the severe code of that period a serious occupation; indeed, the very materials for carrying on the art were difficult to obtain, and Fulton was indebted to a schoolfellow for the first which came into his possession. Possibly the example of Benjamin West, who was born in the adjacent Chester county twenty-seven years before Fulton, had actually lived in Lancaster for some time, and had even now carved out a career for himself in England, was not without influence.

[1] The deed is still preserved in the Court House of Lancaster.

Many are the stories, mostly improbable and therefore not reproduced here, of Fulton's experiments and attainments in various branches of mechanics during his boyhood—so greatly does subsequent success cast a glamour over early recollections of schoolfellows and others who thus shine, as it were, with a reflected glory.

Fulton's boyhood coincided with stirring times in the world at large, and particularly so in New England, where the colonists, whose discontent had been fomented by the treatment meted out to them by a short-sighted Government at home, at last broke out in 1775 into open rebellion, resulting finally in the loss to Great Britain of these colonies. Lancaster was geographically in the theatre of war, and was a place of manufacture and depot for rifles, blankets, and clothing for the colonist troops. As many as 2000 British prisoners were under guard there at one time, among the officers being the unfortunate Major John André. In 1777 Congress held session in the Court House at Lancaster. Can it be wondered at that the boys of the neighbourhood followed these events with the keenest interest? At this period were sown in Fulton's mind the seeds of that strong leaning towards the republican and dislike of the monarchical form of government which distinguished him in after years.

CHAPTER II

ENTRY INTO THE WORLD — PAINTS MINIATURES—LEAVES FOR ENGLAND—EXHIBITS AT THE ROYAL ACADEMY—GIVES UP PAINTING

IN 1782, when seventeen years of age, Fulton left his native town for Philadelphia, there to seek his fortune. That city was the capital of the State of Pennsylvania, which, under the mild and beneficent rule of members of the Society of Friends, enjoyed the distinction of being the pioneer in the arts of peace among the States of the Union. Hither came men of science and scholarship, finding the atmosphere congenial to work and study. In Philadelphia were founded the first American Philosophical Society, the first public library in America, the first medical and law schools; the first printing press in the middle colonies was set up there, and prior to the Revolution more books were published in Pennsylvania than in all the other colonies combined. It is not surprising that Fulton should develop quickly in the new field of thought and activity which opened before him.

Not much is known of his doings during the first three years of his stay in the Quaker City. It is said that he was apprenticed to a silversmith, but he would be too old for that; another statement which is much more probable is that he was glad to turn his hand to almost any kind of work in drawing plans, designing buildings, and painting portraits. Already in 1785, by his application and industry, he had established himself as a miniature painter,[1] and during the next two years he met with a considerable

[1] White's *Directory of the City of Philadelphia*: "Fulton, Robert: miniature painter, Corner of 2nd and Walnut Streets."

measure of success. Several miniatures and one or two portraits of some merit remain to this day to prove his proficiency. Charles Willson Peale was then the principal painter in the city, and Fulton may have had lessons from him.

Fulton was a personable youth of agreeable manners, and appears to have embraced the opportunities for social intercourse that the city of Philadelphia afforded. Among the number of those whose acquaintance he made was Benjamin Franklin, who not only allowed him to paint his (Franklin's) portrait but also gave him introductions to people of consequence from whom he received commissions.

Franklin himself as a young man had gone to England to improve himself in his trade of printer, and, having greatly benefited from his stay there, was ready to encourage others to go and do likewise. Besides his example, there was that of Benjamin West, who had now attained to an eminent position among English painters. Small wonder then that Fulton should be fired by a similar ambition, and cherish the thought of visiting the Old World.

Having this object in view he had an incentive to save something from his earnings; but, like a dutiful son, as a first charge on his savings he made provision for his mother by buying a farm for her in the township of Hopewell, Washington County, Pa., for the sum of £80. The choice of locality seems to have been determined by the fact that his maternal uncle, the Rev. Joseph Smith, had acquired land and was in charge of the Presbyterian congregation there. The deed,[1] dated the 6th day of May 1786, is too long to reproduce in full, but the more interesting points in it can be briefly summarised.

The parties to the deed are "Thomas Pollock and Margaret his wife" of the one part and "Robert Fulton,

[1] County of Washington Record Book, C., vol. i. p. 56, quoted at length in Reigart's *Life of Fulton*, p. 41.

miniature painter, of the city of Philadelphia and State aforesaid, Yeoman," of the other part. The estate—the area of which is given as 84¾ acres—is described as "a certain parcel of land on the waters of Cross Creek, it being part of a tract of land granted by the Commonwealth of Pennsylvania the 12th day of December A.D. 1785 to the Reverend Joseph Smith his heirs and assigns called Wiliome." It would therefore seem as if the reverend gentleman had sold part of his original grant to the Pollocks. Fulton's purchase brought it back, as it were, into the family.

At Hopewell Fulton's mother spent her declining years till her death in 1799, watched over by her widowed daughter Elizabeth. The latter continued to reside there with her children, and was eventually confirmed in the ownership of the estate by her brother's will.[1]

Fulton also, on September 18, 1786, bought from John, Elizabeth, and William Hoge,[2] four building lots in the neighbouring town of Washington, Pa., just then being laid out; he made the purchase, doubtless, with the idea of giving one lot to each of his sisters and one to his brother.

About the time of the purchase mentioned above, Fulton had a serious attack of inflammation of the lungs, accompanied by spitting of blood, which must have warned him that he was not robust physically. He went to the warm springs of Virginia to recuperate, and incidentally made new acquaintances. It appears that it was during his stay there that his decision to make the journey to Europe was finally arrived at.

At length his preparations were made, and Fulton, shortly after he had attained to man's estate, sailed for England, buoyant and hopeful. It must have been at the end of the year 1786 or the beginning of 1787 that he arrived

[1] See p. 271.

[2] The Indenture is still in existence, and is in the possession of Mrs. Frank Semple.

in the mother country. He had but forty guineas in his pocket—not a large sum truly to start life with, but lack of money has never been an obstacle to a young man with energy and enthusiasm. He was not friendless exactly, for he had brought with him a letter of introduction from Franklin to West. When he arrived in London and presented this letter, he met, as might have been expected, with a warm welcome; the Wests were noted for their hospitality to their fellow-countrymen, and in this case there was between them the additional bond of relationship. We can hardly doubt that they invited Fulton to stay with them till he found lodgings. West recommended him to rooms at Mr. Robert Davy's, 84 Charlotte Street, Rathbone Place, just vacated by William Dunlap. Probably Fulton went there, but he could not have afforded to stay long, as the terms were a guinea a week.[1] He did not, as has been often stated, reside with the Wests during his art student days. This is proved incidentally in a letter to his mother quoted below, wherein he says of West and himself, "we live near each other."

It is almost certain that Fulton, like Gilbert Stuart before him, was working under West's direct supervision. Merely to have been allowed to frequent his studio must have been an inspiration for any young man, apart from his art studies, for West was already very high in his profession and was visited by the most famous people of the day. What Fulton's impression on his entry into this new world must have been may be imagined from the description given by one[2] who had preceded him by a few years:

"The impression made upon an American youth of eighteen by the long gallery leading from the dwelling-house to the lofty suite of painting rooms—a gallery filled

[1] William Dunlap, *History of the Arts of Design in the United States*, 1834, p. 256.

[2] *I.e.* William Dunlap, *loc. cit.* p. 67.

with sketches and designs for large paintings—the spacious room through which I passed to the more retired attelier —the works of his pencil surrounding me on every side—his own figure seated at his esel, and the beautiful composition at which he was employed, as if in sport, not labour ;—all are recalled to my mind's eye at this distance of half a century, with a vividness which doubtless proceeds in part from the repeated visits to, and examination of, many of the same objects during a residence of more than three years in London."

A period of close attention to art now ensued—so close that it is uneventful. The only serious problem that Fulton had to face during this time was how to secure the wherewithal to pursue his studies. Many an anxious hour did he spend pondering over ways and means ; how he did manage to support himself we can only guess, but although often on the brink of want he never actually lacked a meal. This Bohemian life, although not altogether to his liking, broadened his sympathies and increased his knowledge of the world. No doubt poverty also inculcated self-restraint, but it should be put down principally to his early training and moral character that, placed at a critical age amid the temptations of the metropolis, he did not yield to the attractions of profligacy and vice.

It must have been a great comfort to Mrs. Fulton to have received such a reassuring letter as the one that has been preserved, dated July 25, 1788, from a friend named George Sanderson, who had just returned to America. He commends Fulton's progress "in the liberal Art of Painting" and also mentions the influential friends that "his personal accomplishments and prudent behaviour" had won for him.

Those were the days when letters were few and far between, on account of the prohibitive cost of postage and the lack of postal facilities, so that people used to take advantage of the occasions when friends or acquaintances were travelling in order to get their correspondence forwarded. Some of the affectionate and dutiful letters that reached Mrs. Fulton by such roundabout channels have been preserved and make continual references to the difficulties in the way of letter-writing. In one letter,[1] dated July 31, 1789, Fulton asks his mother "to write small and close that you may say a great deal in small cumpas for the ships often put the letters ashore at the first port they make. They then come post to London And I have often paid half a guinea for a small package of letters—the better to accomplish this you better buy letter paper as it is thin for we pay according to the weight and not the size so if you can send me a pound of news upon an ounce of paper I shall save almost a guinea by it."

Fulton also remarks, "I am frequently Changing my Lodgings to suit my Convenience": indicative no doubt of his Bohemian existence during his stay in London. The Royal Academy records show that he lodged at 67 Margaret Street, Cavendish Square, in 1791, and at 18 Newman Street in 1793.

Another letter[2] of earlier date tells of his prospects, and makes mention of the way he intends sending correspondence. It is as follows:

LONDON, *April 14th*, 1789.

DEAR MOTHER,—It being so short a time since I wrote my last letter to you—this will consist of very little more than an account of my very perfect state of health And good prospect of succeeding in my profession. My pictures have been admitted this year into the Royal Academy And I hope in time to be a proficient in the Art. Painting Requires more studdy than I at first imagened in Consequence of which I shall be obliged to Stay here some

[1] Reproduced by permission of Mrs. Frank Semple from the MS. in her possession.

[2] *Ibid.*

time longer than I Expected—But all things work together for good in the end and I am Convinced my exertions will have a good tendency. In your next letter please to give me a very particular account of everything you know particularly how you like the little farm if you have a good garden And what kind of Neighbours you have got. And in fact I should like to know every thing that will give you pleasure or promote the happiness of the family—There is nothing Interupts my happiness here but the desire of seeing my Relations but time will bring us together. And I hope at my return to see you all happy as the day is long. I hope Mr. Smith is well—Please to present him my kind Love—Allso to Polly, Abraham, Bell, Cook and Children—The gentleman who carries this letter and many others of mine to Baltimore—is not a very particular friend therefore I cannot trouble to take a large Package—in this case Polly, Abraham and Bell must excuse my not writing to them by this opportunity—What letters I do send will be delivered to George Sanderson Baltimore—he sends them to Turbitt and so on to you—Please to give my Compliments to Mr. and Mrs. Hoge and friends in generall and believe me to be with the most Sincere regard for my Relations a loving Brother and Affectionate Son,

ROBERT FULTON.

We are unable to reconcile Fulton's statement that pictures of his were admitted into the Exhibition of the Royal Academy of 1789, with the fact that he does not appear as an exhibitor there till 1791; possibly up till then his paintings had been rejected. The pictures that he exhibited in the latter year were two "portraits of young gentlemen": lest it might be thought that he owed the distinction not to his own merits but to his having a friend at court in the person of Benjamin West, who was a Royal Academician, we hasten to add that Fulton also had four other pictures in the Exhibition of the Royal Society of

British Artists in the same year. Although Fulton in a subsequent letter says that "these exertions are all for honour," it is difficult to believe that the portraits, at least, were not commissions for which he received payment.

At any rate, the fact that he had been "hung," or, more likely perhaps, the recommendation of West, induced Viscount Courtenay[1] to commission a portrait of himself from Fulton, and for this purpose the latter left London in June for Powderham Castle, Lord Courtenay's seat near Exeter, where he was for the time being the guest of the steward of the estate.

His stay in London had been broken only by a three months' visit to France in 1790, of which we have no details, so that this trip to Devonshire must have been very welcome, especially as the part of the county that he was visiting was noted even then for its salubrity.

Lord Courtenay was so pleased with his portrait that he introduced Fulton to all his friends, who gave him commissions which enabled him to pay off some debts he had contracted and lay by a little money for the future.

The details of Fulton's life during this period are gleaned largely from a letter which he wrote to his mother from Devonshire on January 20, 1792. As it is so important, we give it in full:[2]

MY DEAR MOTHER,—This Morning I Recd a package of letters from Philadelphia among which were one from you one from Abraham and two from Mr. Morris one of which was for Mr. West. In Consequence of my leaving London on June last for to do some business for Lord Courtney In Devonshire which is about 200 Miles from London The letters by some accident have not reached me till now. As you rely on it I should have answered

[1] William Courtenay, b. 1768. Succeeded his father, 1788, as 2nd Viscount Courtenay and *de jure* 9th Earl of Devon. Was successful in establishing his right to the dormant earldom 1831. Died unmarried in 1835.

[2] By kind permission of Mrs. Frank Semple, who possesses the original MS.

them by the first Conveyance—But I Recd them with Infinite Pleasure as they come from you and Informed me of your good health. And now I will attend to the particulars As I am well convinced every Incidant Relative to my life will Communicate pleasure to you. You express much desire to know how my pictures were Recd at the Royal Academy—this I believe I answered before but posibly the letter has miscarryed you will be pleased to hear that I sent eight pictures which Recd every posable mark of Approbation that the Society could give but these exertions are all for honor—there is no prophet arising from it. It only tends to Create a name that may hereafter produce business—My little tour through France proved very agreeable and was of some service to me as a painter in as much as I saw the works of some of the most able masters in the art—which much improved my eye and taste.

Mr. West and me are on a very familiar footing and when he is in town pays me much attention which is extremely agreeable as we live near each other. This evening I forwarded Mr. Morris's letter to him which I have no doubt he will be very happy to receive And I shall call on him immediately on my going to London which I Suppose will be in about six months. When I wrote you last I beged you would Settel everything to You(r) mind relative to the Lotts and after Regulating everything with Mr. Hoge and putting me on the way how to act I would transfer my Right in the manner you Can best Settel among yourselves—tho I could wish one of them were sold to pay pollock—For I Realy feel my honor Concerned in keeping the poor man so long out of his money nor had I the least idea of its remaining so long unpaid or I should have endeavored by some means to have it done—but I hope when I hear from you next in Answer to these letters you will have everything so Situated so as I may transfer them to your wish And if no other method can be found one lott ought to be sold to pay pol'k—It gives me much

Pleasure to hear of Abrahams attention to you tho I am sorry he has run away with the Idea of my Getting Rich —I only wish it was true—but I Cannot Concieve from whence the Report arose—And I must now Give Some little history of my life since I Came to London. I Brought not more than 40 Guineas to England and was set down in a strange Country without a friend and only one letter of Introduction to Mr. West—here I had an art to learn by which I was to earn my bread but little to support whilst I was doing it And numbers of Eminant Men of the same profession which I must Excell before I Could hope to live—Many Many a Silant solitary hour have I spent in the most unnerved Studdy Anxiously pondering how to make funds to support me till the fruits of my labours should sifficant to repay them. Thus I went on for near four years—happily beloved by all who knew me or I had long ear now been Crushed by Poverties Cold wind—and Freezing Rain—till last Summer I was Invited by Lord Courtney down to his Country seat to paint a picture of him which gave his Lordship so much pleasure that he has introduced me to all his Friends—And it is but just now that I am beginning to get a little money and pay some debtt which I was obliged to Contract so I hope in about 6 months to be clear with the world or in other words out of debt and then start fair to Make all I Can. You see dear mother this is very different from being Rich (?) not that I can say I ever was in absolute want heaven has been kind to me and I am thankfull—hoping now to go on Smooth and happy as the absance from my friends will admit of. My Poor Sister bell I hope she and her little family will be happy I hope she will not think I forgot her because I dont write her She may believe me she Occupies much of my thoughts And I wish much to know why Poyton left the situation of the saw mill but none of you have informed me. I am happy to hear that all relations are well I shall write to them seprately. I enjoy excelant health which I hope will Continue till I may have the happiness of seeing you. Please to remember me kindly to Mr. Smith and all friends And may Heaven Continue its blessings towards you is the most unfeigned wish of your Obedient Son

ROBERT FULTON.

The "Lotts" referred to in this letter were the building lots in Washington township, whose purchase has already been mentioned. Fulton thought that the time had now arrived to transfer them into the names of his sisters, who had married in the meantime: Elizabeth to one Scott, Isabella to one Cook, and Mary to David Morris, the nephew of Benjamin West. There are references to these transfers in several letters, and it appears as if some difficulties occurred in the process.

The "pollock" who is mentioned was the one from whom Fulton had purchased the Hopewell Farm. One would almost have thought that Fulton's brother, Abraham, would by this time have done something towards paying off the debt on his mother's farm, but there is a hint that instead he was content to build on the hope that Robert would become rich.

Preoccupation with commissions in the West Country, lasting till about the middle of 1792, did not give Fulton much opportunity to exhibit in London, so that his absence from the Royal Academy in that year is explained. Several historical paintings,[1] known to us only through engravings published early in 1793, may have been part of the fruits of his labours during this period. At any rate, he did get back to town in time to send to the Academy Exhibition of 1793 a portrait of a Mrs. Murray.

Fulton was in good spirits and apparently still engrossed in his work, when he wrote to his brother-in-law a "business" letter, dated London, May 21, 1793; it contained a eulogy on Benjamin West which is worth quoting:[2]

[1] Appendix B, p. 280.

[2] By courtesy of the Chicago Historical Society, who possess the original.

"MARY QUEEN OF SCOTS UNDER CONFINEMENT"

"Your Uncle West is now at the head of his proffession and Presides at the Royal Academy over all the Painters in England—But he is a Great Genius and merits all the honour he has obtained—he has stedily persued his Course and Step by Step at length Reached the Summit where he now looks Round on the Beauties of his Industry—an Ornament to Society and Stimulis to young Men."

It is obvious that Fulton was now fairly launched on an artistic career. At a time when wealth had increased, but no more rapid means of portraiture than the artist's personal touch was known, there was plenty of scope in this branch of art, at least, and miniature painting then reached its highest development. Fulton seems to have done a fair share of portrait painting, but no miniatures of this period, if any were painted by him as would seem likely, are known to exist.

As Fulton now threw up his artistic career suddenly, it may not be out of place to say a few words as to his technique and attainments as an artist. On these points we cannot do better than quote the opinion of an eminent art critic,[1] based on what little material is available at the present day. Speaking of Fulton's miniatures,[2] he says:

"Apart from a curious flatness that he gave his miniatures, which can be recognised even in the reproductions, they are good, yes, remarkably good, for so young a man with so little instruction. They are well drawn, good in design, delicately coloured, as miniatures should be, and well executed technically. From some of the qualities that they possess, I should not be surprised if he had had some instruction or help from Charles Willson Peale, who, at Fulton's time, was at the top of the profession here."

This is quite probable, as they were well acquainted

[1] Mr. Charles Henry Hart, of Philadelphia, in a letter to the author.

[2] A list of Fulton's paintings, as far as they are known, is given in Appendix B, p. 280.

with one another. As regards his larger paintings, judging by the few authoritative pictures remaining, the same critic says: "Fulton's work showed strong characterisation and breadth, a firm brush and good colour sense. He had not yet developed a style of his own, and while he gave some promise, it is doubtful whether he would ever have equalled Benjamin West: decidedly he would not have attained to the stature of John Singleton Copley, Gilbert Stuart, and John Trumbull, to mention only those who were his contemporaries and compatriots."

It is not easy to give a plausible explanation of why Fulton gave up his career as an artist. He may have admitted to himself reluctantly that he did not possess talent of that high order which was necessary then, as now, to bring a man into the front rank of artists; it is more probable that he was dissatisfied with the pecuniary results so far achieved, which, for a man who had turned thirty, were somewhat meagre. To leave at that age the profession of art to begin that of engineering, then only in its infancy, although such a change was not so difficult then as it would be now, must have appeared to his friends to be the height of rashness.

It is unnecessary to enlarge upon the close association that exists between these two professions when we reflect that each involves both the imaginative and constructive faculties. In rare cases these faculties have been united in one person—Leonardo da Vinci is perhaps the best known instance. In modern times, specialisation has rendered such a union impossible, but many engineers have had the artistic feeling highly developed; we may instance the cases of Fulton's own countryman Samuel F. B. Morse, the electrician, and in this country of James Nasmyth, the inventor of the steam hammer, himself the son and brother of eminent artists.

Fulton's was a like case; in him the artist and the engineer struggled for expression, but the latter was undoubtedly the stronger. His early training was by no

"LADY JANE GREY THE NIGHT BEFORE HER EXECUTION"

means wasted, however, for his skill and rapidity in putting ideas on paper were of the utmost value to him.

When, in subsequent years, Fulton had occasion to turn his attention to painting, whether for profit or recreation, he found to his delight that his hand had not lost its cunning—indeed he was wont to say that his technique was superior to what it had been in his younger days.

CHAPTER III

PROJECTS FOR MARINE PROPULSION—STUDIES THE ENGLISH CANAL SYSTEM—DIGGING MACHINE—PATENT FOR INCLINED PLANE—WRITES ON CANAL NAVIGATION

WHATEVER Fulton's reason was for giving up the profession of art, he seems to have come to the decision quickly, and that too while he was in Devonshire. Apparently one of the first things that he put his hand to was a design for a "mill for sawing marble or other stone," which was set to work near Torbay, Devon. In 1794, when he was back in London again, he sent a model of this mill to the Society for the Encouragement of Arts, Commerce, and Manufactures, who awarded him their silver medal for his ingenuity. The model was in existence in the Society's Repository as late as 1813, but it has since been lost sight of so that we are unable to say in what the improvement consisted.

We turn now to Fulton's connection with systems of canal construction and with the problem of moving vessels by means of steam-power—both of them destined to have far-reaching influence on his own career, and one of them on the course of the world's history.

Fulton's thoughts were drawn to the first of these questions by "perusing a paper descriptive of a canal projected by the Earl of Stanhope in 1793."[1]

This canal was one intended to join the Bristol and the English Channels, passing from Bude Haven through the hilly district about Hatherleigh and touching Holsworthy, the lord of the manor of which was Lord Stanhope himself. The difference of levels was upwards of 500 feet, and water was scarce.

[1] Introduction to his *Treatise on Canal Navigation*, xiii.

While staying at Torquay, Fulton wrote to his Lordship a letter, dated September 30, 1793, enclosing a sketch of a scheme for doing away with the necessity for locks and minimising the loss of water; it was to consist of a preponderating cistern of water to draw the canal boat up an inclined plane from one level to another. He also informed his Lordship that he had a project for moving ships by steam.

We need not necessarily suppose that Fulton had already made the acquaintance of Lord Stanhope, although it is quite likely that they had met in West's studio. In any case it could hardly be considered presumption on Fulton's part, because the great interest that the Earl took in all that related to mechanical and physical science was well known; in fact, he was an inventor of a high order himself: the Stanhope levers in printing presses and the Stanhope lens in optics may be quoted as examples of his genius. Just at the moment he was interesting himself in navigation by steam.

He replied to Fulton's communication in a courteous letter, dated Holsworthy, October 7, 1793, informing him that his idea of the inclined plane was the same as described by Mr. Edmund Leech about sixteen years earlier. Then, for the first time, Fulton "discovered that the idea of a preponderating body of water was by no means new." His Lordship, however, expressed a wish to receive the ideas on steam-boats, saying: "it is a subject on which I have made important discoveries."

The "discoveries" referred to were really a revival of a proposal that had been made by Genevois of Berne in 1759, and are embodied in two patents (Nos. 1732 and 1771) taken out by Lord Stanhope in 1790 for a double-ended vessel which was to be driven by a propeller operating like the foot of an aquatic bird; this was to work through a trunk in line with the keel and be operated by a steam-engine. Experiments with models had proved successful, and Lord Stanhope had succeeded in 1792 in obtaining the assistance of the Navy Board to further his schemes.

A vessel of 200 tons burden was under construction in Deptford Dockyard (*Gent. Mag.*, 1792, i. 956), the cost of which was to be reimbursed by Lord Stanhope should it prove unsuccessful.

Fulton's reply[1] was as follows:

MY LORD,—I extremely regret not having received your Lordship's letter in time to have the pleasure of an interview at Exeter as a Mechanical conversation with your Lordship would have been infinately interesting to a young man. To atone for such loss and conform with your Lordship's wish I have made some slight drawings descriptive of my Ideas on the Subject of the steamship which I submit with diffidence to your Lordship. In June '93 I began the experiments on the steamship; my first design was to imitate the spring in the tail of a Salmon: for this purpose I supposed a large bow to be wound up by the steam-engine and the collected force attached to the end of a paddle as in No 1 to be let off which would urge the vessel forward. This model I have had made of which No. 1 is the exact representation and I found it to spring forward in proportion to the strength of the bow, about 20 yards, but by the return of the paddle the continuity of the motion would be stoped. I then endeavoured to give it a circular motion which I effected by applying two paddles on an axis, then the boat moved by jerks. There was too great a space between the strokes; I then applied three paddles forming an equilateral triangle to which I gave a circular motion by winding up the bow. I then found it to move in a gradual and even motion 100 yards with the same bow which before drove it but 20 yards.

No. 2 is the figure of my present model in which there are two equilateral triangles, one on each side of the boat acting on the same shaft which crosses the Boat or Ship and turns with the triangles; this, my Lord, is the line of experiment which led me to the triangular paddles which

[1] Stanhope MSS.

FULTON'S FIRST SKETCH FOR A STEAMBOAT, 1793

at first sight will convey the Idea of a wheel of perpendicular oars which are no longer in the water than they are doing execution. I have found by repeated experiment that three or six answer better than any other number as they do not counteract each other. By being hung a little above the water it allows a short space from the delivery of one to the entrance of the other; it likewise enters the water more on a perpendicular as the doted lines will shew its situation when it enters and when it is covered the circular dots exhibit its passage through the water. Your Lordship will please to observe in the small wheel with a number of paddles A. B. C. and D. strike almost flat in the water and rise in the same situation whilst E. is the only one that pulls, the others act against it which renders the purchase fruitless; while E. is urging the Ship forwards B. A. is pressing her into the water, and C. D. is pulling her out: but remove all the paddles except E. and she moves on in a direct line. The perpendicular triangular Paddles are supposed to be placed in a cast Iron wheel which should over hang above the water—it will answer as a fly and brace to the perpendicular oars. This Boat I have repeatedly let go and ever found her to move in a steady direction in proportion to the original purchase. With regard to the formation of ships moved by steam I have been of opinion that they should be long, narrow and flat at bottom, with a broad keel, as a flat Vessel will not occupy so much space in the water; it consequently has not so much resistance. A letter containing your Lordship's opinion of this mode of gaining a purchase on the water and directed for me at the post office, Exeter, will much oblige your Lordship's most obedient and

Very humble servant,

ROBERT FULTON.

TORQUAY, *November 4th*, 1793.

THE RIGHT HONORABLE
THE EARL OF STANHOPE.

This letter is interesting not only as showing the date—June 1793—at which Fulton began his consideration of the problem of moving vessels by mechanical means, but also because of the insight it gives into the careful and methodical methods of experimenting which were characteristic of him. From their elementary character, it seems obvious that Fulton did not know anything about the work on this subject that had been done previously. To us at the present day this is an advantage, for it affords an interesting and unique insight into the progress of an invention from its birth in the brain of the inventor right up to the time of its maturity. We can easily imagine that Lord Stanhope was disappointed, if indeed he had expected any assistance—no wonder that he still adhered to his duck-foot propeller! The experiments with his vessel, which he named the "Ambi-Navigator Kent," fitted with an engine of 12 H.P. supplied by Messrs. Boulton & Watt of Birmingham, were prosecuted in Greenland Dock, Rotherhithe, in 1795, but no greater speed than three miles per hour was attained.

We can conjecture that Lord Stanhope told Fulton that the problem of moving vessels mechanically had got far beyond the stage shown by the latter's sketches. At any rate Fulton dropped the subject for the time being to devote himself to the study of canal engineering.

The most likely reason why he decided to do so was because canal construction in England was then in its heyday. The opposition and distrust that were encountered when Brindley was constructing the Duke of Bridgewater's Canal in 1767, the Grand Trunk Canal in 1772, and other later canals, had given place, owing to the financial results achieved, to the wildest speculation. The premium on shares in existing canals was as much as 1000 per cent., and, in consequence, numberless worthless schemes were launched upon a gullible public. "In the course of the four years ending in 1794, not fewer than eighty-one Canal and Navigation Acts were obtained; of these, forty-five were passed in the two latter years, authorising the expenditure of not less than £5,300,000."[1]

In passing, it is interesting to note how closely history repeated itself half a century later in the case of railways.

It is somewhat strange that, in his letters home, Fulton did not mention a word about his canal projects. One letter written just at this time[2] to his brother-in-law shows Fulton rather in the light of a keen student of foreign affairs and a strong friend of republican institutions. This portion of the letter is as follows:

"Since I Last heared from you I have been much troubled by the Repeated Accounts in the London papers of the Inroads of the Indians on the Frontiers. I Sincerely hope this has not Been in your Nighbourhood So as to Interrupt the Progress of improvement in the Rising town of Washington. As to Europe it is all in alarm, the united efforts of England, Prusia, Spain, Holland, Germany, Rushia and all the Allied Powers have not been Able as Yet to Mount Another King on the Back of the French Nation. It is almost incredebl with what Vigor the French meet their enemies while *Live the Republic is the Constant Song; and Liberty or death their Motto.* Thus determined to Establish Republickism they have at this moment five hundred thousand Men under Arms Ready for the ensuing Campaign.

"The Allies Seeing so much unshaken firmness Ready to meet them begin to dispair of King making. And think it time to Look to their own Safety, As the discontended enumrate fast in all the Belligerent States, the People Contemplate the Nature of a Republic, And the more they think the more they admire it. When a Revolution once takes place in the mind it will Soon make its

[1] Smiles, *Lives of the Engineers*, i. 297.

[2] *I.e.* April 1, 1794. Original in possession of the Chicago Historical Society, and reproduced by their permission.

appearence externely, And I Can assure you there Are numbers who do not hesitate to Say that Monarchial Governments are going out of Fashion. Things being thus situated it is the Report of the day that the King of Prussia, has withdrawn from the alliance. The Empres of Rushia, has Certainly found work at home with the turks—And thus the french Are eased of two powerful adversaries—how things will terminate god only knows, But as far as Man Can penetrate into events it is believe(d) the French will prove Sucesful and establish a Republic the Natural Consequence will be Republicks throughout Europe, *In time*, It has Been much Agited here Whether the Americans would join the French—But I Believe every Cool friend to America Could wish them to Remain nuter. The americens have not troubelsome neighbours they are without foriegn Possessions, and do not want the alliance of any Nation for this Reason they have nothing to do with foriegn Politics, And the Art of Peace Should be the Study of every young american—which I most sincerely hope they will mantain."

Fulton advocated canals of small size partly because of cheapness in construction, but also to facilitate speed of transport with light loads. To overcome differences of levels, especially where water was scarce, he proposed to do away with locks and substitute either inclined planes along which the boats might be drawn on rails or else vertical lifts or hoists. The inclined plane was not new; indeed it is supposed to have been in use for canals in China a thousand years ago; in its simplest form it is to be seen at many of the locks on the upper Thames. Nor was the idea new to England, for William Reynolds, of Ketley Ironworks, had in 1792 constructed several inclined planes on the Shropshire Canal.

For his improvements Fulton took out his one and only English patent (No. 1988); it is dated May 8, 1794, and was sealed on the 3rd of June following. In it he

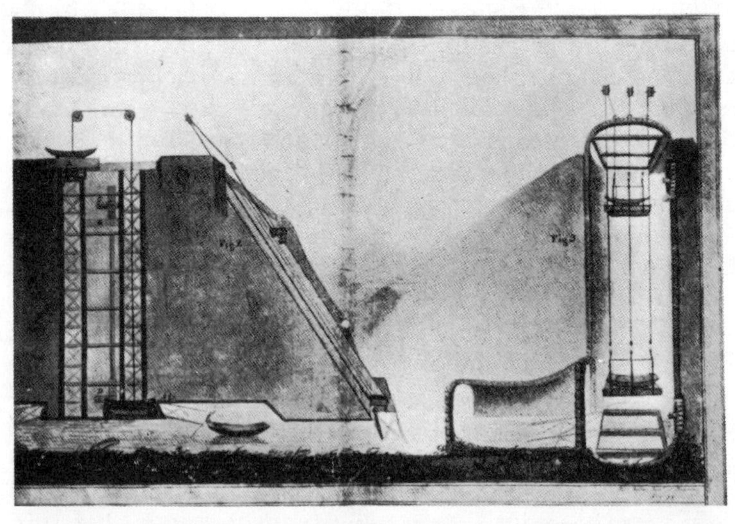

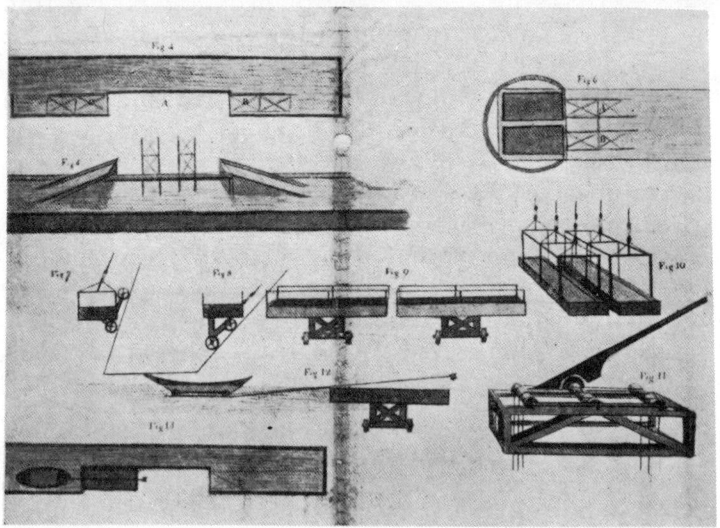

FULTON'S CANAL INCLINED PLANE, 1794

describes himself as "late of the City of Exeter, but now of the City of London, Gentleman." The title of the invention is "A machine or Engine for conveying Boats and Vessels and their Cargoes to and from the different levels in and upon Canals, without the Assistance of Locks or the other Means now known and used for that purpose." The Specification runs to six printed pages, and is accompanied by a coloured drawing (reproduced herewith). An inclined plane of any angle between 20° and 90° was to be used; it was to have rails on which were to run "cisterns" each capable of carrying one wheeled boat, which was to be drawn on to it by inclines as seen in Figs. 4 and 5, 12 and 13. One cistern was to balance the other (see Figs. 1 and 2) the direction of motion to be determined by letting water by suitable means, if necessary, into the topmost cistern. If the lift were perpendicular a tunnel or level with a vertical shaft would be necessary as in Fig. 3. The plan of this is shown in Fig. 6 and of the cisterns in Fig. 10. For checking the speed of descent of the cistern, a friction brake (see Fig. 11) was to be used. It is difficult even for a trained mind to see in this specification anything more than a crude idea, ill digested; better methods, worked out in a more practical manner, were already in use.

The preparation of the specification and drawing must have occupied him some considerable time. The expenses of obtaining a patent in those days amounted to £100 or more, and, as we shall see subsequently, Fulton disposed of a sixteenth share, probably to assist in meeting this outlay.

For the next five or six years, problems of canal construction occupied Fulton's attention almost exclusively. He himself says:[1] "I passed three years at various canals in England, to obtain practical knowledge on the manner of constructing them, and to make myself familiar with

[1] Report of the Board of Commissioners of the Western Canal, dated Feb. 22, 1814.

their advantages, and was well acquainted with some of the best engineers."

It was natural that, in prosecuting these inquiries, Fulton should direct his steps to the scene of Brindley's first triumphs; accordingly it is not surprising to find him shortly after in Manchester, whence he wrote the following letter[1] to Messrs. Boulton and Watt:

MANCHESTER, *November 4th*, 1794.

GENTLEMEN,—I shall esteem it a favour to be informed of the Expences of a Steam Engine with a Rotative movement of the purchase of 3 or 4 horses which is designed to be placed in a Boat. You will will [*sic*] be so good as to mention what sized boat it would occupy, as I wish to have it in as little Space as Possible and what you concive will be the Expence when finished compleat in the Boat. Whether you have one ready of the dimentions specified or how soon one might be finished. With the Weight of Coals which it will Consume in 12 hours—and what Quantity of purchase you allow to Each horse as I am anxious to apply some Engines of the above dimentions as soon as Possible. Your Emediate Answer will much oblige Your
most obedient and very humble Servant, ROBT. FULTON.

BRIDGEWATER ARMS
MANCHESTER

There is an amount of unconscious assurance about this letter that is refreshing. The writer wants a business firm to quote for an engine of special design to fit a boat which he also wants designed for him; he wants to know also what to expect from the engine when he has got it, and what it would cost to instal and operate it! This was too large an order, and the firm did not send any reply—at least there is no record of one. They were

[1] Boulton and Watt MSS.

too busy with the remunerative work of stationary engine building under their patent monopoly to trouble with speculative business.

It is interesting to note, however, that this letter gives the first indication that Fulton had realised the importance of keeping down the space and displacement needed by a steam engine when used in a boat for propulsion. What the occasion of writing was we do not know, but experiments had been made about this time by a certain John Smith with a paddle-wheel boat worked by an atmospheric beam engine on the Bridgewater Canal between Runcorn and Manchester.[1] A speed of two miles per hour only was attained. A man like Fulton, with a grasp of general principles, would easily see the defects of such an engine for the purpose, and the idea of employing Watt's patent engine might easily occur to him.

Although the letter is dated from an inn, Fulton was at the time living in a boarding-house at 8 Brazennose Street, Manchester. One of his fellow-boarders there was Robert Owen,[2] just then managing some cotton mills in Manchester, but afterwards owner of the cotton mills at New Lanark, Scotland, where he carried out among his workpeople his celebrated schemes of social reform. The young men were nearly of the same age, and not dissimilar in tastes; no wonder, then, that they should be mutually attracted. Just as on previous occasions in Philadelphia and London, Fulton's personal gifts had stood him in good stead, so now, in the same way, he made the acquaintance of many cultured people; "while . . . forming one of a circle of inquiring friends who very frequently met, he was considered a valuable addition. The late Dr. John Dalton was one of this circle, and Coleridge came occasionally from his college during vacations to join us."[3]

Dalton was just about Fulton's own age, and was then

[1] *Mechanics' Magazine*, xvii. 261.

[2] *Life of Robert Owen*, written by himself, 1857, p. 64, *et seq.*

[3] *Ibid.*, p. 72.

carrying out the chemical experiments which led to his enunciation of the Atomic Theory. Samuel Taylor Coleridge was seven years Fulton's junior.

Fulton had now almost exhausted his resources. In his extremity he confided to Owen,[1] "that, in prosecuting an invention which had occurred to him, for more expeditiously and cheaply digging or raising earth in forming canals . . . he had expended all his funds, and he knew not, except by disposing of part of the interest in his patent, how to obtain more, for all his means and credit were exhausted. He said there was a canal to be constructed near Gloucester, and if I [*i.e.* Robert Owen] could supply him with funds to go there and see the Commissioners appointed to carry it into execution, he might perhaps succeed in obtaining a contract for digging a portion of it, and might then bring his new patent into notice and profitable action, and he would give me half of the interest in the invention." Although Owen considered the success of this venture to be "very problematical," he eventually supplied Fulton with funds with which to go to Gloucester.

The canal was the Gloucester and Berkeley Ship Canal, 16½ miles long, the Act for which was obtained in 1793; work was commenced in 1794, but, owing to long delays due to insufficient capital, the canal was not opened for traffic till 1827.

Owen gives no details of the digging machine; indeed it would appear that it had only just taken shape in the fertile brain of Fulton himself. However, as he communicated particulars of it, together with a sketch,[2] to Lord Stanhope about a year later, when his plan was more mature, we are not in doubt as to his ideas.

Owen's first written communication from Fulton, dated November 20, 1794, was "filled with curious calculations respecting his new digging machine." Owen, either con-

[1] *Life of Robert Owen*, written by himself, 1857, p. 64.

[2] See p. 36.

vinced of success or his fears of failure overcome, now agreed to finance Fulton and entered into articles of agreement of partnership with him. Owen recites this agreement in full; but, as it occupies 2½ octavo pages, we will spare our readers by giving only the salient facts. It opens thus:

"Minutes of agreement made this seventeenth day of December 1794, between Robert Fulton of the City of London, Engineer of the one part and Robert Owen of Manchester in the county of Lancaster, cotton manufacturer of the other part.

"Whereas the said Robert Fulton hath lately invented and obtained His Majesty's Royal Letters Patent for the exclusive exercise for a term of fourteen years of a certain machine for transferring boats and their cargoes to and from higher levels and lower levels in and upon canal navigations, independent of locks, of which machine thirty parts or shares (the whole into thirty-two parts being divided) are now vested in the said Robert Fulton. And also hath invented and shortly intends to make application for letters patent for a certain other machine for removing earth out of canals to the banks thereof, in cases of deep digging, without the use of wheelbarrows, the sole and whole property of which is now vested in the said Robert Fulton. And whereas the said Robert Fulton and Robert Owen have agreed to become co-partners in the said machines and in the exercise thereof at the time and upon the terms hereinafter mentioned. . . ."

The terms, succinctly stated, were, that Owen was to advance immediately £60 towards the digging machine to get it into operation. When either the inclined plane or the digging machine business reached a certain specified success the two were to become copartners equally interested in both inventions. Owen was to advance £400 to the said copartnership to be repaid out of the first profits. Fulton agreed "from the date hereof and after the commencement of the said co-partnership to the end of the same to apply his whole time and exertions in the said business."

Fulton now appears to have left Manchester—a sociable person such as he would never lack an invitation for the Christmas season—for we find that the first letter Owen received from him was dated December 26, 1794. In it he intimated his intention of going to Gloucester about the first of January 1795, gave additional calculations, suggested new improvements in his digging machine, and ended by saying, "I will send you a sketch and description after digesting the subject," and "Please to write to me immediately and let me know how the improvement in the model succeeds."

The next paper among Owen's MSS. was an account of a debt owing to a Mr. Thomas Lenning by Fulton, which he requested Owen to pay for him. Then followed a long letter from Fulton "with new calculations and diagrams of more improvements on his former invention," and concluding "When the rhino is gone, I will write to you." The last touch is delightful, and no one can fail to appreciate it. This letter was succeeded by seven more in rapid succession, dated from Gloucester, from the 14th January to the 26th of February 1795, "with new calculations, various sketches of new machines and improvements, and asking for more money." The latter, we may be sure, was needed.

The next incident in the intercourse between these two men is perhaps best given in Owen's own words:

"He had had a previous unsettled contract with a Mr. McNiven, a canal contractor, to whom he had requested me to send a letter from him to Mr. McNiven, with proposals for a settlement, but Mr. McNiven would not agree to the conditions Mr. Fulton had proposed. I had therefore to write to Mr. Fulton to advise him to come from Gloucester, whence his letters were dated, to Manchester to settle this business, as Mr. McNiven had threatened to adopt strong measures to enforce a settlement. It seems that he then came to Manchester and made new proposals to me, to continue the partnership, or to make my advances to him a debt, which he would repay me with five per cent. interest, and it appears that I preferred and accepted the latter condition. The following is the Memorandum of proposals made by Mr. Fulton, dated 17th March 1795":

MANCHESTER, *17th March*, 1795.

Memorandum—Mr. Robert Owen having advanced the sum of £93, 8s. in part towards promoting the two projects of running boats independent of locks and removing earth out of canals—it is hereby agreed that the said Robert Owen shall advance to the said Robert Fulton a further sum not exceeding £80, to enable him the said Robert Fulton, to make a fair experiment on the earth removing apparatus; that on finishing such machines, should the said Robert Owen think proper to proceed in the partnership as per contract, he shall be at full liberty so to do. But should a partnership be presented to the said Robert Fulton previous to finishing the said machine, he shall be at liberty to accept of the same on the proposal of the said Robert Owen. And in such case, the said Robert Fulton to pay to the said Robert Owen five per cent per annum, for the monies advanced until the said Robert Fulton shall be enabled to refund the principal.

ROBERT FULTON.

Fulton's next letter to Owen is dated November 2, 1795, and in it he regrets his inability to pay any part of the debt. He does not mention the digging machine, but it is reasonable to assume that he had expended the further sum advanced by Owen in bringing it to as great perfection as the apparatus admitted of. We hear no more about it till early in the following year, when, in a letter[1] to Earl Stanhope, he describes it fully and illustrates it by a sketch (*see* next page).

[1] Stanhope MSS.

This letter contains, we may suppose, Fulton's final ideas on the subject, and is such a good example of his lucid style that we give it in full:

LONDON, *Jan. 6th,* 1796.

MY LORD,—The enclosed is some thoughts on an engine to Ajust in Cutting Canals; the Idea is to have a Cutter which will take up a furrow of Earth about 4 inches Square—Which in the first drawing it pushes into a Segment of a Circle About one foot from the Ground, And a movement being taken from the Axel of the Hind wheels, which puts the Flies in motion, *they by the Velocity which they acquire are to Strike the earth out of the Segment or Stage on the Bank of the Canal.* Each fly is Calculated to Strike off about half a pound at a time, And the distance which the Earth will move through will be in proportion to the force with which it is Struck. Possibly it may be necessary as in the Second Figure to Raise the earth by *endless scrapers,* to some heighth on the machine, that it may be struck to the proper distance with the greater Ease, while Figure 3 shows that Such Machine may Cut into the Corners and give the proper Slope.

This being the principle the Question is whether it will answer any good purpose which I Conceive it will on the following Considerations. First that as it takes a small Quantity at a time it will work any place where you Could Plough; then if the force of the flies are equal to strike of the earth the Quantity which one man and 4 horses would deliver per day would stand thus: Supposing a horse to Walk 15 miles per day—every 81 lenial yds would be one Cube, 21 Cube yards per Mile in 15 miles 310 yards:—

Expense	4 horses . . .	16/–
	man	4/–
Wear of machine	. . .	2/–
		22/– or 264 pence

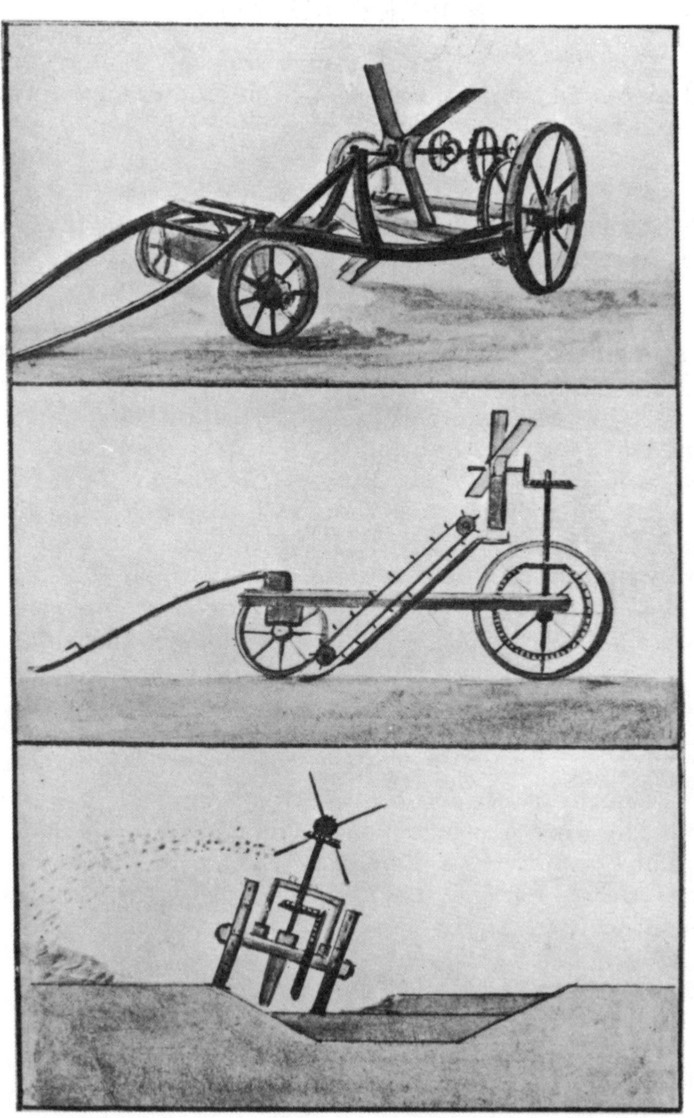

FULTON'S DIGGING MACHINE, 1796

This is not one Penny per Cube Yard, Which in all Cases that I know would be 3d.

But if Such a machine or Any other Can be made to Answer, it will Give further advantages by expedition and Set one independent in a great measure of Canal diggers. But in America where Manual Labour is of So much Importance Something to Assist In Cutting would be a most material improvement. Therefore as I am anxious for some such Machine your Lordship will oblige me by an opinion on these thoughts. And as I am convinced a Machine may be made which may be Very usefull, your Lordship be so good as to throw some hints Into the Scale, and you will oblige Your Lordship's most sincere

ROBT. FULTON

P.S. In America many of our Lines will be through forests, and full of huge Stumps, hence the following will be a Capital mode of Drawing them out of the ground, and out of the way:

A small Capstain built on a sledge which a horse may draw any place on a pair of 6 or 8 Round blocks. Being fixed to two stumps and the horse Set in motion the weakest stump must give Way—And if the Machine is fixed to a tree on or near the Canal bank the stump may be Drawn out of the Line of Canal.

Thus every little helps. Please to direct to No. 3 Frith Street, Soho.

A brief consideration of the sketch and the calculations will show that the digging machine was a crude and impracticable apparatus. The power for cutting the earth was to be obtained through the axle of the machine from the four horses employed in dragging it. The number of cuts works out on Fulton's figures (assuming that a cubic yard weighs 1 ton) at 28 per lineal yard traversed. At this rate the velocity of the flies would be so great that they would deal a shattering blow instead of the slow motion necessary with a shovel. Nevertheless this is the first attempt we have met with to solve the problem of mechanical excavation, the solution of which in our own time has made practicable such an engineering feat as the construction of the Panama Canal.

Fulton must have realised that his machine was a failure, because he neither proceeded to a patent (that might have been, of course, from lack of funds), nor does he mention the machine in the book he was now occupied in writing—his *Treatise on the Improvement of Canal Navigation*. This was Fulton's first appearance as an author. In order to "boom" his book, as we should now term it, Fulton wrote a signed article on "Small Canals," which was published in the *Star* newspaper July 30, 1795, in which he announced the forthcoming publication. His idea was, of course, to bring his system of Small Canals, wheeled boats, and inclined planes before the public; but the book was not confined to this alone, as it includes designs for aqueducts and bridges, engraved on copper from drawings made with his own hand. None of these designs are from actual practice, as has been asserted and as might be inferred from his styling himself on the title page "Civil Engineer." Although the title was at that time assumed rather loosely—civil engineering not being a definite profession—yet Fulton had no right to use it, for he had not been in practice, nor had he assisted in carrying out any engineering works.

The dedication of the book is dated March 1, 1796; it was published by I. & J. Taylor, from whom it is not unreasonable to suppose that Fulton received enough to put him in funds again for the time being.

The work was replied to by William Chapman[1] in the

[1] William Chapman (b. 1749, d. 1832), civil engineer (associated with Rennie as engineer to the London Docks and in sole charge for construction of docks, canals, and harbours), patented among other things the chain-driven locomotive, A.D. 1812.

following year in his *Observations on the Various Systems of Canal Navigation*, 1797, 4to, wherein he pointed out how old a device the inclined plane was, and also how unsuitable the small canal was to a country like England, where population was so dense.

CHAPTER IV

CORRESPONDENCE WITH LORD STANHOPE—BUDE CANAL—LEAVES FOR FRANCE

SHORTLY after getting ready for the press his *Treatise on Canal Navigation,* Fulton left for the North. Why he returned is not stated. It could hardly have been to see Robert Owen, or the latter would have mentioned it. It is most likely that it was to show his fellow-countryman, Joshua Gilpin,[1] the canals in the neighbourhood. Another suggestion is that Fulton had some hope of obtaining employment there. Some colour is lent to this suggestion by the statement,[2] founded only on hearsay however, that "the Duke of Bridgewater employed Fulton to construct an inclined plane for the underground canal at Walkden, near Manchester, which enabled boats full of coal to descend to a lower level canal by means of windlass and ropes: their weight caused the empty return boats to be drawn up to the canal on a higher level."

The statement is not inconsistent with other facts, although confirmation from the papers of the Bridgewater Trustees is not forthcoming. The work is stated to have been done in 1794, but could not have been till 1796—only a slight discrepancy, however.

Fulton kept up his correspondence with Lord Stanhope, and, though the whole of it has not been preserved, enough remains to show that the latter was taking a very keen interest in the Bude Canal, both in the route to be followed and in the method to be adopted in working it.

As already explained, the country to be traversed was

[1] See p. 61.

[2] Sir W. H. Bailey, *Notes on Canal Boat Propulsion,* Fourth International Congress on Inland Navigation, 1890, p. 3.

hilly, but water was scarce. Since the bulk of the trade expected—sand, manure, and coal—would be an ascending one, it was evident that enough water was not to be found for ordinary locks. Early in 1796 Lord Stanhope had schemed a method of getting over this difficulty by an invention which he called the "pendanter." Briefly, this consisted of two caissons or boat-carriers worked up and down vertically; they were to be about 50 feet apart, and be connected so as to counterbalance by a set of chains passing over pulleys. To allow for the weight of the chain, which would disturb the equilibrium except when the pendanters were in the mean position, other chains were to be hung from the under-sides of the pendanters, to be picked up from the ground, just as in the Koepe system now so commonly adopted when winding from deep mines. In the extreme position, one caisson was to be level with the lower reach of the canal, and the other caisson was to be at the higher level, where it was to make a junction with the upper reach.

Obviously, unless a perpendicular cliff were available to which to bring the two reaches of the canal, two pendanter pits or shafts would have to be sunk, and the lower reach of the canal brought to the bottom of the pit by a level or tunnel.

Lord Stanhope, with his usual broad-mindedness, hastened to make known his ideas to all those who had become interested in the Bude Canal, among whom were John Rennie, the celebrated civil engineer, and Fulton. The latter replied in the following letter,[1] which is reproduced in its entirety in order that the reader may get an idea of the voluminous nature of his communications:

At Mr. Washington's
STOCKPORT,
April 24th, '96.

MY LORD,—Being in an obscure part of the Country for a few days, I did not Receive your three letters till

[1] Stanhope MSS.

Last evening, Or they should each have been emediately Answered. I have now perused them three times, And I believe become sensable of the Various designs, Which gives me great pleasure to find your Lordship's mind so Intent on Improving navigation by Canals. And as I know it of Infinite Importance that the system should be improved By Constructing a Canal which may Act as Model to Convey Conviction, and Remove the Ignorance of the present practice, I shall feel particularly happy in the assistance of your Lordship's experience, in order to Minutely Investigate any Ideas which may arise In me. And on the other hand, I will Remark on your plans According to the best of my Judgement, hoping by this means a System of real benefit may be produced. In this I Conceive Canals should be Considered generally not Locally. I will therefore View the plans as to General use. And afterwards Consider the application to the particular trade of the Bude Canal.

First the pendanter Balanced by Weights.

This idea is new to me, As to the mode of Working —But in the Course of my experiments I once made use of a similar Carriage or Boat Carrier, with two Gates In the Carriage and one in upper and lower pond of Canal which I Relinquished for the following Reasons:

1st. That all water leaking from the upper Canal Gate would descend the pit, keep it continually disagreeably Wet and Injure the goods in the Boats. 2d. It would be Impossible to keep the gates of the pendanter from leaking particularly after some wear. 3d. The dispatch was not sufficient And the expense much greater, then the Inclined plane. The size of the pit, *which to admit a Carrier that would Receive* 12 *Boats*, must be 60 feet long of an oval shape that the sides might stand, And a tunnel of sufficient width for two Boats to pass with the expence of the materials to support heavy Weights Will be very Costly, And Attended with much difficulty In working. Tunnels and deep pits are usually wet added to which the leakage of the gates or even the dripings from the Bottom of the Pendanter would be an awkward Circumstance, And to Avoid this I adopted a Cage to Receive the Boat as in my 10th and 11th Plates with a Carriage to pass under the Cage in order to transfer the Boat into the upper Canal; thus I had but one gate In the whole Apparatus—placed in the upper Level And even that was extremely troublesome. The Pendanter must also have Balance Chains

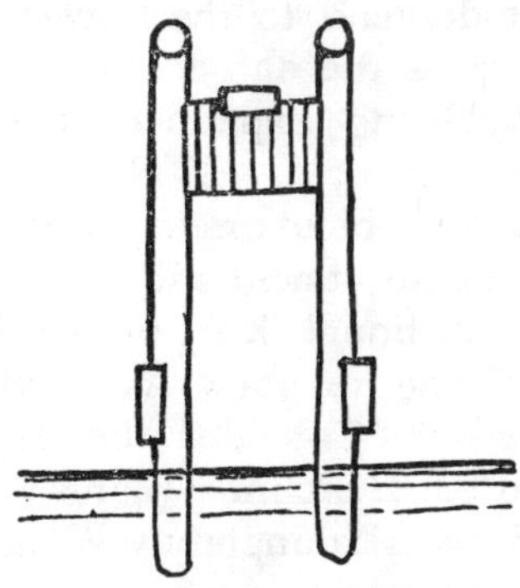

thus to preserve the Equal poize in passing through the space.

2d. The double pendanter as per your last, Is an improvement on the single as one is a Balance to the other. But here are double the gates, double the leakage, nearly double the expense. Though double the quantity of trade may be performed yet the above difficulties appear to me to operate Against a general trade and I Believe a much better Will be devised by your Lordship. This last machine if I Recollect Right is similar to one for which Dr. Anderson has a patent as explained in the *Repertory of Arts.*[1]

[1] Vol. ii. pp. 21–35, giving a review of "General View of the Agriculture and Rural Economy of the County of Aberdeen." *Board of Agriculture*, 1794, 4to, by Dr. James Anderson, LL.D., of Edinburgh. The author merely suggests the application of two counterbalanced caissons to pass canal boats from one level of a canal to another. It was only an idea, however, and never got to the patent stage.

4th. The Cassoon. As your Lordship seems to have abandoned it for the Pendanter I will not say much on its formation. It has all the objections as to leakage, tunnel, and pit, And is much more expensive In Consequence of the great depth of Pit And framing which must be in hight equal to the Ascent, nor do I see how the poize is preserved in passing, particularly In descending as the more wood Immersed the greater pressure it will Require to make the Boat descend to the Lower dry locks. This Apparatus I believe is the subject of a patent to Messrs. Rowland and Pickering explained in the *Repertory of Arts*.[1]

Having stated my objection to these three engenious thoughts as to expence, time, and the very disagreeable circumstances of Continual Wet, Each of Which I hope your Lordship will be so good As to deliberately Consider—

I now come to your Inclined plane With Rollers And this mode I Consider as Infinately the Best. As far as my experiments have extended or what I have seen of others I prefer the Inclined plane to perpendicular Ascents—the plane fits every kind of ground And at much less expence than driving tunnels; The Boats will ascend the plane In near a[s] little time as they Could enter the tunnel, They are free from all wet or damp, there is no leakage, and it is pleasant to work above ground.

It therefore appears to me that the object is to Render the operation of the plane Perfect, and that mode which on Weighing the Various Circumstances will do the most work with the greatest safety for the Least Money will be the Best.

We Agre perfectly as to the size of the Boats, the Business is to mount the Various Levels. And Mr. Leech's

[1] Vol. i. p. 81. E. Rowland and E. Pickering took out Patent No. 1981 (1794). There is no drawing attached, but it is stated in the specification that the necessary well was to be equal in depth to the height of the lift but that pulleys might be used. This therefore was an anticipation of Lord Stanhope's pendanter.

Idea of taking water into the descending Boat I Conceve very Imperfect.

First, Because the Boat would not contain Water sufficient to weigh up the Loaded Boat, the force of the descending Body is diminished In proportion as the Angle is small, for Instance on a Plane of 25 degrees it would Require 4 tons of Water at least to Raise 2 of Cargo, for which the Capacity of the Boat is not sufficient.

Second, the Boat on entering the Lower Canal would be full of Water, In discharging of Which there would be much time lost. But, as a power must be obtained to Raise the Loaded Boat I do not as yet see any mode so good as the tub passing through the pit, Because by this means there is a Certain Power, And you will find In my estimates that this method is not expensive, yet the Operation is easy.

In this, perhaps, I am like a fond father who is pleased with the genious of his friend's Children, yet his affections adhear to his own—But I will endeavour to be open to Conviction should a better mode of obtaining Power Appear.

However, At present this appears to me to be the Best, And the only Question on which I hesitate is Whether Rollers to the Plane or Wheels to the Boats are preferable. On this there has been a Civil War in my Ideas ever since I had the pleasure of seeing your Lordship. At length Rollers have gained some part of the teretory, and I think may be Applied to great Advantage on the Bude Canal, where your Boats are only 12 feet long. Nothing I think, Can surpass Rollers for Boats of that length as to Simplicity, Cheapness, and dispatch, And for your land trade where the Boats may have divisions to give them strength, thus

Because in Passing the Bridge such Boat will not be Injured when at one point It must rest on one Roller.

It gives me great pleasure to see your Lorship disposed to give up the use of horses And give In to my original Ideas, which I think I explained In some of my first Letters from *devon,* of gaining the Power by Reservoirs And Windmills. On the Application of Windmills I have made some drawings Within this few days. Supposing the Mill on an eminence at some distance from the pumps, showing how to extend the Power And Render the Mill perpetual without Attendance. This in Canal works Is indeed extremely Simple And in such works Wind mills Appear particularly Applicable for as on high levels Water is scarce, Wind is powerful and much more Constant; the Canal being the Reservoir to run the water from the Pumps or Buckets, Equal motion is not Required. A Hurrican Could do no harm and the least Breeze would be of service.

Thus Night or Day Without Attendance the mill performs, while the Wind Blows and Deposits a power to be used at pleasure. Hence my Ideas of the Bude Canal At present stand thus:

12 *feet Boats* 2 *tons, Inclined planes and Rollers Tub pit and Sough,* Reservoir *and Windmills where necessary.*

These Juditiously aranged I Conceve will produce a model Canal which will Carry Conviction and exhibit the Superiority of the small scale.

With Regard to fording the Canal Perhaps there may be some difficulty. As it Cannot be less than two feet deep In many Instances, People will not like to wade through to fetch their Sheep, Cows, produce, etc., particularly in Winter or in Case of Ice. To Avoid this Inconvenience I have Constructed a Weigh Bridge which on those narrow Canals may be made for about 14£, And the paving would probably Cost half that Sum.

The Bridge thus: The handels A and B being Weighted have a tendency to keep it open, But may be so balanced

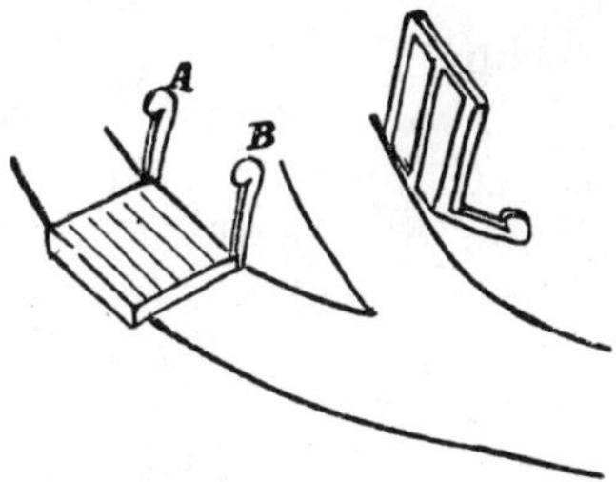

as to open and shut with facility and from either Side by a Small Cord or String.

But these are parts for after Consideration.

Yet previous to your trip to Devon I Conceive it advisable to have the plan which you mean to Adopt well digested, As the Survey should be made Accordingly. To Return to the Inclined plane—I see nothing in Mr. Rennie's objection to the Length of Chain, and even if Chain is objectionable Rope may be used. On the Shropshire Inclined plane, *they work a rope* 600 *yds long* with the greatest ease and this is a Case in point. On the small Canal principle I think the greatest possible Rise should be obtained at one time In order that there may be but few operations; the expence is also less.

I therefore hope the mode will be fully Investigated And that your Lordship will Weigh deliberately the Cassoons and Inclined plane on all points In which you will honour me by further Observations.

If Mr. Rennie is to be of your Party In September, your Lordship will see the necessity of his being at home in the apparatus for transfer or he or any other man *except as a Surveyor* Can be of no use As the Line must In A great measure bend to the apparatus, and Incline plane or Small Canals *by System* is as Novel to the Lock engineer as Machine Spinning was new and Wonderful to the old Women In Sir Richard Arckright's Day.

I hope ere this Your Lordship's Eyes are perfectly well. And Return my thanks for the high opinion you are pleased to entertain of my Conduct and exertions. When time will per[mit] your Lordship to Read my Letter to Genl. Mifflin you will much oblige me by your opinion of my plans for facilitating Conveyances In America by Canals, Also your thoughts on the General System As to Crossing Rivers without aqueducts, etc., etc.

With all possible Respect,
I Remain
Your Lordship's most obedient
ROBT FULTON.

P.S. As I shall Remain In this Country about 3 Weeks any further Communication within that time please to direct to Mr. Washington, Stockport, Cheshire.

THE RIGHT HONBL. EARL STANHOPE.

We think that it will easily be gathered from this letter that Fulton was in hopes that through Lord Stanhope he would have the long-wished for opportunity of putting into practice his ideas on canal construction, and obtain salaried employment in so doing. Unfortunately for Fulton, Lord Stanhope's "pendanter" was designed to overcome exactly the difficulty that the inclined plane had been schemed for. Fulton, therefore, set out to show, conclusively too, how much better the inclined plane is than the pendanter. An interesting suggestion is that of incorporating bulkheads in the boat structure to resist "hogging" stresses; another is that of a bascule bridge for crossing from one side of a canal to the other. The reference to the inclined planes on the Shropshire Canal goes to show that he had been there.

Lord Stanhope replied to this on April 27, 1796, in a long letter, in which he shows that while Fulton's plan only saves one half of the water used in locking, his plan of the pendanter will save it all, on the assumption that the ascending trade in both cases is equal to the descending. Lord Stanhope asks him to furnish an Estimate of the cost of inclined planes to raise a given freight 400 feet high, while he (Lord Stanhope) will get out another estimate to do the same work on the pendanter plan. Further, he suggests a method to catch the inevitable leakage of water.

Fulton replied on May 4th, in a letter longer even than the last, and full of sketches, but not sufficiently interesting to be inserted in full here. He is brimming over with enthusiasm for canals, particularly for his own country, and he discusses the pros and cons of the pendanter and inclined plane in great detail. Perhaps the most interesting thing in the letter is a sketch and description of an arrangement for regulating automatically the area of the sails of a windmill to suit the force of the wind by means of the wind itself. This is the first record, as far as we are aware, of this plan, now well known in connection with pumping windmills. This sketch shows also a tail for moving the sails into the wind; this, although in use at that time, was far from common.

Lord Stanhope replied to this on May 8, 1796, by a letter, in which he announces that he has altered his plan so as to require a sluice-gate on one end of each pendanter only, and also says that he has schemed a method for adjusting the pendanter at its juncture with the canal to within one-hundredth of an inch.

To this Fulton replied in a characteristic letter, again from Stockport, dated May 12th, pointing out the difficulty which would be sure to occur, with seasonal differences, in the level of the upper or of the lower reach of a canal. The most interesting part of the letter is the postscipt, which runs:

P.S.—Has your Lordship heard of a Gent[m] at Mr. Roundtree's factory, Blackfryar's Road, who has constructed an engine acting by the expansion of air, or Inflamible air Created by Spirits of tar. The Ambi-Navigator has just put me in mind of it.

As I leave this on Monday next, Any Communication with which I may be honoured will find me at H. Clarke's Esqr Askham, near York.

The reference in the postscript to "an engine acting by . . . Inflamible air Created by Spirits of Tar," is most probably to the alcohol engine, patented in the following year, of Dr. Edmund Cartwright, D.D., the inventor of the powerloom and an indefatigable experimenter, whose acquaintance Fulton made about this date, possibly in consequence of having gone to look at the engine.

Lord Stanhope, in his reply, dated from Chevening, May 17, 1796, explains how he proposes to allow for possible variations in the canal levels and at the same time how he would guard against possible danger from the acceleration of the moving pendanter. This was to attach to the under-side of each pendanter by a chain, a weight considerably in excess of the difference in weight between two pendanters which would be necessary to enable them to be set in motion. This weight comes to rest on an iron stop a short time before the level is reached at which it is desired to stop the whole system. The pendanter, although still descending, is now lighter than the counterbalancing pendanter, and therefore comes to rest, then slowly rises again until equilibrium is established. The length of the chain and consequently the level at which the system stops are to be regulated by a screw. Lord Stanhope instances an experiment he had made at Chevening House to prove the truth of this scheme.

He followed up this letter quickly by another, dated May 24, 1796, "On board the Ambi-Navigator Ship."[1]

In this he informs Fulton of a method he has just schemed for anti-friction rollers for inclined planes. On

[1] *i.e.* the "Kent," see p. 26.

the ascending plane the carriage supporting the boat is to be on rollers which roll upwards with the boat and then roll back by gravity to a fixed stop. On the descending plane each roller is attached by a cord over a pulley to a weight moving vertically. After being rolled down by the passage of the boat, the weight causes it to roll up again.

He also discusses the application of these to the Bude Canal, and at the end he says, "Your Book abt Canals has set me you see on fire; particularly the Part about America and your note about the enormous expence of Horses. So I hope that at last I shall burn to some purpose; provided you keep on blowing the fire, as you have done." If Fulton replied to this, the letter has not been preserved; but it was fairly obvious that he could expect little from the Bude Canal, for Lord Stanhope would naturally endeavour to have one or more of his own inventions tried to the exclusion of others. As we hear no more of the Bude Canal in connection with Fulton, it may be interesting to note that the canal was actually constructed, but not till after Fulton's death—*i.e.* between the years 1819 and 1826. It is still in existence, but is now partly disused. The canal commences by a tidal dock or basin at Bude Haven, and passes by Marhamchurch to Red Post Inn, where it divides—one branch going to within 1½ miles of Holsworthy, with a "feeder" from Virworthy reservoir, and the other branch going to within a mile of Launceston, following very closely the course of the river Tamar, a total length, including branches, of 34 miles. From Launceston the river is navigable to the Hamoaze and Plymouth Sound, thus giving a route from the Bristol to the English Channel.

The chief point of interest in the canal, from our point of view, is that differences of level are surmounted by inclined planes to the number of seven, and also that a modification of Fulton's endless chain of buckets, described in his letter of May 4th, is made use of. The inclined planes are usually worked by water-wheels, but that at Habbacott Down, 2½ miles from Bude, is unique. This plane is 900 feet in length, with two lines of rails dipping into the canal at each end. The barges are provided with small wheels, and are drawn up or lowered down the plane by an endless chain, to which they can be hooked. At the top of the incline this chain winds and unwinds on a drum which is set in motion by the weight of one of two buckets, 8 feet diameter full of water, descending alternately in wells 225 feet deep. As soon as the full bucket reaches the bottom of the well, it strikes a stop which raises a plug in the bottom and allows the water to run out, an operation taking one minute only. The waste water is delivered by an adit level to the canal below. In case of accident, the plug can be actuated by a chain which winds and unwinds on the same barrel as the buckets so as to be always of the proper length. A steam-engine is also held in reserve in case of emergency. The principal traffic on the canal is in the sand from the haven, which, as also at Padstow, is peculiarly rich in carbonate of lime, and is used as manure on the fields. The amount taken up is 50 to 200 tons a day.

For the next few months practically nothing is known of Fulton's movements, but it is almost certain that he was trying to arouse interest in his "system of creative canals" by means of his book. He sent copies to prominent men, among them being General John F. Mifflin, Governor of Pennsylvania, the letter to whom is printed in the book. On September 12, 1796, Fulton presented a copy "to His Excellency George Washington, President of the United States." In the covering letter[1] he enumerates the advantages of canals, and hopes "that your Excellencie's Sanction will awaken Public Attention to the Subject."

This elicited an acknowledgment on the 14th December

[1] In possession of the Historical Society of Pennsylvania.

1796[1] from George Washington, in which he says: "As the Book came to me in the midst of busy preparatory scenes for Congress, I have not had liesure yet to give it the perusal which the importance such a work would merit."

Nothing, however, was done officially; the State of Pennsylvania continued to adhere to its plan of turnpike roads, probably more generally useful than, although as costly, as small canals would have been.

To come back now to England, we find Fulton writing to Owen on September 19, 1796, regretting his inability to pay any part of the debt he owed, but informing Owen that "his new speculations were beginning to be successful in some tanning improvements, in addition to his canal contracts, which continued to give him prospect of ultimate success." What this improvement in tanning was we have been unable to discover; but the optimistic tone was hardly borne out by actual facts, for a letter addressed to Lord Stanhope a few months later reveals the fact that at this period Fulton was in dire straits—without doubt he was at the very lowest ebb of his fortunes. The letter is a human document of pathetic interest, and reading between the lines we can only gather that Fulton had spent anything but a merry Christmas—in fact, that he was in actual want.

LONDON, *December 28th*, '96

MY LORD,—Your Lordship's Goodwill towards men, and your Public Spirit I See extend itself even to America, for your Lordship appears to have taken in the Idea, that I am about to Sacrifice Public Good to private Gain; And In doing this that I am deviating from my first principles of small and Creative Canals. But as I should be extremely sorry that your Lordship should Receive such an Impression, I must beg Leave to Explain And to Assure your Lordship that I do not deviate from the Creative

[1] Washington papers—Library of Congress.

Canals.—On the Contrary It Shall be one of my Principle exertions to get it Introduced and I hope I shall Live Long enough to Set them In Motion; they will then move onward, Stretch Into distant Regions, And Bending their Branches Round Each hill, Millions of Intelectual Beings Will Glide on their Smooth Surface and Draw Comfort from the System—When Fulton shall be Long, Long Lost to the memory of man.—No, my Lord, that System is sacred, By me it shall not be Violated, nor will I tamely stand by and see it mutilated or frittered away by others. Yet others may Improve it, hence how Applicable your Lordship's Inclined Plane—and of how much Importance in facilitating the Plan. Relative to which plane I hope I shall be Able to make some Contract with your Lordship. Now, My Lord, having I hope Assured you of my Care Over the Creative System—Still there Are some few Situations which I formerly Aluded to Which do not Come within the Creative System; Because there is not Room for Extension, the short Cut for Instance from New York to Phila^d and again from Phila^d to Baltimore —the one About 30 the other 5 miles which will prevent about 500 miles of a coasting voyage: As to the Size of those Canals, that would depend upon circumstances but from what I Recollect of the Country, I think it is flat, with few difficulties. Land is Cheap, Water plenty And Cutting would be the principle Expence; hence those things would be Compared with the Transfer of Cargo. Now my Lord I plainly See that these and a few other Similar points will never be Brought Into the Creative System. I also see that those points will ear long be Laid hold of by some of our enterprizing Americans Who Perhaps would not give the public such good terms As I propose, for In my Calculations I have Charged only one penny halfpenny per ton per Mile—yet I Can make it appear that the Projectors would Receive 4,000 per Annum for the expenditure of 1,000 £ which is 400 per cent; yet the Subscribers would receive 20 per cent:

Now my Lord Am I not Right to endeavour to obtain these advantages which would otherwise fall Into the hands of other Individuals—And on these Just and Lucrative points, And In Contemplating your Lordship's great talents for such Works I Wished a union with your Lordship. My personal emolument is Also a Weighty Consideration; for unless I can acquire a Comfortable Mentainance and am Rather Independent, It will be almost Impossible for me to devote sufficient time to Combatt prejudices And introduce the Creative System. Works of this kind Require much time, Patience and application. And till they are Brought About, Penury frequently Presses hard on the Projector; And this My Lord is so much my Case at this Moment, That I am now Sitting Reduced to half a Crown, Without knowing Where to obtain a shilling for some months. This my Lord is an awkward sensation to a feeling Mind, which would devote every minuet to Increase the Comforts of Mankind, And Who on Looking Round Sees thousands nursed in the Lap of fortune, grown to maturity, And now Spending their time In the endless Maze of Idle dissipation. Thus Circumstanced My Lord, would it be an Intrusion on your goodness and Philanthrophy to Request the Loan of 20 guineas Which I will Return as Soon as possible, And the favour shall ever be greetfully Acknowledged By your lordship's

Most obliged

ROBERT FULTON.

P.S.—On Reading over this Letter I See that much may be gained by obtaining the Situations Aluded to; your Lordship will therefore be so good as to Reconsider the plan.

I have also pondered much on the Liberty of Requesting a favour of your Lordship Which Realy gives me pain but my Lord Men of fortune Can have no Idea of the Cries of necessity—And I must Rely on your Lordship's Goodness.

The age in which this letter was written must be taken into account, and the earlier portion, which we might now term bombastic, was then in the most approved style. Lord Stanhope's usual practice was to make his inventions public property, but Fulton makes it clear that he could not afford to be so generous, but must "acquire a comfortable mentainance" out of any work he undertook. The request for the loan of money is so delicately made that we need not doubt that it was successful. There seems to be some suggestion that he was trying to float a company to undertake operations in the United States. His calculations are quite as optimistic as those of the company promoter of to-day.

This idea of forming incorporated bodies to carry out canal navigations in the several American States seems to have been revolving in Fulton's mind during the next few months, for the scheme is elaborated with further calculations in a letter[1] which he addressed to President Washington, in reply to the latter's acknowledgment of the receipt of his *Treatise on Canal Navigation*. We give it in full:

LONDON, *February 5th*, 1797.

SIR,—Last evening Mr. King presented me with your Letter acquainting me of the Receipt of my publication on Small Canals, which I hope you will soon have time to Peruse in a tranquil retirement from the Buisy operations of a Public Life. Therefore looking forward to that period when the whole force of your Mind will Act upon the Internal improvement of our Country, by Promoting Agriculture and Manufactures: I have little doubt but easy Conveyance, the Great agent to other improvements will have its due weight And meet your patronage.

For the mode of giving easy Communication to every part of the American States, I beg leave to draw your Particular attention to the Last Chapter on Creative Canals; and the expanded mind will trace down the time when

[1] Washington papers—Library of Congress.

they will penetrate into every district Carrying with them the means of facilitating Manual Labour and rendering it productive. But how to Raise a Sum in the different States has been my greatest difficulty. I first Considered them as National Works. But perhaps an Incorporated Company of Subscribers, who should be bound to apply half or a part of their profits to extension would be the best mode. As it would then be their interest to Promote the work: *And guard their emoluments.*

That such a Work would answer to Subscribers appears from such Informations as I have Collected, Reletive to the Carriage from the neighbourhood of Lancaster, to Philadelphia. To me it appears that a Canal on the Small Scale might have been made to Lancaster for 120 thousand £ and that the carriage at 20 shillings per ton would pay 14 thousand per annum of which 7000 to Subscribers and 7000 to extension. By this means in about 10 years they would touch the Susquehanna, and the trad would then so much increase as to produce 30,000 per annum, of which 15,000 to Subscribers, the Remainder to extension; Continuing this till in about 20 years the Canal would run into Lake Erie, Yielding a produce of 100,000 per annum or 50 thousand £ to Subscribers which is 40 per cent.; hence the Inducement to subscribe to such undertakings.

Proceeding in this manner I find that In about 60 or 70 years Pensilvania would have 9360 miles of Canal equal to Bringing Water Carriage within the easy Reach of every house, nor would any house be more than 10 or 14 miles from a Canal. By this time the whole Carriage of the country would Come on Water even to Passengers —and following the present Rate of Carriage on the Lancaster Road, it appears that the tolls would amount to 4,000,000 per year. Yet no one would pay more than 21 shillings and 8d per ton whatever might be the distance Conveyed; the whole would also *be Pond Canal* on which there is an equal facility of conveyance each way. Having made this Calculation to Show that the Creative System, would be productive of Great emolument, to Subscribers, it is only further to be observed that if each State was to Commence a Creative System It would fill the whole Country, and in Less than a Century bring Water Carriage within the easy Cartage of every Acre of the American States,—conveying the Surplus Labours of one hundred Millions of Men.

Hence Seeing that by System this must be the Result, I feel anxious that the Public mind may be awakened to their true Interest: And Instead of directing Turnpike Roads towards the Interior Country or expending Large Sums in River Navigations—Which must ever be precarious and lead [no where] I could wish to See the Labour, and funds applied to Such a System As would penetrate the Interior Country And bind the Whole In the bonds of Social Intercourse.

The Importance of this Subject I hope will plead my excuse for troubeling you with So long a Letter, And in expectation of being Favoured with your thoughts on the System and mode of Carrying it into effect, I remain with the utmost

Esteem and Sincere Respect,
Your most obedient Servant
ROBT. FULTON.

HIS EXCELLENCY GEORGE WASHINGTON.

The idea here thrown out by Fulton of applying profits, in excess of a certain percentage, from a work of public utility, to extending its operations—what we may designate 5 per cent. philanthropy—is decidedly in advance of his time, and is only feebly exemplified so far in municipal undertakings.

The most interesting suggestion contained in the letter is that of constructing a canal between Philadelphia and Lake Erie, and is the first record that we have of such a project. The canal was actually carried out, with some assistance from Fulton himself,[1] and is the well-known Erie Canal. Fulton shows clearly that he realises that improved means of transit are the key to progress and the greatest leveller of international dissensions.

On the day of his first writing to George Washington, he wrote[2] also to his brother-in-law, David Morris, explaining that he had given up painting some time ago on account of his new pursuits: "Seeing the necessity of an Easy Communication with the Marts of trade I have devoted much time in order to Contrive a means of effecting it; which I believe I have Accomplished and having Published a Book on the Subject, I have sent you one by Dr. Edwards. On this publication I will not Remark but hope it will give you some pleasure to peruse it. Also Some Satisfaction to my mother to see that I have made an exertion to Serve my Country by the [book]. In Consequence of this new pursuit in the Canal enterprise, I have laid aside my panels, and have not painted a picture for more than two years—As I have little doubt but Canals will answer my purpose much better and of which you will Judge."

How Fulton managed to exist during the next few months we do not know. Fortunately the negotiations hinted at in his letters to Lord Stanhope and George Washington appear to have borne fruit, for in the April following he wrote the following enthusiastic letter[3] to Owen, announcing a great change in his fortunes:

LONDON, *April 28th*, 1797.

DEAR SIR,—Yesterday Mr. Atheson presented me with your kind letter, and I beg you together with all my old companions, to accept my most sincere thanks for all the

[1] Gallatin, A., *Report of the Secretary of the Treasury*, 1808, *on Communications.*

[2] The letter is in the possession of Mrs. Frank Semple, by whose permission it is made use of.

[3] *Life of Robert Owen*, written by himself, 1857, p. 70.

friendly sentiments and good wishes they entertain in my favour.

It was my intention to write to you about the 18th of next month, at which time I shall have a bill due and I hope to be in possession of cash.

The agreement I have now made, I hope will crown my wishes; having sold one fourth of my canal prospects for £1,500 to a gentleman of large fortune, who is going to reside at New York. Of this £1,500, I shall receive £500 on the 17th of next month, £500 in six months and £500 on my arrival in America which I hope will be about June '98.

Now my friend, this being the state of my money prospects, it becomes necessary that I should deal equal with all my creditors whose patience in waiting the result of my enterprise I shall long remember with the most heartfelt satisfaction in which *Thank Heaven* (some men would say *please the pigs*) I have succeeded.

In the appropriation of the first £500 it is stipulated between my partner and me, that I should go to Paris and obtain patents for the small canal system—this I calculate will cost me about £200. Of the remaining £300, I will send £60 as your portion and pay you the remainder in six months which I hope will answer your purpose. I shall also be happy to pay any loss you may sustain by paying interest.

In about 3 weeks I mean to set out for Paris, and hope to return in time to be with you at Christmas; and about this time next year I expect to sail for America, where I have the most flattering field of invention before me, having already converted the first characters in that country to my small system of canals. My *sensations* in the business are consequently pleasing—and I hope it will please all my friends; to whom remember me kindly. To the Mr. and Mrs. Marsland, Moulston, Clarke, Jolly, and the whole assembly of Worthies remember me good *Owen*. Adieu my friend for this time,

believe me, sincerely yours,

ROBERT FULTON.

The only "canal prospects" that he could possibly have to sell, one would suppose, were shares in his patent for his inclined plane. How anyone "going to reside at New York" could consider that one fourth in this was worth £1,500 passes comprehension. We can only make the suggestion that Fulton had persuaded his client that his invention was one that would be found indispensable everywhere. Now in France, following on the Revolution, the constitution of 15 Jan. 1790, among other things swept away the old division of the country into provinces and brought into the public domain all waterways previously belonging to them; this was followed in 1791 by the confiscation of nearly all the canals in private hands. A period of progress in public works ensued, and as a patent law had been brought into operation in 1791, Fulton may have thought it advisable to reap whatever benefits France might afford before going to the United States, where there were several canal projects afoot and where also a Federal patent law was in operation.

It would be interesting to know who "the gentleman of large fortune" was. If we may hazard a guess, we should say it was Joshua Gilpin [1] of Philadelphia. His father's great scheme was to cut a canal between Chesapeake Bay and Delaware Bay, but he did not live to see its inception. His son took up the scheme with enthusiasm, and in fact devoted his life to its furtherance. As a necessary preliminary, he came to England in 1795 to study the canal system, remaining till 1801. Fulton and he were within a few days of the same age. They were engaged on the same business, and Gilpin's evidence, given in his *Memoir*,[2]

[1] Joshua Gilpin, b. in Philadelphia 8th Nov. 1765; d. there 1840; son of Thomas Gilpin (b. 1728 d. 1778), member of the Society of Friends. While in England he married an English lady.

[2] Gilpin, *Memoir on the Rise and Progress oj the Chesapeake and Delaware Canal*, 1821, p. 49. Acts for the construction of the Chesapeake and Delaware Canal were passed between 1799 and 1801, but it was not till 1803 that sufficient funds were subscribed to make a start; work was suspended in 1805, but the canal was finally completed in 1820.

is conclusive on this point: ". . . having imbibed an interest in this work from the labours of my father, and a local knowledge of the country almost from my infancy I availed myself of seven years' residence in Europe, to obtain correct practical information of works of this kind, by visiting most of the existing canals, and collecting such a mass of documents as is not often done, even by professional men. A large part of my investigations were pursued in concert with the late Col. Tatham and Mr. Fulton, particularly with the last, both in England and on the Continent."

This, however, is only circumstantial evidence. The fact that locks, and not inclined planes, were adopted on the canal in question, might be considered presumptive evidence that Fulton's statement that he had "converted the first characters in that country" to his "small system of canals" could not have referred to Gilpin. We have, however, the decision that the Directors of the canal arrived at quoted in the *Memoir*,[1] and it is to the effect that: "to have adopted plans, however ingenious, were untried, and might have failed in execution, was to subject this great work to a hazard that would have been an unpardonable dereliction of their duty." This surely refers to Fulton's schemes.

Robert Owen had one more letter from Fulton, dated London, May 6th, wherein he enclosed the £60 which he had promised, and said also that he would send the remainder in five months. This, however, he did not do, nor did he even send the money when leaving England for the last time, when he could well have afforded to have done so. Owen, however, took the will for the deed, for he says: "I consider the little aid and assistance which I gave to enable him to bestow so great advantage on his country and the world as money most fortunately expended." A broad-minded and charitable view!!

Towards the latter part of Fulton's stay in London he

[1] *Loc. cit.* p. 32.

made the acquaintance[1] of the celebrated Dr. Edmund Cartwright, M.A., D.D., F.R.S., whom we have already mentioned. He had invented a power loom and the first wool-combing machine. Just at this present moment he was engaged in perfecting a closed cycle alcohol engine. These two men, although in such different walks of life, were kindred spirits in all that related to mechanical invention.

Dr. Cartwright's daughter says: [2]

"Amongst other ingenious characters who frequented Mr. Cartwright's house may be noticed one who was then deeply engaged in pursuits similar to his own, but whose claims to originality of invention have not been very willingly admitted on this side of the Atlantic. This person was Robert Fulton. . . . The coincidence of their respective views produced, instead of rivalship, intimacy and friendship between the two projectors, and Mr. Fulton's vivacity and original way of thinking rendered him a welcome guest at Mr. Cartwright's house. . . . The practicability of steam navigation, with the most feasible mode of effecting it became a frequent subject of discourse."

[1] Cartwright's son, Edmund, subsequently stated (see *Gent. Mag.* 1832, i. 108), that the date was 1799, but this is obviously incorrect.

[2] *A Memoir of Edmund Cartwright*, by M(ary) S(trickland), 1843, p. 132.

CHAPTER V

ARRIVAL IN PARIS—CANAL PATENT—SUBMARINE PROJECTS

FULTON did not get away quite so early, nor perhaps quite so easily as he had anticipated. France, at this moment, having outlived the horrors of the Reign of Terror, was now ruled by the Directory, the most noted members of which were Carnot and Barras. Napoleon Bonaparte had been at the head of the army since 1795, and was just at this time in the midst of his brilliant Italian campaign. France had been at war with England since 1793, and was now facing a coalition of Russia and Austria. In 1797, however, there was a short armistice with England, which afforded the necessary opportunity to cross the Channel.

That Fulton's journey through France was not quite an easy matter may be inferred from a letter which he wrote to Dr. Cartwright, in which he details his experiences *en route*. Writing from Paris in July 1797, he says:[1]—

"After being detained at Calais three weeks, waiting for a passport, I made a circuit of about three hundred miles, and on arriving at Paris, I found the Directory had given a special order for my passport, which was sent to Calais after my departure; thus there is every symptom of my remaining here in peace, although the Americans are by no means well received or suffered to rest in quiet.

"The country through which I travelled is like a continued field, in excellent cultivation, and all the districts of France are said to be in an equally good state; thus plenty

[1] *A Memoir of Edmund Cartwright*, p. 138.

will relieve the burthens of war. *But what do I say of war?* In Paris one would suppose they had never heard of it for all is gay and joyous. As to business I cannot yet say much; but I have reason to believe there will be good encouragement to men of genius, and improvement will be rapid on the termination of the war. Please to let me know the state of your ideas relative to the steamboat . . . ."

We conclude from this that Fulton landed on French soil at the latter end of June or the beginning of July 1797. As usual, he is optimistic as to his prospects.

He was fortunate in securing lodgings in the same hotel at which were staying his fellow countryman, Joel Barlow, statesman, philosopher, and poet, and his wife Ruth Baldwin. Probably Fulton bore letters of introduction to the Barlows, or he may have met them in London, where they had resided from 1790 to 1792. However that may be, it was a most happy circumstance for Fulton, and gave rise to a lifelong friendship. Perhaps the intimacy would be more correctly likened to that of father and son, although Barlow was only eleven and his wife nine years older than Fulton, but the fact that they were childless may explain the way in which they treated him. They even had a nickname—Toot—for him, the origin of which, like that of most nicknames, is obscure. Concerning this period, we cannot do better than quote this eulogy: "Here commenced that strong affection, that devoted attachment, that real friendship, which subsisted in a most extraordinary degree between Mr. Barlow and Mr. Fulton during their lives. Soon after Mr. Fulton's arrival in Paris, Mr. Barlow removed to his own hotel and invited Mr. Fulton to reside with him. Mr. Fulton lived seven years in Mr. Barlow's family, during which he learnt the French and something of the Italian and German languages. He also studied the high mathematics, physics, chemistry and perspective and acquired that science which, when united with his uncommon natural genius, gave him so great a superiority over many of those who with some talents but without any sort of science have pretended to be his rivals."[1]

Or, as another writer,[2] with less accuracy but more vividness, says: "During the seven years that Fulton remained in Paris, a room in the poet's house, and a seat at his fireside were always reserved for him." This house was in the rue de Vaugirard, No. 50.

Fulton at once settled down to the work of getting out his specification and preparing his drawings for the French patent for the canal inclined plane. This appears to have occupied him during the winter which was spent in Paris. We have glimpses of him in his correspondence with Dr. Cartwright by letter,[3] of which we give only the more important parts. Writing on Sept. 20th, 1797, he says:

"I have not had an opportunity of answering your letter of the 20th August until now. I am much pleased with your mode of making houses fireproof [*i.e.* English Patent No. 2194, Oct. 11th, 1797] and should be happy to see it extended to America. . . . On these points that I have mentioned to you, that providing me with descriptions and powers, I shall be happy to do my best for you in America; but if you could sell the invention for a reasonable sum, I should think it advisable. My idea of many of those things which may be considered as only the *overflowings of your mind* is to convert them into cash, and adhere firmly, even without partners, to some of your more important objects, such as the steam engine, boat moving by steam, or cordelier. I have a great objection to partners. I never would have but one if I could help it, and that should be a wife."

Fulton, judging by this and subsequent letters, is still

[1] This is quoted by C. D. Colden in his *Life of Fulton*, p. 26, as "the warm language of one who participated in the sentiments expressed." This can be none other than Mrs. Barlow herself, who was still alive and residing within a short distance of Colden when his book was written

[2] Todd, C. B., *Life and Letters of Joel Barlow*, 1886 p. 177.

[3] *Memoir of Cartwright*, p. 140.

apparently on the eve of proceeding to America. His advice about converting unimportant patents into cash is shrewd enough, and is exactly what every one would like to follow. His determination not to go into partnership was to be broken through on more than one occasion.

The next letter is from Paris, on Nov. 28th:

"I have received yours of the 12th instant and am happy to hear of the success of your steam engine, and other improvements, for the extension of which I will endeavour to make an arrangement when I have the pleasure of seeing you. In this country there are but few engines and the principal are at the collieries near Valenciennes. . ."

On Feb. 16th, 1798, Fulton wrote a long letter[1] from Paris, in which, after mentioning the unlikelihood of his return to England, the pleasure he had had in the society of Cartwright's family, and the circumstance of his being "like a wanderer in life," he says: "It would give me much pleasure to make the produce of your mind productive to you. You will therefore consider what part of your inventions I may be intrusted with. The steam engine, I hope, may be useful in cutting canals and moving boats, so that it will be directly in my line of business. By the by, I have just proved an experiment on moving boats with a fly of four parts similar to that of a smoke jack, thus:

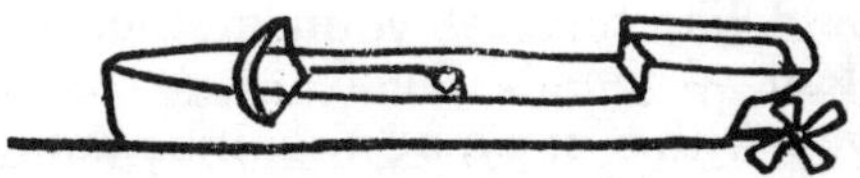

I find this apply the power to great advantage and it is extremely simple. . . . My small canals are making many friends; which business I shall leave under the guidance of a company."

In this letter Fulton mentions also Montgolfier and his hydraulic ram, then just invented.

[1] *Loc. cit.* p. 142.

It is interesting to note that his mind was still casting a thought or two to marine propulsion. The sketch shows that his experiment was exactly that which he had made in 1793, except that he had substituted a screw for the paddle, an alteration that did not advance the solution of the problem in any way.

Eventually, on 14th February 1798, a patent (No 289) for fifteen years was granted to "Sieur Fulton," for "Des nouveaux moyens de construire des canaux navigables."[1] In the printed copy there are sixteen pages of descriptive matter, including numerous tables of expenses showing some considerable knowledge of local possibilities. This matter is elucidated by four engraved plates containing no less than fifty-six figures; on these plates his name appears in full.

In pursuance of his previous practice, Fulton endeavoured to interest persons in high places in his schemes by means of letters. One of such letters[2] is addressed to the great Napoleon himself, just then starting on his expedition to the East, which ended in the occupation of Egypt.

(*Translation.*)

To General Bonaparte.

Citizen General,—Citizen Périer having informed me that you would like to make acquaintance with my work on the System of Small Canals, I take the liberty of presenting you with a copy, and shall be happy if you find therein some means of improving the industries of the French Republic.

To this copy I have added two memoirs which I propose to submit to the Directory. One relates to the absolutely new system of Small Canals, which, if it be adopted, will produce the most considerable part of the

[1] *Descriptions des machines*, 1e Série, vol. iv. p. 207.

[2] Preserved in Lenox Library, N.Y

public revenue. In the other I try to show the favourable results of this system, and at the same time the necessity of an entire liberty of Commerce.

These plans of improvement and my reflections upon Commerce, are elaborations of the following ideas, which I regard as the basis of political welfare, and which seem to me worthy of the consideration of all republicans, and of all friends of humanity. Labour is the source of wealth of all kinds; it follows that the more numerous the industrious and useful class, the more a country should gain in riches and comfort. It is therefore to the interest of each nation to draw from its natural advantages every feature possible. To that end Governments must apply themselves above all to internal improvements and seek continually to increase the number of useful individuals; only by eliminating as far as possible the causes of war will men be enabled to devote themselves to industrious works and reduce mendicancy.

Among all the causes of wars, it is true each day sees disappear that which relates to Kings, Priests, and the things which accompany them. But nevertheless, Republics themselves will not be exempt from melancholy quarrels, inasmuch as they do not separate themselves from the erroneous system of exclusive commerce and distant possessions. Therefore all who love their fellow-men should try and seek to destroy these errors. Ambition itself should not ask for glory further than to show to men the way of truth and to set aside the obstacles which hinder nations from arriving at a lasting peace—for what glory can survive that does not receive the sanction of Philosophy.

To liberate the nations, Citizen General, you have embarked on great enterprises, and the glory you have achieved should be as durable as time. Who then could render a more efficacious approval of the projects which can contribute to the general welfare? It is with this idea that I submit my work to you, hoping that if you find there some useful truths you will grant the support of your powerful influence, and in fact favour projects, the execution of which would render happy millions of men. Could virtuous genius find a more delightful satisfaction! It is from this point of view that internal improvement and freedom of trade become of the highest importance.

If success crowns the efforts of France against England, it will only remain for her to terminate this long war gloriously by granting freedom to trade and by compelling other powers to adopt this system. Political liberty would thus acquire that degree of perfection and of scope of which it is susceptible and Philosophy would see with joy the Olive Branch of Eternal Peace sheltering Science and Industry.

With salutation and respect,

ROBERT FULTON.

PARIS, 12 *Floréal*, *an* VI (1 *May* 1798).

Apart from the rhetorical flourishes which, while sincere enough on Fulton's part, were only the stock modes of expressions of the period, this is quite a remarkable letter. The recognition of the essential or root fact that labour is the ultimate source of all wealth, and that therefore it should be encouraged by unrestricted trade intercourse, stands out in marked contrast to the narrow ideas of the mercantile system of that day. The advice to Governments to turn their attention to "internal improvements" rather than to "distant possessions," is one that might be listened to at the present day, not from any conviction of its truth perhaps, but because nearly all the area available has been seized already and the policy of "opening up new markets" has been found to be but barren.

Fulton, like so many others at this time, looked upon Napoleon as the strong man intent only on his country's welfare. Actually his letter was a waste of paper and ink, for Napoleon had just tasted the intoxication of success in war, and may even then have been meditating the ambitious idea of establishing himself in supreme power. The establishment of a canal system did not go far in the direction of furthering that idea !

But we proceed too fast, for the period had already arrived when Fulton had turned his attention to the subject of exploding gunpowder under water and to the design of a submarine boat to carry these mines to their destination unobserved. Why Fulton left the canal question is not known. Perhaps the arrangement, whereby he was to receive from his partner in November 1797 the second instalment of £500, had fallen through; we can surmise also that he found it, if anything, more difficult to realise his plans in France than he had done in England. Surrounded as he was by wars and rumours of wars, he may have thought that he would be most profitably employed if he turned his attention to engines of war.

It may not be out of place to give a brief summary of what had been done in the direction of submarine warfare prior to Fulton's taking up the subject.

Of course the idea of destroying a vessel by attack below the water line, *i.e.* by ramming, is old and was practised in classical times, while the use of combustible matter or missiles under water is hinted at. The most noteworthy development of the last method took place when Antwerp was besieged in 1584 by the Spanish. Giambelli, an Italian, who had vainly submitted his schemes to Philip II of Spain and in disgust had entered the service of the Dutch, blew up by means of bomb ships with clockwork detonators the bridge that the Duke of Parma had built to close the entrance to the City from the seaward. Had it not been for cowardice of the Dutch admiral the siege would have been raised. After the fall of Antwerp, Giambelli went to England—the parallel with Fulton's career, as will appear later, is curious—and was engaged in fortifying the Thames. When in 1588, the

English fireships came among the Spanish fleet in Calais roads, the fear that they were Giambelli's infernal machines caused such a panic that the fleet stood out to sea; this incident was undoubtedly a factor in the defeat of the Spanish Armada.

Navigation under water is quite a different and much more serious problem. We find the first intelligible description of a submarine boat in William Bourne's *Inuentions or Deuices: Very necessary for all Generalles and Captaines, or Leaders of Men, as wel by Sea as by Land,"* published in 1578. The alteration in displacement of the boat to cause it to sink or rise was to be effected by admitting water into, or forcing it out of, side compartments, is by means of screws working a form of bellows—a method hardly practicable.

It would weary the reader to refer to all subsequent schemes for submarine navigation, but we may mention one that seems to have been put to a practical test. It was that of Cornelius van Drebbel, an ingenious Dutchman, who is credited with having in 1624 "built a ship which one could row and navigate under water from Westminster to Greenwich . . .; even five or six miles or as far as one pleased."[1] Unfortunately only the vaguest descriptions and no plans of this vessel have been preserved.

We now come to the work of a man who achieved the first real practical results. This was David Bushnell (b. 1742, d. 1824) of Saybrook, Conn., who as early as 1771 conceived the idea of a submarine boat which should carry with it the explosive compound or magazine intended for the destruction of an enemy's vessel. No doubt he was led to think about warlike engines owing to the War of Independence, which was being waged at that time. He submitted his invention to the Governor and Council of the state of Maine, who in 1776 advanced £60 to help him to further his enterprise. He built a

[1] Boyle, *New Experiments Physico-Mechanical*, 1660, p. 578.

boat of wood shaped like a turtle, which "was provided with an oar placed near the top of the vessel and formed like a screw." It was steered by a rudder, behind which was a magazine to contain a powder case. There was a hatch on the top and just sufficient room for a man to stand upright. The vessel, owing to its shape, had practically no manœuvring power, and was really intended to drift just awash with the tide to the enemy's ship, and there the occupant was to attach the explosive. An unsuccessful attack was made on H.M.S. *Eagle*, 64 guns, when lying at anchor in the river Hudson at New York. In 1777, an attack on H.M.S. *Cerberus*, at anchor at New London in the Connecticut River resulted in the blowing up of a schooner astern of her with the loss of several men. Bushnell subsequently went to France and carried on experiments there, but with little more success.

Fulton's scheme, as will be seen shortly, somewhat resembled Bushnell's. This resemblance would be explained if the former had been acquainted with what the latter had done, which is probable because a description of the invention had been published in 1795.

Fulton's work in France on the submarine and torpedo boat has only recently been disentangled from his subsequent experiments in steam navigation, and exhibited in their true light through the researches of French investigators in the National Archives at Paris. The documents concerning Fulton were brought to light in 1896 by the exertions of Lieut. Emile Duboc. Since then they have been studied closely by others.[1]

It is now found that Fulton had already in 1797 conceived the idea of a submarine boat, and had so far matured his plans that he was able to submit definite

[1] We acknowledge our indebtedness to the valuable treatise by G. L. Pesce, *La Navigation Sous Marine*, 1906, p. 165 *et seq.* (2nd edition, 1912), and the almost equally valuable work by the late Lieut. Delpeuch, *Les Sous-Marines à travers les siècles*, 1908, p. 74 *et seq.*

propositions to the French Directory on 22 Frimaire an VI (13 Dec. 1797).

These propositions he sent to one of the Directors, La Réveillère Lépeaux, with a covering letter dated 2 days later, in which he says he is willing to explain his engine to a technical man such as General Bonaparte, whom he has been told is "a good engineer." As these propositions formed the basis of all the subsequent negotiations with the Directory, and the Government which succeeded it, we give them in full:

TO THE EXECUTIVE DIRECTORY.

PARIS, *22d Frimeire, 6th Year of the Republic.*

CITIZEN DIRECTORS,

Considering the great importance of deminishing the Power of the British Fleets, I have Contemplated the Construction of a Mechanical Nautulus. A Machine which flatters me with much hope of being Able to Annihilate their Navy; hence feeling confident that practice will Bring the apperatus to perfection; The Magnitude of the object has excited in me an Ardent desire to Prove the expirement; For this Purpose, and Avoid troubeling you with the Investigation of a new Project, or the expence of Carrying it into effect; I have Arranged a Company who are willing to bear the Expence, and undertake the Expedition on the following Conditions

First

That the Government of France Contract to pay the Nautulus Company 400 Livers per Gun for each British Ships over 40 Guns which they may destroy; and 2000 Livers per Gun for All vessels of war under 40 tons which they destroy, that the sum be paid in Specie within six months after the distruction of Each Vessel.

Archives Nationales, Dossier Marine D[1] 21, fol. 07.

Second

That all prizes of British Vessels and Cargoes taken by the Nautulus Company; shall be the Property of the Company; nor meet with any Interruption from the Agents of Government further than to Ascertain that they are British Property—

Third

That the Government Give to the Nautulus Company the exclusive Right to Use this Invention from all the Ports of France: Except when it is the desire of Government to Construct Such Vessels to Act against the Enemies of the Republic. In Such Case the Government, to be at Liberty to Build and Multiply the Mechanical Nautulus, on paying to the Company One hundred thousand Livers for Each Nautulus which they may Construct or use in the Service of the Republic.

Fourth

As a Citizen of the American States; I hope it may be Stipulated that this Invention, or Any Similar Invention, shall not be used by the Government of France Against the American States, Unless the Government of America First apply the Invention Against France.

Fifth

That if Peace is Concluded with England within three Months from the date hereof Government will pay to the Nautulus Company the Amount of the expences which they may have Incured In the experiments, Such payment to be made within three Months after the declaration of Peace.

Sixth

And whereas fire Ships or other unusual means of destroying Navies are Considered Contrary to the Laws of war, And persons taken in Such enterprise are Liable to Suffer death, it will be an object of Safety if the Directory give the Nautulus Company Commissions Specifying that all persons taken in the *Nautulus or Submarine expedition*

Shall be treated as Prisiners of War, And in Case of Violence being offered; the Government, will Retaliate on the British Prisiners in a four fold degree.

Citizens hoping that this engine will tend to Give Liberty to the seas; it is of Importance that the experiment Should be proved as soon as Possible in order that if Successful the terror of it may spread before the descent on England, and that it may be brought Into use to facilitate that descent.

Submitting these proposals to Your deliberations and waiting your Command, I remain with all possible Respect your most Obedient

ROBERT FULTON.

NO. 556 RUE DU BACQ.

It will be noticed that no hint is given in the letter as to the construction of the *Nautilus,* and as the scheme must have appeared to men of that time quite visionary, the fact that the communication was considered at all, leads to the supposition that some influence had been brought to bear upon the Directory possibly by members of the "Company" which Fulton had formed.

The propositions were transmitted on the 11th Nivôse (31 Dec. 1797) to the Minister of Marine[1] who appears to have entertained them favourably, for on the 18th Nivôse he handed his report to the Directory and on the 24th gave his reply to Fulton himself. This was to the effect that the inventor's propositions were accepted in general, with the following amendments to the clauses enumerated;—

(1) The sums proposed as prize money for the destruction of the enemy's ships, being too great, were to be halved.

[1] The Minister at this moment, Georges René Pléville-le-Pelley, was quite one of the old school—He was born at Granville 26th June 1726, commenced his career in the merchant marine, where he saw much service and in 1744 had a leg shot away. This did not prevent his entering the naval service. In 1788 he was with d'Estaing in the North American campaign and was made captain. Rear-Admiral in 1797, he was envoy plenipotentiary to the congress of Lille. In the following year he was Minister of Marine, then Vice-Admiral, Senator, and grand officer of the Legion of Honour. Died 1805.

(3) The construction of as large a number of *Nautili* as deemed necessary was authorised, the place of construction, however, to be far removed from all the war ports.

(5) The reimbursement of the expenses of the Company that was asked for in case of conclusion of peace was refused unless due to fear inspired by the construction of the *Nautilus*.

(6) Finally, the Minister absolutely refused Fulton's request for commissions in the French Navy, because he did not think that it was "possible to grant commissions to men who made use of such means to destroy the enemy's forces and, even so, that such commissions could be any guarantee to them. For the reprisals with which the French Government could threaten the English Cabinet would be useless, since there existed in England three times more French prisoners than English prisoners in France."

It would have been surprising had an old salt like Pléville-le-Pelley shown anything but the repugnance which existed universally at that time, to the employment of what were considered such unfair methods of warfare. His dictum was that the agents must be considered outside the pale of civilisation and as no better than pirates. History has often repeated itself, and just such prejudice met the introduction of the crossbow and again of the harquebus. Nowadays it is different: the dirigible balloon and the aeroplane had been modified to act as destructive engines of war before an opportunity had arisen where they could be so employed in actual warfare.

Fulton's reply[1] to the communication of the Minister was an acceptance of the amendments made by the Directory with the exception of that to clause 5, which he stipulated should read that the total sum to be reimbursed to the Company on the conclusion of peace should be a sum not exceeding 25,000 francs, the reason given being

[1] Archives Nationales, Dossier Marine D[1] 21, fol. 23.

that the construction and trial of the *Nautilus* would take three months. Fulton also held to his original demand for commissions for the crew. He proposed to construct his submarine at Paris and test it at Havre.

These revised conditions, with minor additions as to terms of payment, he embodied in his "Third proposals relative to the mechanical Nautulus," which he forwarded to the Minister on the 1st Pluviôse an VI (20 Jan. 1798).

A draft decree was drawn up and submitted by the Minister to the Directory; but it was never issued, for, on the 27th Pluviôse (5 Feb.) Fulton received from the Minister a letter[1] telling him that all his proposals were rejected.

Judging from a marginal note by the Minister on the report, there is no doubt that it was the question of their recognition as belligerents that proved the stumbling block.

Fulton, however, was not to be discouraged by this check, but took advantage of a change of ministers a few months later to urge once more his invention upon the Directory, this time with rather more success.

[1] Delpeuch, *loc. cit.* p. 78.

CHAPTER VI

SECOND ATTEMPT TO INTRODUCE THE SUBMARINE—REPORT OF A COMMISSION THEREON—PAINTS PANORAMAS FOR A LIVING—CONSTRUCTS AND OPERATES THE SUBMARINE

WE must now follow rapidly the vicissitudes of Fulton's second attempt to influence the French Government to adopt his proposals for making a submarine boat. A new Minister of Marine and of the Colonies had been appointed on April 28, 1798, in the person of Eustace Bruix,[1] a man then only in his fortieth year, and therefore not so hide-bound as his predecessor by traditions of the service.

On the 5th Thermidor, an VI (July 23, 1798), Fulton renewed the encounter by submitting to Bruix his propositions.[2] In the covering letter, he states that the project has been examined and approved by citizens Monge, Dufalga, Montgolfier, Pérrier, and other distinguished savants, and, after offering once more to make the experiments at his own expense, he ends by saying:

"The destruction of the English Navy will ensure the independence of the seas and France, the Nation which

[1] Eustace, Comte de Bruix (b. 1759, d. 1805), entered the French Navy in 1778 as a volunteer and took part in several battles in the American War. Under the Revolution he took part in the engagement of 13 Prairial, as chief of the staff of the fleet. He was appointed Minister of Marine, April 28, 1798, and Vice-Admiral the following year, when he performed a series of voyages in the Atlantic and Mediterranean, although pursued by several English squadrons. In 1801 Napoleon appointed him Admiral; then in 1803 gave him the command of the Boulogne flotilla. Unfortunately the activity he displayed in organising this enterprise and his excesses hastened his death.

[2] Archives Nationales, Dossier Marine D^1 21, fol. 44. This is the first letter written in French from Fulton to the Government; only the signature and date are in his own writing, however.

has most natural resources and population, will alone and without a rival hold the balance of power in Europe."

Bruix, "relying on the opinion of enlightened citizens," *i.e.* those cited above, transmits these propositions once more to the Directory. Apparently the result was favourable, for, a week later, the minister appointed a commission of experts to examine Fulton's project, and at the same time he convened a meeting of them to take place on the 15th Thermidor (August 2), at Fulton's residence. One of these letters of appointment has been preserved;[1] it bears a curious device symbolising the liberty of the seas, with the words "Liberty," "Equality," on either side of it.

(*Translation.*)

PARIS, 13*th Thermidor, Year VI. of the Republic One and Indivisible.*

EUSTACE BRUIX,
Vice-Admiral to Citizen Adet,
810 RUE DU REGARD, PARIS.

CITIZEN,—Citizen Robert Fulton having invented a machine for the destruction of the enemy's marine forces, you are informed that I have appointed you one of the Commissioners for examining the same. I invite you in consequence to the residence of Citizen Fulton, No. 515 Rue du Bacq, on the 15th of this month at 11 A.M.

The other Commissioners will also attend, and you will come to an agreement with them as to the report which you will make to me relative to Citizen Fulton's machine.

(Signed) E. BRUIX,
Minister of Marine and of the Colonies.

TO CITIZEN ADET,
810 RUE DU REGARD,
PARIS.

[1] In the MS. collection of Mr. A. M. Broadley, to whom I am indebted for permission to use it. See F. B. Wheeler and A. M. Broadley, *Napoleon and the Invasion of England: The Story of the Great Terror*, i. 302.

The experts were Rosily,[1] president of the Commission, for navigation and seaworthiness; Adet[2] for the chemical questions involved; Périer[3] for practical mechanics; Prony[4] for hydrostatics; and Forfait[5] for naval architecture. The names of citizens Gautier,[6] Cachin,[7] and Burgues-

[1] Comte de Rosily-Mesros (b. about 1750, d. 1833) entered the Navy in 1771, made a voyage round the world with Kerguelen, was abandoned on the island named after that Admiral and nearly perished. He took part in the famous encounter between the frigates *Arethusa* and *La Belle Poule.* He was promoted Rear-Admiral in 1793, and Vice-Admiral in 1796. In 1805 he was sent by Napoleon to relieve Villeneuve of his command of the Mediterranean fleet, the news of which precipitated the latter to his destruction at Trafalgar. After three years' blockade in Cadiz Roads, the remains of the fleet fell into the hands of the Spaniards, and Rosily returned to Paris, where he founded the corps of hydrographical engineers. Grand Cross of Legion of Honour, member of the Academy of Sciences, of the Bureau of Longitude and of other societies.

[2] Adet (b. 1763, d. about 1822), distinguished chemist, author of *Traité de leçons élémentaires sur la chemie,* but all his life an ardent politician.

[3] There were two brothers—A. C. Périer and J. C. Périer—both celebrated mechanicians; probably the elder of the two (b. 1742, d. 1818) is meant. They launched a company in 1778 for supplying Paris with water by means of Watt's pumping engine. During the Revolution, they were nearly ruined with making warlike material for which they did not get payment. They confined themselves subsequently to supplying machinery for works and manufactories.

[4] C. C. F. M. R., baron de Prony (b. 1755, d. 1839), engineer and mathematician. He entered the Corps des Ponts et Chaussées and had charge of the construction of the Pont de la Concorde, which was finished in 1790. For this he was promoted to the rank of engineer-in-chief. He was then set to revise the trigonometrical tables, to adapt them to the new decimal notation. In 1798 he was appointed director of the Ecole des Ponts et Chaussées. Napoleon, who had a very high opinion of Prony, sent him several times on missions into Italy. Under the Restoration he accomplished the embankment of the Rhône, labours which brought him the title of baron.

[5] P. A. L. Forfait (b. 1752, d. 1807), naval architect, educated under d'Estaing. He designed a type of transatlantic pacquet remarkable for its speed and the burden which nevertheless it could carry. By his advice Antwerp was made into a maritime port. By going from Havre to Paris in sixteen days in a lighter furnished with dipping masts, he proved the possibility of ascending the Seine. He was Minister of Marine from 24th Nov. 1799 to 1st Oct. 1801. He was then appointed Councillor of State, Inspector-General of the flotilla of Boulogne, Commander of the Legion of Honour, Maritime Prefect of Havre, and then of Genoa. Died embittered by the degradation which he considered he had undergone.

[6] G. M. B. Gautier du Var (b. 1769, d. 1824), deputy of department of Var at the council of 600 in 1798. Political writer.

[7] Cachin (b. 1757, d. 1825), civil engineer. He specialised in canal and harbour engineering. To him is due the harbour of Cherbourg, the inner portion of which was inaugurated in 1803.

Missiessy[1] appear also at the foot of the report; they must have been appointed subsequently. It would have been difficult to have nominated men better qualified in their respective spheres to undertake such a task.

The report[2] of the Commission, which is dated 19 Fructidor (5 Sept. 1798), exhibits in consequence, as might be expected, remarkable thoroughness and is instructive even at the present day, because it illustrates so well the growth of an invention; space, however, precludes us from giving it in full.[3] The first part of the report is occupied with a description of Fulton's plans for the construction of his *Nautilus*, which, it will be seen, was of the type which takes in water ballast until the weight of the volume of water displaced equals that of the boat—a type which is most difficult to keep in adjustment and which can give only an erratic depth line. With the report there is a drawing which is here reproduced as a help to the reader.

The Hull was to be of the shape of an imperfect ellipsoid 6.48 m. (21.25 ft.) long and 1.94 m. (6.43 ft.) diameter. Below this hull there was to be another hull of metal 0.52 m. (1.7 ft.) deep, terminating 1 m. (3.28 ft.) from the bow with the curve of which it was to "fair." The sides of this hull were to be similarly "faired" to the sides of the ellipsoid while the after end, fashioned like the stern of an ordinary vessel, was to terminate 0.75 m. (2.46 ft.) from the end of the ellipsoid. The middle of the hull was to

[1] Eduard, Comte de Burgues-Missiessy or Missiessy-Quiès (b. 1756, d. 1837). Entered the Navy at the age of ten. Later he distinguished himself during the American War. He developed a code of signals, and also did work on the stowage of ships, afterwards published. In 1805, with a squadron of five ships, he did great damage to English commerce in the Atlantic. In 1802 he was appointed to command the fleet of the Scheldt, and was made Vice-Admiral. He was commander-in-chief of the port of Antwerp, and repulsed the attack of the Walcheren expedition in 1808. Maritime Prefect of Toulon in 1815. Grand Cross of the Legion of Honour and of the Order of Saint Louis.

[2] Archives Nationales, Dossier Marine D^1 21, fol. 48–58.

[3] It is to be found in full in Pesce, p. 124.

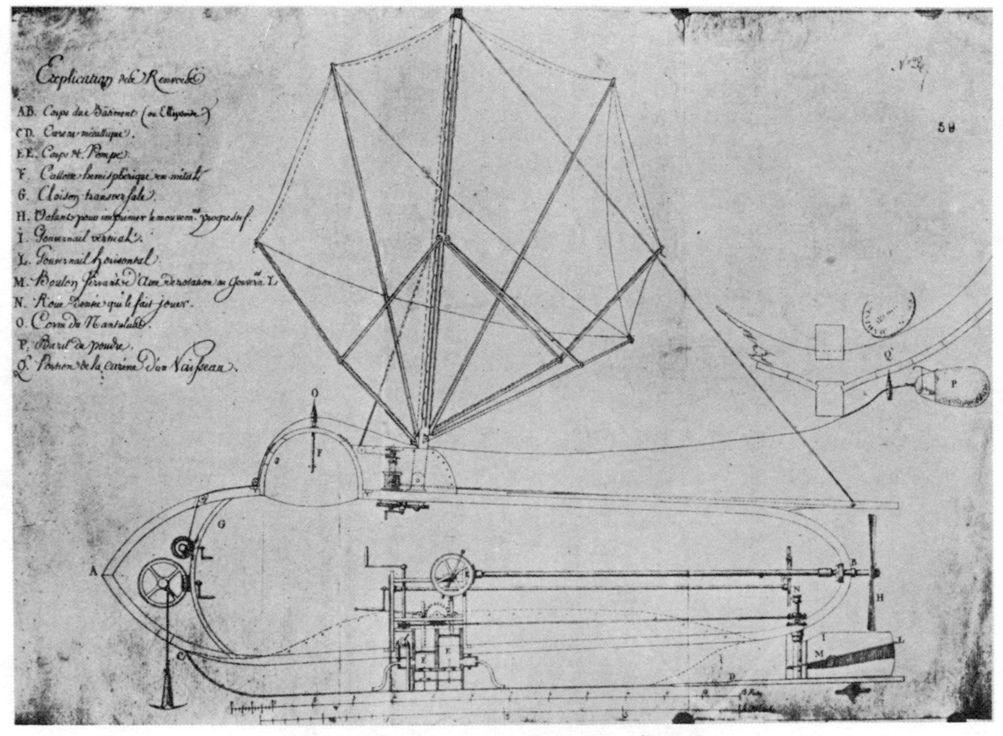

FULTON'S SUBMARINE "NAUTILUS," 1798

have a flat floor. The object of this hull, which was also to serve as a keel, was to accommodate such a quantity of water ballast as would make the difference between the weight of the whole submarine boat and the weight of the water displaced by it not more than 4 to 5 kilos., so that the introduction of this small quantity of water would be all that was necessary to make the submarine sink or rise to the surface. This was to be accomplished by a suction and force pump worked by lever, pinion, and racks, very much like the air pumps of the period. In the words of the report:

"Citizen Fulton, who had in view particularly the object of imitating the mechanism by which fish make their movements in the water, has, by means of the pump just referred to, taken the place of the swim bladder which by its spontaneous dilations and contractions increases or diminishes the volume of the fish and makes it approach the surface or sink to the bottom of the water, at will."

At the bow of the ellipsoid, on the upper surface, there was to be a metallic dome or conning tower pierced with sidelights of thick glass and furnished with a manhole serving as an ingress for the crew and stores.

At about 1 m. (3.28 ft.) from the bow of the ellipsoid, a water-tight bulkhead cut off a compartment which enclosed the anchor gear and a small winch the use of which will be explained later. Both were worked by shafts passing through stuffing boxes in the bulkhead. The anchor was of the stockless type, the shank being drawn up the hawse-hole leaving the flukes resting against the hull.

Propulsion—which, after all, was the most important point—was to be effected by means of a screw, called by Fulton a fly, actuated by cranks and gearing. The diameter was to be 1.34 m. (4.4 ft.), and there were to be four wings about $\frac{2}{3}$ m. (2.2 ft.) wide. He hoped to obtain when at full speed 240 revolutions, and at ordinary times 120 revolutions, of the screw.

The rudder was to be of the usual unbalanced type projecting 1 m. (3.28 ft.) from the stern and 0.50 m. (1.64 ft.) deep. It was to be worked by a sprocket chain from a crank in the centre of the boat, where the commander of the vessel stood. A second horizontal rudder, intended to maintain the vessel at a predetermined immersion, was hinged on a pin on the vertical rudder and at right angles to it so that it could turn through an angle of 30 deg. half above and half below the horizontal line. It was to be actuated by a pinion working a sleeve on the vertical rudder spindle on which was a collar. The latter came against a hook or stop on the extremity of the horizontal rudder.

For propulsion when at the surface, and instead of using the screw, a hinged mast was to be arranged at a point about one-third of the vessel's length from the bow. To this mast was to be bent a sail like a fan, furled by sheets on the ribs. After furling the sail, the mast was to be lowered against the hull and two envelopes shaped like the sheath wings of a fly were to close over it. Three men were to suffice for working the *Nautilus*, and with a lighted lamp were expected to be able to stay for three hours under water.

The attacking apparatus of the *Nautilus* was to consist of a submarine mine or torpedo,[1] which was merely a copper barrel intended to hold a quintal (100 lbs.) of gunpowder and furnished in front with a gun-lock the trigger of which was to be pulled off by a lanyard. To get this into position and fire it the following apparatus was schemed. Through the conning tower of the *Nautilus*, by means of a stuffing box, passed a shaft. The outer end of this terminated in a screw eye, called by Fulton "the horn

[1] Fulton himself adopted this word for his apparatus, although it was not a torpedo in the modern sense of the word. The analogy of course was with the torpaedo or cramp fish, whose peculiar mode of attack was known at an early period; *cf.* Sir Thomas Herbert's *Travels* (ed. 1638), p. 349, where he describes it as "evaporating a cold breath to stupefie such as either touch or hold a thing that touches it."

of the Nautilus." Through the eye passed the tow rope attached to the torpedo from a small winch inside. The *Nautilus* was to be navigated till under the keel of the ship which it was intended to blow up and the horn was to be embedded in the planking by a few blows on the end of the shaft so that it could then be screwed firmly into the wood. The *Nautilus* was then to set off, leaving the horn behind, till the tow rope brought the torpedo into contact with the ship's bottom. In the words of the report "la poudre fait une explosion terrible qui, ne pouvant agir sur l'eau à cause de son incompressibilité exerce tout son effet contre les flancs du vaisseau et le brise." It must be remembered that it was not generally known at this time and indeed till many years later that an explosive would act under water in this way. The Commission did not consider that this apparatus would act satisfactorily, and were of opinion that experiments were necessary to determine the point.

The cubic content of the boat was calculated at 10.37 cub. m. (366 cub. ft.). Allowing one-third of this space for the accommodation of men and stores, the remaining 6.92 cub. m. would suffice, according to Lavoisier's experiments that a man consumes $2\frac{5}{7}$ cub. m. of air per hour, for 3 men for $12\frac{1}{2}$ hours. But to allow for the necessary lamp-light and the fact that the carbon dioxide from combustion and the men's lungs would render the air irrespirable long before this point had been reached—the Commission put it down at 6 hours. It will be seen later that Fulton and his assistants only remained 3 hours under water.

With regard to the equilibrium of the boat, the Commission remarked that it would not do that the conning tower should come flush with the water merely, in order to renew the air by opening the side lights; but that it would be necessary for the conning tower to emerge 3 or 4 decimetres. It would then be necessary to deal with 500 kilos of water instead of the 4 or 5 spoken of by the inventor. Fulton proposed a pipe to the other extremity of the hull in order to establish a current of air.

Fulton showed to the Commissioners in action, a model of the boat in which the screw was worked by a spring, but they were of opinion that there was no comparison between it and an actual boat, because the spring was in proportion at least three times the strength of three men working cranks. We shall see later that the Commissioners were right. In his means of propulsion Fulton was following Bushnell, who had employed a single threaded screw of one complete turn. Fulton's propeller, however, was a short portion only of a quadruple threaded screw. It is worthy of remark that when, half a century later, the screw was applied to steam navigation, exactly the same evolution was gone through. Had Fulton's work been made known, a considerable amount of experimenting might have been dispensed with.

After approving of the ordinary rudder, they were of opinion that the horizontal one for controlling the rise and descent of the *Nautilus* would not be effectual. Fulton at once proposed a second screw[1] under the keel. This was approved, as it was considered that it would give a means of more effectually controlling the vertical speed.

The Commission approved the anchor gear, but criticised the sail arrangement on the ground that the largest surface was at the upper part, and would therefore diminish the boat's stability.

They remarked that the force with which a floating body tends to resist inclination is proportional to the cube of the ordinates of the plane of flotation. Here the plane of rotation is zero, because the difference between the weight of the entire system and that of the volume of water which it would displace is only 4 to 5 kilos. Therefore, theoretically, the breath of a child would suffice to capsize the boat. Either the sails must be omitted or the *Nautilus*

[1] The idea was borrowed from Bushnell, and we find it cropping up again regularly in more recent times, *e.g.* in the boats of Tuck, 1884, of Nordenfelt, 1885, of Baker, 1892, of Holland, 1892, and of Pullico, 1896.

must have greater emersion, which means dealing with a larger quantity of water.

Further difficulties were suggested, *e.g.* the enemy might furnish their vessels with nets[1] wherewith to fish for the torpedoes. The *Nautilus* might be surprised, and it would take the crew some time to furl the sail and plunge. There would be a difficulty in knowing the distance run under water and the depth below the surface. For the latter contingency, Fulton proposed a barometer, but the Commissioners show that it was not practicable.

The report terminates thus:

(*Translation.*)

"The arm conceived by citizen Fulton is a terrible means of destruction, because it acts in silence and in a manner almost inevitable. It is particularly suitable to the French, because, having a weaker navy (we should say necessarily) than their adversary, the entire destruction of both navies is of advantage to them.

"This arm is without doubt imperfect; it is the first conception of a man of genius. It would be very imprudent to risk coming out of the workshop and crossing the high seas to attack the English ships in their harbours. The inventor, who undertakes to command the boat himself and find the necessary crew, should practise with them, so that he may acquire confidence by experience, perfect his steering, and make experiments to find out the best means of piercing or blowing up sides of vessels; this is certainly not the affair of a day. A convenient spot where there is at least a depth of water of 5 metres is necessary, since the machine is 3 metres deep. There should be still water and also currents, so as to learn to make headway against them and to calculate the leeway. Workshops suitable for the preparation of the necessary apparatus secretly are wanted. . . .

[1] This is not quite the same idea as modern torpedo netting, which is protective merely, but the germ of that invention is here.

"The Commission invites the Minister of Marine and of the Colonies to authorise citizen Fulton to make the machine, the model of which he has produced, and grant him the necessary means. It cannot be doubted that, with the same brains that have been put into its conception, the elegance and solidity of the different mechanisms comprised in it, he who has executed the model would be able to construct the full-sized machine in a manner equally ingenious."

Now at last, one would have thought that Fulton's end was gained; but the difficulties in his path were far from being removed. On the 27 Vendémiaire, an VII (18th October 1798) he sent the Minister, on behalf of the Company, an amended scheme which, however, differed only from the first proposal in two of the articles. Article 2 was amended to read:

"Since the taking or destruction of the first English war vessel will justify the experiments and will prove the importance of the invention, I stipulate that, as soon as the government shall have received certain intelligence of the taking or destruction of the first English war vessel by means of the Nautulus, immediately there shall be paid to me or my order five hundred thousand francs in French money, with which sum I engage to build a fleet of Nautuli in order to put into execution my plan against the English fleet."

Article 4 read:

"That the government engage to pay to me, my heirs and assigns the sum of a hundred francs in cash for each pound of calibre of the guns of the English vessels destroyed during the war by the Nautulus or put out of commission. That is to say, for a gun of 5 lb. weight of shot there shall be delivered to me five hundred francs; for a gun of 10 lb. weight of shot a thousand francs, and so on. The cash shall be paid to me immediately on the receipt of certain intelligence."

The business, however, hung fire, and, as a last resource,

Fulton appealed to one of the Directors, the notorious P. J. N. F. Barras, in the following letter,[1] dated 27th October 1798:

ROBERT FULTON AU CITOYEN DIRECTEUR BARRAS.

CITOYEN DIRECTEUR,—D'apres le repport des commissaires nommés par le ministre de la marine il parait que la Machine et les moyens que j'ai proposés pour détruire la flotte Angloise sont prononcés praticables, permettez-moi donc de rappeller à votre consideration les consequences [qui] doivent résulter du succes de cette entreprise. Le commerce énorme de l'Angleterre, ainsi que son Gouvernement monstreux, dépend de sa marine militaire. Quelques vaisseaux de guerre détruits par des moyens si nouveaux, si cachés et si incalculables, la confiance des matelots est anéantie et la flotte rendue nulle de l'époque de la première frayeur. Dans cet état des choses les républicains en Angleterre se leveront, pour faciliter la descente des français, ou pour changer eux-mêmes leur governement, sans verser beaucoup de sang, et sans aucunes depenses pour la France. L'Angleterre républicanisée les mers seront libres; la liberté des meres devendra le garant d'une paix perpetuelle à toutes les nations maritimes; d'une telle paix la France gagnera plus que toute autre nation à cause de sa grande population et de l'immensite de ses ressources. Ce ne sera qu'alors que le génie humain sentira géneralement le prix des principes pour lesquels les français se sont montrés si prodigues de leur sang dans tous leurs miracles de bravoure.

Si, au premier coup d'œuil, les moyens que je propose paraissent revoltons, ce n'est que parce qu'ils sont extraordinaires, ils ne sont riens moins qu'inhumains, certainement c'est la manière la plus douce et le moins sanguinaire que le philosophe puisse imaginer pour renverser ce

[1] British Museum, Add. MSS. 36747. It is the only Fulton document preserved there, and we have thought, therefore, that it was worth while to give the original text.

systeme de brigandage et de guerre perpetuelle qui a toujours vexé les nations maritimes;—pour donner enfin la paix à la terre et pour rendre les hommes à leur industrie naturelle, et à un bonheur jusqu'ici inconnu.

Salut et Respect.

ROBT FULTON.

6 *Brumaire, An* 7.

(*Translation.*)

CITIZEN DIRECTOR,—From the report of the Commissioners named by the Minister of Marine it would appear that the machine and the means which I have proposed to destroy the English fleet are pronounced to be practicable. Permit me then to recall to your consideration the consequences which should result from the success of this enterprise. The enormous commerce of England, no less than its monstrous government, depends upon its military marine. Should some vessels of war be destroyed by means so novel, so hidden and so incalculable the confidence of the seamen will vanish and the fleet rendered useless from the moment of the first terror. In this state of affairs the Republicans in England would rise to facilitate the descent of the French or to change their government themselves without shedding much blood and without any expense to France. With England republicanized, the seas will be free. The liberty of the seas will become a guarantee of perpetual peace to all maritime nations.

By such a peace France will gain more than any other nation because of her large population and of the immensity of her resources. Only then will humanity perceive how priceless are the principles for which the French have shown themselves so lavish of their blood, in all their miracles of bravery.

If, at first glance, the means that I propose seem revolting, it is only because they are extraordinary; they are anything but inhuman. It is certainly the gentlest and the least bloody method that the philosopher can imagine to overturn this system of brigandage and of perpetual war which has always vexed maritime nations: To give at last peace to the earth, and to restore men to their natural industries, and to a happiness until now unknown."

This is a holograph letter, but it is not certain whether it was Fulton's own composition or whether he was helped in it by Barlow or some other friend; if the former it bears out the statement[1] that he studied the language assiduously. In his earlier negotiations with the Government, he wrote in English, then he signed letters written by another person in French; finally, he wrote entirely in the latter language.

This letter to Barras was of course meant to be propitiatory, but really Fulton must have known that his statements about republicanizing England were altogether wide of the mark. The general feeling here with regard to the French Revolution was one of horror and a dread lest similar excesses should take place. The vast results for good that were to flow from this social upheaval had not yet begun to show themselves. However that may be, the appeal was quite a failure, and nothing whatever was done to carry out the recommendations of the Commission. The cup was dashed from Fulton's lips apparently in the very hour of victory.

Fulton communicated a knowledge of his doings to his friends in England. Joshua Gilpin, writing on August 28, 1798, from London, to Lord Stanhope, says:[2]

"I hear from France that Mr. Fulton has not yet gone to America; and probably it may be some time before he gets away, as an embargo rests on our vessels; besides which the Government and he are amusing each other (I think, however, to little purpose) on his new invention of the submarine boat. I fear this will keep him from more useful pursuits."

[1] See p. 65.

[2] *Century Magazine*, vol. lxxvi. p. 935.

Fulton refers to it again in a letter[1] written to Mr Gilpin from Paris, November 20, 1798—evidently a reply to friendly criticism:

"I thank you for. . . Mr. Chapman's observations on my system of small canals[2] which observations will tend to bring the subject to discussion and Render its importance understood. . . But for the pleasure of Seeing my Canal system stand in its true Light I look to America, and to America I look for the perfecting of all my plans.

. . . .

The plan of my *Nautilus* you say is not liked, this must be because its consequences are not understood. The Idea is yet an Infant, but I think I see in it all the nerve and muscle of an Infant hercules which at one grasp will Strangle the Serpents which poison and Convulse the American Constitution.

Every man who has the least pretension to expanded Reflection and a Knowledge of the interest of nations must admit that a perfect free trade is of the utmost importance, but a free trade or in other words a free Ocean is particularly Important to America. I would ask anyone if all the American difficulties during this war is not owing to the Naval systems of Europe and a Licenced Robbery on the ocean? How then is America to prevent this? Certainly not by attempting to build a fleet to cope with the fleets of Europe but if possible by rendering the European fleets useless. A letter has not Room for much on this head, my Reasons on the Subject shall make their appearance in time, and I hope in manner which will carry Conviction. From what I have heard, some of my friends fear that I may become an instrument in the hands of party—but of this I believe there is not the least danger. . . . I cannot unite with any party or polity, nor will I aid them unless I Clearly see that an obstacle between Society

[1] Sutcliffe, *Robert Fulton and the Clermont*, p. 316.
[2] See p. 38.

and a Lasting Peace or improvement Can be Removed. . . . I am happy Ralph has gone to America where I hope to return early in the Spring.

"Remember me also to Mr. Cartwright's family; with Regard to his engines I will write him."

This letter shows that Fulton had already relinquished the active pursuit in France of his canal projects. His treatise on canal navigation was however translated by M. de Récicourt and was published in Paris the following year. It is interesting to note that it was also translated into Portuguese and published in Lisbon in 1800. It is probably on the strength of this book that Fulton is referred to in contemporary French technical literature as an authority on canals.

Fulton is very explicit also in this letter as to the course he intended to pursue with regard to the submarine, and his subsequent conduct was in accordance with it. Clearly, he shared the view which has been held by many other enthusiasts in like case, that ultimately his inventions would do away with warfare altogether by rendering it impossible.

It was all very well, however, to write letters in lofty strains, but he had no assured income, and by this time his funds were once more at a low ebb: he was obliged, therefore, to look round for some means of livelihood. It was only natural that his thoughts should turn to his late profession of art, so that we find a few portraits, such as the one of his friend Barlow, dating from this period. Barlow seems to have been a good friend to him financially, and probably gave him this commission as a delicate way of putting him in funds once more. But Fulton's execution was excelled by that of many other artists in Paris, and there was but small demand just then for the art of portraiture. Small wonder that the field of mechanical invention should occur to his mind as a suitable one to delve in; in fact, he became a prolific patentee. He had already turned his attention to the problem of making rope by machinery, instead of by hand as then almost exclusively practised, as is shown by the following letter [1] to Cartwright:

PARIS, *June 20th*, 1798.

MY DEAR SIR,—Still I continue in France and thus take the opportunity of writing to you by my friend, Mr. Gilpin, who will convey to America anything you have to communicate to me on mechanical subjects. In a long letter I wrote to you on mechanics on March 5th, I mentioned some ideas of a machine for making ropes, the model of which is now finished, capable of making a rope one inch diameter. By Mr. G. I send you a piece of rope fabricated on the engine by which you may judge of its state of perfection. But still I conceive you have superior ideas on the movement of such an engine, particularly the means of giving equal tension to the strands.

It was for this machine that Fulton, in conjunction with Nat. Cutting, a compatriot, obtained on 18th May 1799, a patent for fifteen years for "Machines à fabriquer toutes espèces de cordes, câbles et cordages en général." [2]

The machine that Cartwright had invented—his "cordelier"—which is referred to by Fulton in this letter, was patented by the former in England in 1792 (No. 1876). Fulton's machine was no improvement upon his, but it was much superior to the hand methods then in use in France, and therefore had considerable vogue. It must have brought in some addition to his means, especially if it is true, as has been stated, that his machines were introduced into the French Government Dockyards.

The success of Fulton's rope-making machine, however, was quite insignificant when compared with that of another of his ventures in which his artistic training stood him in good stead. This was when he hit upon the happy idea of

[1] *Memoir of Cartwright*, p. 146.
[2] *Description des machines*, vol. v. p. 62.

painting a panorama, then quite a novelty, and therefore just the thing to attract the attention of the versatile Parisians and to bring him prominently before the public. So true it is that any way of amusing, or again of feeding, one's fellowman is appreciated whereas any proposal for improving his condition, the advantage of which requires a little thought to grasp, is generally rejected.

The Panorama was, however, not original with Fulton, for it was introduced by Robert Barker, a portrait painter of Edinburgh, who patented the invention in Great Britain in 1787 (No. 1612). No doubt the idea of panoramic representation was older still, but Barker was the first to bring it before the public on a large scale. His Panorama of Edinburgh was exhibited in the Haymarket in 1789; this, however, was only a small affair, 25 feet diameter. He then painted a view of London which was shown in 1792. Finally, in 1793, he took a lease of ground in Leicester Square and erected three panoramas, the largest being 90 feet diameter. This was opened early in 1794 and was succeeded during subsequent years by others—in fact it proved a very remunerative enterprise.

Such an exhibition, touching so closely on his then intended profession of art, besides being so close to where he was residing at the time and being a fashionable resort of the town, could not have been unknown to Fulton. It is just possible that he had come to some arrangement with the inventor, just as he had proposed to Dr. Cartwright in regard to one of the latter's inventions,[1] but if so we have no record of it.

However that may be, a French patent[2] was taken out on April 26, 1799 for the term of ten years by "Robert Fulton of the United States." On 17 Frimaire an VIII (Dec. 8th, 1799) he disposed of his patent rights "par acte notaire" to James W. Thayer, a compatriot, and his wife Henriette, née Bec.

[1] See p. 66.

[2] *Description des Brevets*, 1e Série, vol. iii. p 44.

A plot of land situated in a central position in Paris, on the south side of the Boulevard Montmartre, was secured, and upon it was erected a large building 14 m. (46 feet) diameter, to contain the Panorama. The site is now indicated by the "Passage (*i.e.* an arcade, with shops) des Panoramas,"—with the exception of the "rue Fulton"[1] near the Jardin des Plantes—the only vestiges in the city to remind those who know the facts, of Fulton's long stay there. The subject of the Panorama that he painted and completed early in 1800, was the "Burning of Moscow," not, of course, the fire which signalised Napoleon's invasion of Russia, for that did not take place till 1812, but an earlier one, of which so many are recorded in the history of Moscow in the seventeenth and eighteenth centuries. Doubtless Fulton chose this subject for this very reason, because he would be on very safe ground, and also because it offered an opportunity for a very lurid production. This was succeeded by another on the same site.

As indicating how popular[2] the Panorama was, outlasting even the Republic itself, it is interesting to note that the concessionaires on March 9, 1809, obtained a prolongation of their patent for five years, just when it was about to expire, so that it remained in force till April 27, 1814. It

[1] There is a "rue Fulton" in Havre also, close to the Bassin de l'Eure.

[2] The Panorama was even the theme of a Parisian street ballad or music-hall song. One verse goes

Paris pas plus grand que cela
Jouit de succès légitime
Un savant vous le montrera
Pour un franc cinquante centimes
Et tout le monde donne ou donnera
Dans le pano, pano, panorama.

(Paris more than any place
Rejoices in a legitimate success.
A clever man will show it you
For one franc fifty centimes.
And everybody goes or is going
To the pano, pano, panorama.)

is interesting also, to find that Fulton, on 26th April 1801, obtained a second patent for fifteen years, for improvements in panoramas.

Notwithstanding these pre-occupations Fulton continued in an insistent way to importune the Directory to listen to his proposals on submarine navigation. One of these appeals is as follows: [1]

To the Citizens composing the military Committee of the executive Directory of the French Republic.

PARIS, 29 *Messidor, an* vii. (17 *July* 1799).

Citizen Fulton, American, presented to the Directory 18 months ago, the model of an engine intended to destroy, in the open sea and even in their ports, English vessels and, in consequence, to wipe out their military marine.

This project was sent to the Minister of Marine, who nominated to examine it, a commission composed of citizens Borda, Perrier, Adet, Prony, Forfait, Rosily, and Barthélemi: the report of the commission was as favourable as the author could desire: the principles of this engine were found to be simple and in accordance with those of mechanics and augured the happiest success if carried out.

Citizen Fulton offered to the Directory to execute the first engine; he did not even ask government for an advance for any expenses if they did not think fit to make them; he only asked for permission to construct this engine at Paris and to make trial of it against some English fleet blockading our ports.

Citizen Fulton has never been able to obtain that permission, but he has not ceased to beg for it with all the zeal of a disinterested patriot, who asks neither for place nor money.

. . . .

[1] Archives Nationales, A. F. III. 152*a*, quoted in Desbrière, vol. ii. p. 256.

He proceeds to deduce the conclusion that the motives for refusal were humanitarian and then goes on:

Citizen Fulton asks the executive Directory to authorise him to construct at Paris the engine of which he is the inventor and to make trial of it against the enemy. He undertakes to make the trial himself and begs no other compensation after more than 18 months of work, expense, and entreaty than the happiness of having contributed to the re-establishment of peace, the freedom of the seas and of commerce, and to the consolidation of the Republic.

Health and respect,
ROBERT FULTON.

This letter was duly considered by the Committee and their report thereon contains this significant remark:

"The inventor is no charlatan—he proposes to captain his engine himself and thus gives his head as a hostage for his success."

They go on to comment on the delicate mechanism of the engine and the need for actual trial against the enemy before any conclusion can be arrived at. They conclude with the pious opinion that "philosophy would not reprove a means of destroying the destroyers of the liberty of the seas."

Fulton's request was simple and demanded a like answer, instead of which nothing was done. Such treatment reminds one of the policy of "masterly inactivity" depicted in Dickens's "Circumlocution Office" rather than that of a young Republican government armed with "new brooms," so quickly does bureaucracy creep in with its red tape.

There is now a gap in Fulton's life of some months, during which we have no documentary evidence as to his movements. It is asserted, however, by his biographers with every appearance of the truth, that, disgusted with his treatment by the Directory, he approached the executive of the Batavian Republic through the intermediary of their Ambassador in Paris—M. Schimmelpennick, with the offer of his submarine *Nautilus*. This led Fulton to visit Holland, where a commission reported on his plans with such lukewarmness that nothing was done. One gentleman alone—a M. Vanstaphast—was on his side and offered to back him up with capital.

Fulton was not away from Paris very long, because on 13 Vendémiaire an VIII (5 Oct. 1799) he wrote to the Minister of Marine a letter[1] in English, enclosing a very long statement, in French, of "observations upon the moral effects of the Nautilus in case it should be employed with success," and "Reflections upon the general effects which the success of the Nautilus would produce for the extension of the principles of Liberty and the establishment of a lasting peace among the nations." He does this because he considers that it is necessary to refute certain objections that he imagines must be held in high quarters.

Five days after its receipt a report is called for and the same day Fulton submits amended conditions, among which he reiterates once more his request for a commission.

But a change had come over affairs in France by the Revolution of 18 and 19 Brumaire (Nov. 9 and 10, 1799), which resulted in the overthrow of the Directory. In its place Napoleon constituted the Consulate, with himself as First Consul; practically he was in supreme power, because the Second and Third Consuls were merely figureheads.

Fulton, who, as we have already seen, had always had the greatest confidence in Napoleon, lost no time, we may be sure, in calling upon the new Minister of Marine: this was none other than Forfait, who had been a member of the first Commission that had reported so favourably on Fulton's plans.

[1] Archives Nationales, Dossier Marine D[1] 21, fol. 61.

Forfait's observations on Fulton's request for a commission dated 25 Germinal an VIII (15 April 1800), are as follows:

"It cannot be disguised that the Nautilus is a machine not yet in use and that it infringes in several points the laws of war. It would be dangerous, especially at this moment when so great a number of Frenchmen are in the power of the English, to express any kind of menace in the Commission. In granting it pure and simple, that is to say, in acknowledging as combatants the men serving on the Nautilus and the Nautilus vessel itself, I think that that ought not to create more fear than the menace of reprisals can give security for."

Whether Fulton obtained permission to build a submarine or only had a tacit understanding with Forfait we do not know; but Fulton's next letter,[1] dated 20 Germinal (10 April), announces that the *Nautilus* which he is having made in the workshop of C. Perrier is on the point of being finished. He requests the minister to place before Napoleon his conditions, and begs for a prompt and favourable decision. Then follow his 3 conditions which are of similar tenor to those which he had before submitted. He concludes: "I have every reason to hope from Bonaparte the welcome, the encouragement that have so long been refused by Directors and Ministers"—thus showing how hope had sprung up again within him at the advent of Napoleon to power.

On the authority of an eye witness[2] the trial trip of the *Nautilus* is stated to have taken place on the Seine in front of Hôtel des Invalides, but it is possible that his memory was at fault, and that he was confusing these trials with those of the steamboat of 1803, because the official documents suggest that the submarine was built at Rouen—a much more suitable place. Even if the boat was con-

[1] Archives Nationales, Dossier Marine D[1] 61, fol. 77.

[2] Guyton de Morveau, *Bull. de la Soc. d'Encouragement*, 1809, vol. viii. p. 197.

structed at Paris, it was certainly taken to Rouen for completion, because correspondence took place between the Minister and both Fulton and the Commissary of Rouen.

By the month of July the *Nautilus* was nearly finished, when a modification presented itself to Fulton and was at once added. This is described by Quesnel, Commissaire de la Marine at Rouen, in a letter[1] to the Minister, dated 29 Messidor, an VIII (17 July 1800) as "a kind of boat which forms a platform of 6 feet wide by 20 feet long, such that when the *Nautilus* is on the surface it will have the appearance of an ordinary boat." This would in no way hinder plunging, but would give the crew room to stand outside when the *Nautilus* was at the surface. Quesnel continues to report progress to the Minister, and from his letters we condense the account which follows.

The *Nautilus* was launched on the 5 Thermidor (24th July) and five days later commenced her trial trips. These took place "in 25 feet of water in the middle of the Seine between Bapeaume and the shipyard of the late citizen Thibault." Fulton took two people down with him (letter of 5 Therm.) and made two plunges, the first of which lasted 8 minutes and the second 17 minutes.

The trials lasted for three hours, during which the boat changed her position frequently. The current, however, caused Fulton considerable difficulty, and he resolved to proceed to Havre, where he wished to make trials in the open sea. The following evening he wrote to Forfait:[2]

ROUEN, *the* 11 *Thermidor*, *An* 8*th*.

CITIZEN MINISTER,

Yesterday I tryed my experiments with the Nautilus in water 25 feet deep and have succeded to Render the sinking and Rising easy and famelior, the Current which was at least one League per hour togather with the want of suffecient experience, prevented me making the movements

[1] Archives Nationales, *loc. cit.* fol. 83.

[2] *Loc. cit.* fol. 88.

under water which I desired, however time will perfect that part of the operation, having succeded to sail like a common boat and plunge under water when I think proper to avoid an enimy—it may be sufficient at present to render an operation against the enimy successful, this day I propose to set off for havre and hope to arrive there on the fourth, be so good as to send me An order for the powder I may want which will be from 8 to 10 Quintals.

I have not yet heared any thing of the letter of protection from the Primier Consul be so good as to spech to him on that subject and let me know his determination.

Adue, patience and perseverance are the friends of Science. Count on my Zeal—to Render the Nautilus useful.

ROBT FULTON.

The tone of this letter is very confident; but, considering the circumstances, it was justified. The latter part of the letter refers to a passport, or rather a commission, which was to be issued to Fulton.

He lost no time, after coming to the decision, in carrying it out, for on July 31st, at 6 A.M., he set out for Havre, towing the *Nautilus* behind two barges (letter of 12 Thermidor) arriving there four days later.

On the 17th Thermidor, an VIII (5th August 1800)[1] Fulton wrote to Forfait from Havre:

"You will learn with great pleasure that all my experiments on submarine navigation have fully succeeded."

He then gives details of three experiments that he has tried:—

1. Using wings like the sails of a windmill for propulsion (*i.e.* the screw propeller).

2. Plunging by means of lateral wings and retaining the boat at a desired level.

3. Increasing the displacement by means of a weighted anchor so as to make the *Nautilus* sink.

[1] Archives Nationales, A. F. IV. 1049, quoted in Desbrière, vol. iii. p. 307.

On the 26 Thermidor (14 August 1800) Fulton again addressed the Minister,[1] giving the result of three more experiments:

4. Moving the boat in a straight line without oars.

5. Plunging and remaining down 1 hr. 2 m.

6. Finding that the compass acts in the same way below water as on the surface.

It is unnecessary to go into all the details with which Fulton favoured the minister, since he embodied them in a report that he made after he had arrived again in Paris.

Before, however, we go into that report we shall digress slightly in order to show whence came the "sinews of war" that enabled Fulton to prosecute his experiments. For this information and for other scraps of human interest about Fulton's doings we are indebted to the correspondence that passed between Barlow and his wife, who had been ordered by her physician to spend the summer months at Havre for the sake of the sea-bathing, her husband meanwhile staying behind in Paris.

Writing on the 29 Thermidor, an 8 (17 Aug. 1800), Barlow says:[2] "Tell Toot he shall have the [$]1000 in a day or two, but Thayer has not paid according to his promise. The pictures go not well—50 or 60 livres a day for both,—and at this season! But the excessive heat prevents everybody from stirring out, especially on the Boulevards, and in the daytime."

The "pictures" were of course the panoramas, and the money was Fulton's share of profits from the concessionaires.

Fulton was now eager to try his boat on the high seas, and proposed to set out for Cherbourg, whose huge natural harbour would afford ideal facilities for experiment. It was a bold, almost rash undertaking, and so Barlow evidently thought, although he tried to hide from his wife

[1] Dossier D[1] 21, fol. 92.

[2] C. B. Todd, *Life of Barlow*, p. 177.

his worst fears in a reassuring letter[1] to her on the 17 Fructidor (4th Sept.):

"And poor Toot, I suppose, is now gone. I have not believed of late there was much danger in the expedition, especially if they don't go over to the enemy's coast. . . . He is master of all his movements, and it appears to me one of the safest of all hostile enterprises."

As a matter of fact, Fulton had not started, for the simple reason that he had no commission or passport. He wrote to Barlow asking him to use his influence with Forfait to get this.

Barlow replied on the 19 Fruct. (6th Sept.):[2]

"DEAR FULTON,—Your letter of the 16th came yesterday about 4 o'clock, too late to see the Minister, and this morning he seems to have got up wrong end foremost. I went to his porter's lodge at 9 o'clock and sent up a letter concise and clear, explaining the affair and telling him I should wait there for an answer, or for leave to speak to him. . . . I always doubted whether this Government would suffer your expedition to go into effect. It is possible they have reserved to themselves this method to prevent it, always in hopes before that your preparatory experiments would fail, or that your funds and patience would be exhausted."

Barlow's pertinacity was rewarded, however, and he succeeded at length in obtaining a promise of the desired commission for Fulton. His letter of the 20 Fruct. (7th Sept.) runs as follows:

"Toot: I went to the Marine again yesterday at 3 o'clock and sent up a written request for an answer to my letter of the morning. The minister referred me to Forestier who, he said, had orders to attend to this affair. I went to Forestier's *bureau*:[3] his *adjoint*[4] told me that

[1] *Loc. cit.* p. 181.
[2] *Loc. cit.* p. 182.
[3] Office.
[4] Assistant.

the business was done; that the orders were sent that day by post to the *préfet* of the marine at Havre to deliver you the commission and dispense with the caution. Thus if you can rely on a class of men on whom I have learned long ago not to rely at all, the business is done. . . . But if there is any more difficulty, which is altogether probable, explain it to me, and I will go to Forfait with pleasure to get it removed. . . . Your old idea that these fellows are to be considered parts of the machine, and that you must have as much patience with them as with a piece of wood or brass, is an excellent maxim. It bears up my courage wonderfully every time I think of it, and makes me a better part to the machine than I should otherwise be.

I have told it to several persons, who say it is a maxim to be quoted as the mark of a great mind. I will take care that it shall not be forgotten by the writer of your life, who, I hope, is not born yet."

Barlow's letters now cease, but it appears that his fears for once were ill-founded, and that Forfait's passport did actually arrive, thus enabling Fulton to carry out the plan he had so long looked forward to.

The full account of this expedition and the report of his other experiments is dated 16 Brumaire (Nov. 7), and is addressed to his friends Monge[1] and Laplace,[2] who,

[1] Gaspard Monge, Comte de Péluze (b. 1746, d. 1818), mathematician. Early showed mathematical talent, and unfolded a new branch of his subject—that of descriptive geometry. Appointed in 1768 to the Chair of Mathematics at Mezières and in 1780 at the Louvre. Embraced the revolutionary cause ardently, was appointed Minister of Marine in 1792, but retired in the following year. Appointed Principal of the École Polytechnique in 1793. Employed in diplomatic missions in Italy and accompanied Bonaparte to Egypt. After the restoration of the Bourbons he was ignominiously expelled from the Institute.

[2] Pierre Simon, Marquis de Laplace (b. 1749, d. 1827), mathematician and astronomer. His life work was the study of the theory of probabilities and of the mutual attraction of the heavenly bodies. Author of *Mécanique Céleste*, Minister of the Interior after the Revolution of the 18 Brumaire, but held office for six months only—member of the French Academy, and of nearly every learned Society in Europe. Made a Count and a peer of France by Louis XVIII.

together with Volney,[1] were subsequently appointed by Napoleon commissioners to report on the invention.

The report reads almost like a romance, so great were the strides that Fulton had made in these few short months in developing and perfecting submarine navigation—strides greater, it can confidently be said, than any that had been made in the same time either before or since. For this reason we are tempted to give the report in full:[2]

ROBERT FULTON *to* CITIZENS MONGE & LAPLACE, *members of the National Institute.*

CITIZENS,—Not having had the time to busy myself with the drawings and description of the latest changes that I have thought fit to make in my Nautilus, I take the liberty to recommend the model of it to your examination as the best means of enabling you to judge of its fórm and combinations.

Although having exact details of experiments, I shall limit myself to rendering here a succinct account of the most important of them.

First experiment.—The Nautilus is 20 feet long and 5 in diameter and according to the calculations of Cen Guyton it will contain a quantity of air sufficient for 3 men and a candle for three hours.

Second experiment.—On the 6 Fructidor (24 Aug. 1800) I plunged in the basin at Havre to the depth of 15 feet having with me two people and a lighted candle; we remained below the surface for the space of one hour without experiencing the slightest inconvenience.

Third experiment.—On the 7th (25 Aug.) I tried to

[1] Constantine Francis de Chassebœuf, Comte de Volney (b. 1757, d. 1820), traveller and linguist. Travelled in the East 1783–5. He was on the side of the Revolution but deprecated its excesses. Member of National Assembly. Travelled in America and published an account of the climate and soil of the United States. Sided with Bonaparte in the *coup d'état* of the 18 Brumaire. He became senator and count under the empire.

[2] Archives Nationales, Dossier Marine D1 21, fol. 98.

manœuvre the Nautilus by means of wings 4 feet diameter like the sails of a windmill; to this end at first I placed on the bridge two men with oars; they took 7 minutes to row about 90 toises (192 yards), the length of the basin; then I ordered the same 2 men to set the sails and in 4 minutes the Nautilus covered the 90 toises to the starting place;—I proved by this that the speed of sails to that of oars is about 2 to 1 and that these sails are very suitable to manœuvre a boat under water. The success of this experiment has given me several new ideas which I hope will facilitate much the use of carcasses of powder or torpedoes.

Fourth experiment.—On the 8th (26 Aug.) I tried balancing the Nautilus under water in such a way as to prevent it rising towards the surface or descending to the bottom, meanwhile advancing. This is executed by means of a pair of wings placed horizontally on the front of the Nautilus and which communicate with the interior. By turning these wings from left to right the Nautilus is made to descend below the water, in turning them from right to left, it is raised to the surface. My first trial was unfortunate, in not having placed the boat in the necessary trim in order that the wings could act. The next day I had a decided success and I kept my Nautilus below water at a depth of about 5 feet whilst it covered a distance of 90 toises, about from one end of the basin to the other. This day I made several movements under water and I observed that the Compass acts as well under water as at the surface. The three people who have been my companions during these experiments are so familiarized with the Nautilus and have so much confidence at present in the movements of this machine that they undertake without the least concern these aquatic excursions.

Having thus assured myself of the ease of emersion and of submersion of the Nautilus and all its movements as well as the effect on the compass, on the 9th (27 Aug.) I *half filled* an ordinary barrel and placed it at anchor in the harbour at about 200 toises (426 yards) from the jetty; —I seated myself then in an ordinary boat at the distance of about 80 toises and placed in the sea a torpedo containing about 30lb. of powder; the torpedo was attached to a small rope of 100 toises; the current going under the barrel, the torpedo passed without touching it; but turning the helm of the boat in which I sat, I made it go obliquely till I saw the torpedo exactly under the barrel; I then drew back the cable till at last the torpedo touched the barrel; at that instant the battery went off, the powder exploded and the barrel was reduced to fragments being lost in a column of water 10 feet in diameter that the explosion threw into the air to the height of 60 or 80 feet.

On the 25 of the same month (12 Sept.) I left Havre for La Hogue and in this little voyage, my Nautilus sometimes did a league and a half ($4\frac{1}{2}$ miles) per hour, and I had the pleasure of seeing it ride the waves like an ordinary boat.

On the 28th (15 Sept.) I put into a little harbour called Growan near Isigny at 3 leagues from the islands of Marcou. On the 29th the equinoctial gales commenced and lasted 25 days. During the time I tried twice to approach two English brigs which were anchored near one of the islands, but both times, whether by accident or design, they set sail and were quickly at a distance. During one of these trials I remained during the whole of one tide of 6 hours absolutely under water, having for the purpose of taking air only a little tube which could not be perceived at a distance of 200 toises.

The weather being bad, I remained 35 days at Growan and seeing that no English vessel returned, and that winter approached, besides my Nautilus not being constructed to resist bad weather, I resolved to return to Paris and place under the eyes of Government the result of my experiments.

In the course of these experiments there has come to me a crowd of ideas infinitely more simple than the means that I have employed hitherto and in an enterprise so new and without precedent one ought to expect that new ideas should present themselves, tending to simplify the execution of the great object in view.

As to myself I look upon the most difficult part of the work as done. Navigation under water is an operation whose possibility is proved, and it can be said that a new series of ideas have just been born as to the means for preventing naval wars or rather of hindering them in the future; it is a germ which only demands for its development the encouragement and support of all friends of science, of justice and of society.

Health and respect.

ROBERT FULTON.

PARIS, *the* 16 *Brumaire an* 9.

The hardihood of Fulton in going in this cockle-shell a voyage of about 70 miles upon what was really a warlike expedition upon the high seas seems almost incredible. His attempt to blow up the English brigs that were cruising along the coast was frustrated not by accident but by design because Fulton's movements generally were known to the British Admiralty. Captain S. H. Linzie, H.M.S. "L'Oiseau," off Havre, writing on Sept. 21, 1800, thanks the Secretary to the Admiralty for his letter [1] of the 14th "giving an account of Mr. Fulton's Plan respecting the possibility of destroying the ships on this station," and says: "I shall be very much on my guard." So that it is explained why the brigs so quickly slipped from their anchorages.

Fulton followed up his letter to Monge and Laplace [2] by giving on the 27 Brumaire (18 November) answers to their questions and an estimate of what would be the minimum cost of placing the submarine on a war footing. The

[1] Admiralty Sec. In Letters 1, 2067, letter 224.

[2] Archives Nationales, *loc. cit.* fol. 100.

latter, he thinks, would be a quarter of a million francs, the fifth of the cost of a man-of-war. He says:

"Far from being discouraged, I have undertaken the experiments at my own expense. I have succeeded to such an extent as to leave no reasonable doubt as to the success of the whole design. But I have expended as much as my circumstances will permit and more than one individual should do for an object of general interest."

He offers to give up the command of the *Nautilus* and to instruct French citizens in the use of it and to supervise only the construction of submarines. He regards as absolutely necessary prompt advances for the following:

For the construction of a *Nautilus* of 30 feet long and 6 feet diameter	50,000 livres
2 small boats	2,000 ,,
20 torpedoes	2,000 ,,
To descend the river from Paris to Havre and to test the mechanical arrangements . . .	3,000 ,,
Total . .	57,000 ,, (*i.e.* £2,280)

He also asks that the three persons already instructed by him in the work of the *Nautilus* should be retained in Government pay at the rates:

Captain Sergent	600 livres per month
Lieut. Fleuret	400 ,, ,,
Citizen Guillaume	180 ,, ,,

If there should be need of two additional men, they would require 180 livres per month each. As for himself he would accept whatever the Government chose to give him.

Laplace and Monge lost no time in submitting a report[1]

[1] *Loc. cit.* fol. 104.

to the First Consul, for it is dated the next day, 28 Brumaire, an 9 (19 November 1800). It runs:

(*Translation.*)

CITIZEN FIRST CONSUL,—You have charged us to examine the *Nautilus* of Cit. Fulton, and to give you our opinion on the probability of its success.

Instead of giving a description of this machine of which you know the object perfectly well, we beg you to indicate the time when we can see you; Cit. Fulton will bring the model of his *Nautilus* and at one glance you will know its form, the movements of which it is susceptible, and the nature of the operations which it can execute.

We have looked into the projects of Cit. Fulton, his means of execution, and the experiments that he has made already. We do not doubt his success especially if the operation is conducted by the inventor himself who combines with great erudition in the mechanic arts an excellent courage and other moral qualities necessary for such an enterprise.

They then go on to suggest that further experiments on the under water effects of powder in blowing up an actual vessel are needed. When these are proved, experiments can be undertaken against the enemy. For this purpose they recommend a grant of 60,000 livres.

Apparently this letter was submitted to the First Consul at the same time as was Fulton's of the 18th Nov. On the 5 Frimaire the latter document was minuted in the margin and signed by Napoleon: "Je prie Mtre. de la Marine de me faire connaître ce qu'il sait sur les projets du Cn. Fulton."

A few days later Monge and Laplace presented the inventor to the First Consul, warmly recommending him and advising the allowance of the sum he asked for.

Apparently this was the one and only time the two notable men met.

Nothing coming of this interview, however, Fulton called on Forfait on the 11 Frimaire (2 Dec.), and the next day wrote[1] from rue Vaugirard, 50, expressing surprise that nothing had been done and saying:

"You have said a good deal about economy and the lack of positive evidence,—there will be little merit in the Government in adopting this project if it demands that an individual, at his own expense, without protection and without any other encouragement than that it accords to ordinary sailors, should succeed in destroying an English vessel."

Fulton encloses—this is the fifth time of his doing so—his terms which were substantially those which have already been quoted.

Evidently Fulton's interview and letter roused Forfait, and the latter on the following day, 13 Frimaire (4 Dec. '00) wrote a report to Napoleon. He acknowledges that Laplace and Monge commend Fulton's views, but considers that their request for an old hulk wherewith to carry out further experiments is out of the question, not only on account of the initial cost, but also because if they succeed a wreck will be formed which it will be expensive to raise. He proposes that Fulton should destroy an enemy's vessel, and then states that Fulton refuses this because it would be necessary to wait till spring. Apparently the minister's idea was that the submarine function of the boat should be abandoned, and that it should be used merely to convey torpedoes to the vessels. He remarks, hypocritically:

"I have always been the most ardent defender of the plunging boat, and it is with pain that I see it abandoned; for it is abandoned in the new system since it plays only a secondary part."

The vacillation exhibited in this report is only equalled

[1] *Loc. cit.* fol. 95. The letter is in French.

by the myopic refusal to try an experiment on a vessel because the resulting wreck might be difficult to raise! No wonder Napoleon caused such an unsatisfactory minister to be removed from office a few months later.

Laplace and Monge must now have redoubled their efforts at this set-back, and evidently they succeeded, for on the 8 Ventôse, an IX (27th Feb. 1801), Fulton received a letter from the Minister of Marine formally stating that his propositions had been accepted, and that 10,000 francs had been placed to his credit. On the 12 Ventôse Fulton accepted the terms which were recapitulated in the Minister's letter of the 7 Germinal (28 March), which is so explicit that we give it in full:[1]

(*Translation.*)

1st DIVISION,
OFFICE OF THE PORT,
PARIS, *7th Germinal,*
The 9th Year of the One and Indivisible Republic.

THE MINISTER OF MARINE AND OF THE COLONIES.

TO MONSIEUR ROBERT FULTON,
RUE DE VAUGIRARD, NO. 50, PARIS.

I announced to you, Sir, on the 8th Ventôse that the First Consul had authorised me to accept your proposition relative to the *Nautilus*. You will have seen by that letter that you will in consequence be credited with the sum of 10,000 francs to repair this machine, construct the auxiliaries, and to convey at your own expense, the *Nautilus* to Brest.

It has been decreed that you will be allowed for the destruction of the Enemy's vessels, according to their armament, as follows:

400,000 francs for those of more than 30 guns.
200,000 „ „ „ „ 20 „ up to 30 guns.
150,000 „ „ „ from 12 to 20 guns.
60,000 „ „ „ 10 guns.

[1] *Century Magazine*, vol. lxxvi. p. 938, by permission of Mrs. Sutcliffe.

This power is the minimum below which you will have no power to return claim.

By your letter of the 12th Ventôse you declare your acceptance of these conditions and I give the order to put to your account the sum of 10,000 francs by means of which you must put in order the armament, the equipment and the dispatch of the *Nautilus*.

There exist several means of determining in an authentic manner the destruction of the enemy's vessels. The attestations, the declarations and the interrogations put in legal form by competent authorities will serve you as title to claim the payment of the sums which may ultimately be due to you.

Since the navigation which you are about to undertake is absolutely different from others, and also the form of warfare which the *Nautilus* is intended to make upon the enemy, it is not possible to indicate in advance a fixed method of affirming the truth of the facts.

But it will be supplied by the information of the Commissary of the English Government, and by the Maritime Prefects every time it becomes necessary.

(Signed) FORFAIT.

Although Fulton had accepted these conditions it must be confessed that they did not err on the side of liberality. Fulton was, as we have seen, much more than 10,000 francs out of pocket with what he had already done. It is clear, however, that Napoleon intended a further grant in aid to cover the cost of the trials; the prize money in prospect may also have been sufficiently tempting to one of such a sanguine and ardent temperament as Fulton to act as an inducement.

To equip Fulton completely for his journey only a passport was now necessary. On the 14th Germinal, an IX (4th April 1801), Forfait forwards to the Minister of the

Interior for signature two passports, one of which was for Fulton, with these remarks:[1]

"Their duration ought to be for 8 months, and they give to their bearers permission to go at will into the different ports of the Channel or of the Ocean by land or by sea."

It is not difficult to realise what a busy and anxious time it must have been for Fulton during the next few months—what bid fair to be a turning-point in his career. The *Nautilus* had to be taken from Isigny to Brest. How he got it there, whether overland or round by sea we do not know, but we can be almost certain it was the former, for it had been exposed all the winter and was not in a seaworthy condition. What an unwonted sight the unwieldy object 21 feet long and 6 feet diameter must have been for the villages through which the cart passed!!

Sometime in May, however, Fulton arrived at Brest, and at the dockyard there commenced a refit, which occupied him for two months.

Nor was this all, for Fulton was also busy on a plan for carrying his torpedoes not by a submarine but by a pinnace propelled by a screw. It would appear from the records that have been preserved, that the idea was, of the two, the one most favoured officially. Caffarelli, maritime prefect of Brest, who had had instructions to furnish Fulton with everything he wished for from the Arsenal, gave orders for the construction of a pinnace in which was fitted a screw driven by manual power. Although supplied with selected men from the battleship *Océan*, Fulton, instead of his expected 12 knots, only attained 4 when he went out into the harbour.

This and other experiments are described in a letter[2] from Caffarelli to the Minister, dated 14 Messidor, an IX (3 July 1801):

"I have to render an account to you of the trial by Mr. Fulton.

[1] Archives Nationales, Dossier Marine BB[1], 22. [2] *Loc. cit.*, fol. 106.

"When he came here he asked that a pinnace larger than that which he had and of which the sailing was superior should be constructed. Acting on your authority I have had it constructed under his direction. It is 36 feet long and is perfectly made. With a crew of 24 men applied to 4 cranks and placed on both sides, it has a speed of about 4 knots, sails very well, but manœuvres slowly, which is attributed to its length and to the small size of the rudder which is not as long as the stern post. The movement of the wheels can be heard at about 200 toises (426 yards) distance. Mr. Fulton proposes to remedy this and to increase the speed. I think this improvement will be difficult to obtain. I say further that the pinnace is only an accessory in the projects of Mr. Fulton which can be served in many ways as far as I can see.

"There has been no question of a Plunging boat. I believe that it can be dispensed with as well as the pinnace."

He then details the blowing up of an old sloop by a torpedo; but as this is described by Fulton himself, *infra*, we need only note Caffarelli's opinion about the torpedo:

"A mechanically moved pinnace is not necessary for that: one or two light boats like canoes will fulfil the purpose better, because they require less crew and the paddles do not make so much noise as the wheels.

"A plunging boat is not necessary for the operation; for one can be sure always of destroying a vessel with a long enough line by taking a position according to the sea and the wind. . . .

"I think that Mr. Fulton had at one and the same time three ingenious ideas: that of a boat sailing without oars or sails; that of a plunging boat which directs itself and works at will, and that of the Petard; he has wanted to bring them all together as if one alone could not occupy attention enough. The third by itself . . . will suffice for the success of his projects. It is necessary to exercise with the Petard and hook on from a distance under different directions.

". . . An account is being taken of his expenses. . . they are not of great amount. I have promised to instruct him as to the circumstances of the English cruisers, of their anchorages near the coast, and in a word to give him all the facilities which he can desire."

It was now decided that Fulton should attempt to destroy some of the British ships cruising at the entrance to the harbour.[1]

After an interval devoted to experiments with the submarine (detailed below), on August 8th Fulton went to Conquet to lay in wait, and on the 10th to Berthaume, but all to no purpose. The English had been warned of the designs upon them, and not only had lookouts at the masthead scanning the seas with their glasses, but also boats were kept rowing round their vessels when anywhere near the entrance.[2]

All along, Fulton had been of opinion that the submarine was better than the pinnace; but, unfortunately, the former was not, so he considered, in a really seaworthy condition. In a letter[3] to the First Consul on the 19th Fruct. (6th September), wherein he describes at great length his clockwork torpedoes and the means to be employed for blockading English ports and so obtaining command of the sea, he complains that "for lack of a good plunging boat I have been unable to do anything this summer against the enemy."

Caffarelli in the letter of 22 Therm. says: "Mr. Fulton, not making use of the plunging boat, which by its invisi-

[1] Letter to the Minister from Admiral Villaret de Joyeuse, commanding the squadron at Brest, 15 Messidor, an IX (4 July 1801).

[2] Fulton to Villaret and Caffarelli, 21 Therm. (9th August), and latter to Minister, 22nd Therm. (10th August), fol. 111–12.

[3] *Loc. cit.*, fol. 114–5.

bility would assure the success of the operation, does not respond to the expectations of the Government."

But he is not quite consistent, for he says later: "This manner of making war on an enemy carries with it such reprobation, that the persons who undertook it and failed would be lost. Certainly it is not a gallant death."

That there were cross purposes at work here seems obvious.

We must now notice briefly the experiments with the *Nautilus* upon which Fulton, on his return to Paris, wrote a long report,[1] dated 9th September 1801; as it is so lucid, we quote it at considerable length:

PARIS *the 22d fructidore An* 9.

Robert fulton to the Citizens Monge, La Place and Volney, members of the National Institute, and Commissioners appointed by the first Consul to promote the invention of Submarine Navigation.

CITIZENS, yesterday on my return from brest I received your note and will with pleasure communicate to you the result of my experiments, during the summer, also the mode which I conceive the most effectual for using my invention against the enemy. Before I left Paris I informed you that my plunging boat had many imperfections, natural to the first machine of so difficult a combination: added to this I found She had been much Injured by the rust during the Winter in consequence of having in many places used Iron bolts and arbours instead of copper or brass. The reparation of these defects and the difficulty of finding workmen consumed near two months, and although the machine remained still extremely imperfect, yet She has answered to prove every necessary experiment in the most satisfactory manner.

[1] Sutcliffe, *Robert Fulton and the "Clermont,"* pp. 89, 320.

On the 3rd of thermidor (22nd July 1801) I commenced my experiments by plunging to the depth of 5, then 10, then 15, and so on, to 25 feet, but not to a greater depth than 25 feet as I did not conceive the machine sufficiently strong to bear the pressure (*i.e.* 10·8 lb. per sq. in.) of a greater column of water. At this depth I remained one hour with my three companions and two candles burning without experiencing the least inconvenience.

Previous to my leaving Paris I gave to the Cn. (*i.e.* Citizen) Guyton, member of the Institute, a calculation of the number of cube feet in my boat which is about 212. In such a volume of air he calculated there would be sufficient oxygen to nourish 4 men and 2 small candles 3 hours. Seeing that it would be of great improvement to dispense with the candles, I constructed a small window in the upper part of the boat near the bow, which window is only one inch and a half diameter, and of glass nine lines (*i.e.* $\frac{3}{4}$ in.) thick. With this prepared, I descended on the 5th Thermidor (24th July) to the depth of between 24 and 25 feet, at which depth I had sufficient light to count the minutes on the watch. Hence I conclude that 3 or 4 such windows arranged in different parts of the boat, would give sufficient light for any operations during the day. Each window may be guarded by a valve in such a manner that should the glass break, the valve would immediately shut and stop out the water. Finding that I had air and light sufficient, and that I could plunge and Rise perpendicular with facility, on the 7th Therm. (26th July) I commenced the experiments on her movements. At ten in the morning I raised her anchor and hoisted her sails, which are a mainsail and Gib; the breeze being light I could not at the utmost make more than about two-thirds of a league per hour. I tacked and re-tacked, tryed her before and by the wind, and in all these operations found her to Answer the helm and act like a common hull sailing boat. After exercising thus about an hour, I lowered the mast and sails and commenced the operation of Plunging. This required about two minutes. I then placed two men at the engine which gives the Rectilinear motion, and one at the helm, while I governed the machine which keeps her balanced two ways. With the bathometer before me and with one hand I found I could keep her at any depth I thought proper. The men then commenced their movement and continued about 7 minutes when mounting to the surface I found we had gained 400 metres (1,300 feet). I again plunged, turned her round under water and returned to near the same place. I again plunged and tried her movements to the right and left, in all of which the helm answered and the compass acted the same as if on the surface of the water. Having continued these experiments the 8, 9, 10, and 12th (27th, 28th, 29th, and 31st July) until I became familiar with the movements and confident in their operation, I turned my thoughts to increasing or preserving the air. For this purpose the Cn. Guyton advised me to precipitate the carbonic acid with lime or to take with me bottles of Oxygen which might be uncorked as need required; but as any considerable quantity of bottles would take up too much room, and as Oxygen could not be created at sea without a chemical operation which would be very inconvenient, I adopted a mode which occurred to me 18 months ago, which is a simple globe or bomb of copper capable of containing one cube foot to [join to] a pneumatic pump by means of which pump 200 atmospheres or 200 cube feet of common air may be forced into the Bomb, consequently the Bomb or reservoir will contain as much oxygen or vital air as 200 cube feet of common respirable Air. Hence if according to the Cn. Guyton's calculation 212 feet which is the volume of the boat, will nourish 4 men and 2 small candles 3 hours, this additional reservoir will give sufficient for 6 hours. This reservoir is constructed with a measure and two cocks So as to let measures of air into the boat as need may require. Previous to my leaving Paris I gave orders for this machine but it did not arrive till the 18th Thermidor (6th Aug.). On the 19th I ordered two men to fill it, which was an operation of about one hour. I then put it into the boat and with my three companions, but without candles, plunged to the depth of about five feet. At the expiration of one hour and 40 minutes I began to let off measures of air from the reservoir and so on from time to time for 4 hours 20 minutes without experiencing any inconvenience.

Having thus succeeded:

To sail like a common boat,
To obtain air and light,
To plunge and Rise perpendicular,
To turn to the right and left at pleasure,
To steer by the compass under water,
To renew the Common Volume of air with facility,
And to augment the respirable air, by a reservoir which may be obtained at all times,

I conceived every experiment of importance to be proved in the most satisfactory manner. Hence I quit the experiments on the Boat to try those of the Bomb Submarine. It is this bomb which is the Engine of destruction, the plunging boat is only for the purpose of conveying the Bomb to where it may be used to advantage. They are constructed of copper and of different sizes to contain from 10 to 200 pounds of powder. Each bomb is arranged with a Gunlock in such a manner that if it strikes a vessel or the Vessel runs against it, the explosion will take place and the bottom of the vessel be blown in or so shattered as to ensure her destruction. To prove this experiment, the Prefect Maritime and Admiral Villaret ordered a small sloop of about 40 feet long to be anchored in the Road on the 23rd of Thermidor (11th Aug.) with a bomb containing about 20 pounds of powder I advanced to within about 200 metres (628 feet); then taking my direction so as to pass near the Sloop, I struck her with the bomb in my passage. The explosion took place and the sloop was torn into atoms, in fact, nothing was left but the buye (*i.e.* buoy) and cable; and the concussion was so great that a column of water, Smoke, and fibres of the Sloop were cast from 80 to 100 feet in Air. This simple experiment at once proved the effect of the Bomb Submarine to the satisfaction of all the Spectators. Of this Experiment you will see Admiral Villaret's description in a letter to the Minister of Marine.

Fulton then goes on to outline what appeared to him to be the best methods of using the plunging boat and the submarine bomb, without, however, committing himself too precisely, because experience always suggests improvements. This, however, is only an epitome of what has already been rehearsed and it is therefore unnecessary to give it in full. He concludes:

Thus Citizens, I have presented you with a short account of my experiments and Plan for using this invention against the Enemy hoping that under your protection it will be carried to perfection and practised to promote the Liberty of the Seas.

Health and sincere respect,

ROBERT FULTON.

To every impartial mind this plain statement of facts and deductions therefrom at once lucid and logical should have appealed very strongly. Little more than a year had elapsed since the problem of submarine navigation, till then regarded as a chimera, had been tackled on a practical scale, and now it had been solved in all its main essentials. All the principles which govern the construction and operation of submarines had been experimentally demonstrated, and with the only known motor, *i.e.* muscular power, then available, no better results could have been expected.

The Commissioners made a few inquiries on certain

points which Fulton answered in the following letter,[1] dated the 20th Sept. 1801:

PARIS, *the 3rd Complementary Day, an* 9

Robert Fulton to the Citizens Monge, La Place, and Volney, members of the National Institute and Commissionaries appointed by the First Consul to promote the Invention of Submarine Navigation.

CITIZENS: This morning, I received yours of the 2nd Compl. As to the expense of a plunging boat, I believe when constructed in the best manner with every improvement which experience has pointed out, She cannot cost more than 80,000 Livers (*i.e.* £3200). The Bombs Submarine may be estimated at 80 Livers (*i.e.* £3, 4*s.*) each, on an average, independent of the powder.

I am sorry that I had not earlier information of the Counsul's (*i.e.* Napoleon's) desire to see the Plunging Boat. When I finished my experiments, She leaked very much, and being but an imperfect engine, I did not think her further useful,—hence I took her to pieces, Sold her Ironwork, lead and cylinders, and was necessitated to break the greater part of her movements in taking them to pieces. So that nothing now remains which can give an Idea of her combination; but even had she been complete I do not think she could have been brought round to Paris. You will be so good as to excuse me to the Premier Consul when I refuse to exhibit my drawings to a Committee of Engineers. For this I have two reasons: the first is not to put it in the power of any one to explain the principles or movements lest they should pass from one to another till the enemy obtained information: the Second is that I consider this Invention as my private property, the perfectionment of which will give to France incalculable advantage over her most powerful and active enemy, and which invention, I conceive, ought to secure to me an ample Independance. That consequently the

[1] Sutcliffe, *Robert Fulton and the "Clermont,"* p. 84.

Government should stipulate certain terms with me Before I proceed to further explanation. The first Consul is too just, and you know me too well, to construe this into an avaricious disposition in me. I have now laboured 3 years and at considerable expense to prove my experiments. And I find that a man who wishes to cultivate the Useful Arts cannot make rapid Progress without sufficient funds to put his succession of Ideas to immediate proof; and which sufficiency I conceive this invention should secure to me. You have intimated that the movements and combination of so interesting an engine should be confided to trusty persons lest any accident should happen to me. This precaution I took previous to my departure from Paris for my last experiments, by placing correct Drawings of the Machine and every movement with their descriptions in the hands of a friend; so that any engineer capable of constructing a Steam engine, could make the plunging boat and Carcasses or Bombs.

You will therefore be so good as to beg of the First Consul to permit you to treat with me on the business. And on this point I hope there will not be much difficulty.

Health and sincere respect,

ROBERT FULTON.

This letter disposes very completely of the statement that Fulton built two submarines, one at Havre and the other at Brest—a very natural supposition on the evidence previously available. It also satisfies us as to the ultimate fate of the boat.

Unfortunately for Fulton a change now came over the scene. On Oct. 1st, Forfait, who had at any rate not been ill-disposed to him, handed in his resignation as Minister of Marine after two years of office.

The First Consul appointed to succeed him Admiral De Crès,[1] who like Pléville-le-Pelley was quite one of the

[1] De Crès, le duc Denis (b. 1761, d. 1820), entered the Navy at the age of seventeen and saw service in all parts of the world, showing conspicuous bravery. He became lieutenant in 1785, captain in 1793, and vice-admiral in

old school, and consequently bitterly opposed to the new method of warfare; in this he only voiced the prejudices of his time.

Probably it was this change of ministers which put an end to the matter finally, for the Archives of the Marine make no further mention of Fulton or of his project, and all that is to be found is an account of the expenses which had been incurred on his behalf at the arsenal at Brest, amounting to the sum of 6,820 fr. 43.[1]

Thus apparently did Fulton receive his dismissal—with what bitterness of soul we can imagine—cherishing nevertheless the hope that he would yet have opportunities of perfecting submarine navigation.

By many writers, especially in France, Napoleon has been blamed for not adopting the submarine, the assumption being that the destinies of nations would have been changed thereby. There is also an underlying assumption that other nations could not have adopted the new means of warfare almost as quickly as France could have done.

Now Napoleon was above everything a man of affairs—he was ready and anxious to employ any means known to science to further his ends, but it was no part of his policy to take up anything that had not been put into practice successfully. He allowed Fulton to work out his invention just to that point where he could judge whether or not it would be of use to him, and having convinced himself that it could not, dropped the matter without hesitation. And he was right; Fulton's series of experiments, brilliant though they were, only showed that until a motor could be developed capable of working under the restrictions imposed, further progress was impracticable. For this development the world had to wait many years longer.

1798. In October 1801, he received the portfolio of Minister of Marine, and being subservient to Napoleon in all ways, retained office till the latter's downfall—*i.e.* for thirteen years. He was murdered by his valet.

[1] Letter of Caffarelli to the Minister, 26 fruct. an IX (13 Sept. 1801). *Archives Nationales*, Dossier Marine D' 21, fol. 119.

CHAPTER VII

TURNS HIS ATTENTION TO STEAM NAVIGATION—SKETCH OF THE WORK OF PREVIOUS EXPERIMENTERS—STEAMBOAT ON THE SEINE—BRITISH NEGOTIATIONS TO WITHDRAW FULTON FROM FRANCE

WE have now reached the period when Fulton turned his attention in earnest to what was to be his life's work—the solution of the problem of navigation by steam on a commercial scale.

In order to get a clear idea of what this problem was, it must be remembered that overseas commerce had greatly increased, and with it the burden of the ships employed, so that the difficulty of warping or rowing them out of harbour through calms or against the tide had also increased. It was not an uncommon thing to see hundreds of sail weatherbound in harbour for weeks at a stretch waiting for the wind to change. Merely as showing what a long-standing problem it was, we may mention the alleged attempts to propel boats by steam of Blasco de Garay in 1543 and Denis Papin in 1707. These could safely be dismissed on a priori grounds, even if research had not shown that these experimenters employed muscular power only, when we reflect that Newcomen did not introduce his atmospheric engine — the first practical and satisfactory apparatus for employing the power of steam—till about 1710.

Yet Newcomen's engine was far from being suited to marine propulsion, for its weight for a given power was enormous; in fact it would hardly be too much to say that had any such engine been designed capable of developing power enough to propel a boat of a given size, the engine would have sunk the boat by its own weight.

We are not, therefore, in much doubt as to the success of the scheme of Jonathan Hulls, who took out a patent (No. 556) in 1736 for a stern wheel tug-boat actuated by an atmospheric engine. The title of his pamphlet[1] descriptive of his invention published in 1737 shows clearly the widest extent to which it was expected to apply the steam engine at this time; as a general substitute for sails and oars, it was hardly dreamt of.

It was not until the simple pumping engine of Newcomen had been developed between 1775 and 1782 by the celebrated James Watt into the Cornish pumping engine, and lastly into the double-acting rotative engine suitable for all kinds of power purposes, that for the first time the horse-power obtainable from an engine and its boiler, per pound weight and per cubic feet occupied, was reduced within the limits of displacement of a boat that the engine could propel at a reasonable speed.

For the first really important steps to realise practically this new possibility, we must turn our attention to the New World, where the extensive waterways but lack of highways early suggested that transport by water was easier than by land, if it could be made as certain. The impetus may have been due to the removal of trade restrictions by the War of Independence, 1775–1783; what the nature of these restrictions had been is shown by the fact that the art of constructing steam engines was totally unknown in America at that time.

We ought perhaps to refer in the first place to the experiments of James Rumsey of Virginia, in hydraulic jet propulsion, a method which he was the first to bring to a practical issue although it had been proposed in 1730 by John Allen, M.D.,[2] and even earlier by others. All that

[1] "A DESCRIPTION and DRAUGHT of a new invented machine for carrying vessels or ships out of or into any Harbour, Port or River, against Wind or Tide or in a Calm."

[2] *Specimina Ichonographica*, p. 16.

was required was a steam pump to draw in the water at the bow and force it out at the stern, so that the mechanical arrangements were simple and well understood. In 1785 and again in 1787 and 1788 Rumsey exhibited his boat publicly on the Potomac, and succeeded in propelling her against the current at the rate of four miles per hour. In the latter year he proceeded to England, where he hoped to prosecute his invention. In this he succeeded, for, having induced a wealthy American merchant resident in London to finance him, he took out patents in 1788 (No. 1673) and again in 1790 (No. 1738). In February 1793 their vessel was tried on the Thames, attaining a speed of four knots. Unfortunately Rumsey died suddenly in the midst of his experiments. Fulton, who was in London at the time although it is improbable that he was present, knew about these trials, because in one of his note-books[1] there is an entry entitled "Messrs. Parker and Rumsies experiment for moving boats." Fulton's opinion after consideration of the pros and cons is:

"It therefore appears that the Engine was not loaded to its full power, that the water was lifted four times too high, and that the tube by which the water escaped was more than five times too small."

This shows that Fulton did not realise where the cause of Rumsey's failure lay. If water, contained in the boat itself, is forced out through an orifice at the stern at twice the speed at which the boat moves, the efficiency may be as much as 75 per cent.; that is, looked at in another way, the efficiency would be greater than that of any other form of propulsion. The water has, however, to be taken in at the bow and come to rest relative to the boat; this means a loss of energy which greatly reduces efficiency, and this was Rumsey's case.

Even when the water enters the boat and is not brought to rest relative to it, but is accelerated by a centrifugal pump as in Ruthven's system, a jet is less economical

[1] Sutcliffe, *Robert Fulton and the "Clermont,"* p. 330.

than other means of propulsion, as was proved in 1868 in the Admiralty experiments on H.M.S. *Waterwitch*.

A third system remains to be tried, whereby the velocity of the incoming water is converted by a Venturi tube into pressure before it enters the pump, and is finally discharged through a converging nozzle, again acquiring velocity.

Jet propulsion has received a limited application in exceptional circumstances, *e.g.* in steam life-boats and floating fire stations.

Almost if not quite as early in the field as Rumsey was John Fitch of Connecticut, who on September 27, 1785, laid before the American Philosophical Society at Philadelphia a description, drawing, and model of a machine for working a boat against the stream by means of an endless chain of float boards. Although his petitions to the Legislatures of Pennsylvania, Maryland, and New Jersey for financial aid to enable him to make experiments were unsuccessful, yet the last-named State granted him, on March 8, 1786, an exclusive privilege for fourteen years for making and using all such boats within the waters of that State.

In 1786, on the strength of this privilege, Fitch formed a stock company known as "The Steamboat Company." He engaged a mechanic named Henry Voight, and together they constructed a model boat, but it was too small to prove anything. In a larger model, Fitch adapted the idea, borrowed no doubt from the action of Indians in a canoe, of a set of paddles on each side to be moved by cranks. A boat 34 feet long, 8 feet beam, and 3 feet 6 inches in depth was built at Philadelphia and equipped with a steam engine, which by sprocket gearing actuated six oars placed vertically in a frame on each side of the boat. This was tried successfully on the river Delaware on July 27 in that year.

By this time funds were exhausted, and it was not till 1787 that the State of Delaware granted Fitch a somewhat similar privilege to that of their neighbours, on the strength of which a new agreement was drawn up and fresh capital was raised. A boat 45 feet long by 12 feet beam was built and fitted with horizontal double-acting condensing engine "similar to the late improved steam engines in Europe," 12 inch diam. by 3 feet stroke, which moved by cranks six paddles on each side. On the 22nd August 1787—twenty years almost to a day before Fulton's final success—this vessel was publicly tried on the river Delaware at Philadelphia before members of the Convention met there to frame the Federal Constitution. The speed attained was, however, too slow to satisfy the projectors.

The following year saw them with another boat 60 feet long by 8 feet beam, in which the reciprocating oars were placed at the stern. In July she made a trip from Philadelphia to Burlington, a distance of about twenty miles, the longest trip ever made by steam up to that time; later a speed of over six miles per hour was recorded. Even this was not considered satisfactory, and Fitch continued experimenting with different condensers, boilers, and cylinders during 1789 and the spring of 1790. The beam type of engine, with a cylinder 18 inches diam. driving paddle boards at the stern, was finally decided on.

At last, in the words of Fitch's autobiographical MS.:[1] "On the 16th April (*i.e.* 1790) got our work compleated, and tried our Boat again and although the wind blew very fresh at the north east we reigned Lord High Admiral of the Delaware and no boat in the River could hold its way with us, but all fell astern, although several sail boats which were very light, and heavy sails that brought their gunwales well down to the water came out to try us."

The *United States Gazette*, May 15, 1790, contains the following notice: "Burlington, May 11, 1790. The friends of science and the liberal arts will be gratified on hearing that we were favoured, on Sunday last, with a visit from

[1] Preserved in the Philadelphia Library.

the ingenious Mr. Fitch accompanied by several gentlemen of taste and knowledge in mechanics in a steamboat constructed on an improved plan. From these gentlemen we learn that they came from Philadelphia in 3 hours and a quarter, with a head wind with the tide in their favour. On their return by accurate observation, they proceeded down the river at the rate of upwards of seven miles an hour."

The boat was now considered quite successful, and on June 16th, she was tested in front of Water Street, Philadelphia, in presence of the Governor and Council of Pennsylvania and a crowd of spectators. A speed of eight miles per hour was attested to. This vessel was the first steamboat employed commercially, for during the summer she ran, as advertisements in the newspapers[1] of the time testify, a passenger and freight service on the Delaware between Philadelphia and Bordentown.

In this service the boat must have run between two and three thousand miles, but apparently the Company were losing money all the time, since after the vessel was laid up in the autumn she was not again used. It is not unreasonable to surmise that the weight of the propelling machinery left too little displacement for freight and passengers to enable her to pay expenses.

The subsequent history of John Fitch is very sad. He was sent over to France by his friends in 1791, and on November 29 of that year obtained a patent for fifteen years for[2] "Mecanisme propre à faire mouvoir des bateaux par le moyen d'une machine à feu."

[1] Twenty-three of these notices have been found, of which the following from the *Pennsylvania Packet* of Philadelphia, June 14, 1790, is the earliest, and may be considered typical of the rest:

THE STEAM-BOAT

Is now ready to take Passengers, and is intended to set off from Arch street Ferry in Philadelphia every *Monday*, *Wednesday* and *Friday* for *Burlington*, *Bristol*, *Bordentown* and *Trenton*, to return on *Tuesdays*, *Thursdays* and *Saturdays*—Price for Passengers 2/6 to Burlington and Bristol, 3/9 to Bordentown, 5/ to Trenton. June 14.

[2] *Brevets d'invention*, vol. ii. p. 105.

The disturbed state of the country consequent on the Revolution prevented Fitch from doing anything. He returned to the United States, and after a few more attempts to further the introduction of steam navigation, he died in 1798, at Bardstown, Kentucky, a disappointed and broken man.

The large amount of space which we have devoted to Fitch is only in proportion to the regard in which he ought to be held, and to the bearing which his work had on Fulton's subsequent monopoly. The advances he made were very great, but he was unable to build a boat large enough or an engine quite light enough for the work, nor was transportation so important a question then as it quickly became. Fitch realised exactly what was the crux of the problem, as is shown by the following statement and extract from a letter of his: "If he could bring his steam engine to work *in a boat* he would be under no difficulty in applying its force." "It may also be boldly asserted that it would be much easier to carry a first-rate man of war by steam at an equal rate than a small boat; for in such a case we should not be so cramped for room, nor should we so sensibly feel a few pounds weight of machinery."

We do not intend to enlarge upon the experiments of William Henry, Nathan Read, Samuel Morey, Nicholas J. Roosevelt, and other New England inventors, because their efforts did not advance the problem beyond the stage reached by Fitch.

It must not be supposed that during this time nothing was being done in the mother country. On the contrary matters were in an advanced stage: we refer to the well-known experiments of Patrick Miller, the Edinburgh banker, who for some years had been experimenting with double-hulled boats propelled by paddle wheels turned by muscular power. It was suggested to him in 1788 by his son's tutor that he should apply a steam engine instead of men. He promptly commissioned one from

William Symington, who had patented an engine, really an infringement of Watt's, the previous year. The trial, which took place on Dalswinton Loch on Miller's estate in Dumfriesshire, was quite successful, the speed attained being five miles per hour. The machinery, relying as it did on ratchets for obtaining rotary motion, was not much in advance of Hulls's, and was unsuitable for everyday work even in smooth water. The engine has been preserved, and may be seen in the Science Museum, South Kensington. Miller at once decided on a trial on a larger scale; accordingly one of his double boats was brought from Leith to Grangemouth, taken along the Forth and Clyde Canal, and supplied with an engine of similar design to the last, built at Carron Ironworks. The trial, which took place on the Canal, was even more successful than the previous one, for a speed of seven miles per hour was reached. Miller perhaps did not realise that his results could be applied outside the somewhat narrow limits of inland navigation; but, even so, surprise has often been expressed that he did not prosecute his experiments further; there is, however, some evidence to show that he tried, unsuccessfully, to induce the British Admiralty to take up the subject; and when it is reflected that on his public spirited efforts to make improvements in agriculture and other arts he had expended a very large sum—stated by his family to have been £30,000—without pecuniary return, his inaction, far from being surprising, is only natural.

Glancing back upon this long series of partial successes and disappointments, it is not to be wondered at that, in Fulton's own words:[1]

"The repeated failure (*i.e.* to move boats or vessels to advantage by the power of steam engines) of men of science, among whom were the ingenious Earl of Stanhope, gave an impression to the public mind both in Europe and America, that it was impracticable to make a useful steam-

[1] Sutcliffe, *Robert Fulton and the* "*Clermont*," p. 116.

boat, and under this belief those who attempted it were considered as visionaries or madmen."

Still it is not difficult to imagine that it was the force of circumstances which drove Fulton to think upon the problem, because during the summer he had spent at Brest he must have realised that something a great deal superior to muscular power was required to propel his bomb-carrying boats ere they could be a success.

Besides, there would be much talk about Napoleon's projected descent upon England, and the assemblage for that purpose of troops and transports at Boulogne. But, while the English fleet swept the Channel and blockaded the French ports, there was little chance for such an expedition to slip across, even if the French had got what Napoleon said was all they needed, "Let us be masters of the Channel for six hours and we are masters of the world."[1] Rather may it have occurred to Fulton that a dead calm was the desideratum were only the steamboat in existence. The menace of invasion was removed for the time being by the negotiations which led to the Treaty of Amiens in March 1802.

It is doubtful whether Fulton would have done anything in steam navigation, however, had it not been for the arrival in France of Chancellor Robert R. Livingston, Minister Plenipotentiary of the United States to France. The first thing he heard on his arrival in Paris in November 1801 was the news of the cession of Louisiana and the Floridas by Spain to France. Their new neighbour was viewed with great alarm by the States, and it is a matter of history that they succeeded in coming to terms on April 30, 1803, by the payment of eighty million francs, Napoleon thus astutely putting Louisiana in the hands of a power unfriendly to England and at the same time supplying

[1] Thiers, *Hist. of Consulate and Empire*, vol. v. p. 103. This letter, it is true, was written on a subsequent occasion (*i.e.* to Admiral Latouche-Tréville, July 2, 1804), but the circumstances were the same, and the sentiment one that was held in France quite generally.

CHANCELLOR ROBERT R. LIVINGSTON

himself with the funds he needed so badly for carrying on his schemes of conquest.

Now, Livingston was deeply interested in the subject of steamboats; indeed, he had an idea or two of his own, and, as a result of his experiments, had gone so far as to procure an Act to be passed in March 1798 vesting in himself the "exclusive right and privilege of navigating all kinds of boats which might be propelled by the force of steam or fire on all the waters within the territory or jurisdiction of the State of New York for the term of twenty years from the passing of the Act; upon condition that he should within a twelvemonth build such a boat, the mean of whose progress should not be less than four miles per hour."

He mentioned what he was doing in a letter to James Watt,[1] dated November 4, 1798, in which he says: "Having lately turned my attention to the application of this power [*i.e.* the steam engine] to the propelling of boats which I have reason to think (from some experiments I have made with a small 12-inch cylinder making three feet strokes in a boat of 36 Tuns) I have effected on principles that [are] entirely new . . . I propose to carry the business of propelling boats upon our extensive rivers by means of steam to a considerable length—Tho' steam engines are perfectly made here, yet the small number of workmen that understand the business renders it a slow and expensive operation. I beg to know, Sir, upon what terms an engine 24 Inches cylinder making four feet strokes—The furnace only for a wooden boiler (as the boiler can be made here) can be delivered here on 12 months credit with 5 pr. Ct. interest from the time it is delivered. You will oblige me by an early answer to this part of my letter as I am now about to proceed in making them here if they cannot be furnished cheaper by you—I need not observe that for the purpose I want it, the workmanship must be as light and compact as possible."

[1] Boulton & Watt MSS.

He did not get any engines from Boulton & Watt, however; probably there was a difficulty in getting permission to export them. Nor did he succeed as he was anticipating; possibly his official duties prevented that close application which the problem demanded.

Livingston's brother is said to have met Fulton at the Panorama, and to have introduced him to the Chancellor as being just the man he was on the look-out for. Livingston "communicated to Mr. Fulton the importance of steamboats to their common country; informed him of what had been attempted in America, and of his resolution to resume the pursuit on his return, and advised him to turn his attention to the subject. It was agreed between them to embark on the enterprise, and immediately to make such experiments as would enable them to determine how far, in spite of former failures, the object was attainable; the principal direction of these experiments was left to Mr. Fulton, who united in a very considerable degree practical, to a theoretical, knowledge of mechanics. After trying a variety of experiments, on a small scale, on models of his own invention, it was understood that he had developed the true principles upon which steamboats should be built, and for the want of knowing which all previous experiments had failed. But as these gentlemen both knew that many things which were apparently perfect when tried on a small scale, failed when reduced to practice upon a large one, they determined to go to the expense of building an operating boat on the Seine. This was done in the year 1803 at their joint expense and under the direction of Mr. Fulton, and so fully evinced the justice of his principles that it was immediately determined to enrich their country by the valuable discovery as soon as they should meet there, and in the meantime to order an engine to be made in England."[1]

[1] *Amer. Med. and Phil. Reg.*, vol. ii. p. 256, in a paper entitled "An HISTORICAL ACCOUNT of the application of STEAM for the propelling of Boats." This is stated by Colden, p. 148, to have been drawn up by Livingston himself.

Now, Fulton had already experimented with both paddle and screw for propulsion—just at this moment he was most in favour of the chain of paddle-boards—so that he felt himself on pretty safe ground; but as to the provision of suitable engine-power he was not quite so sanguine. However, he recalled his old friend, Dr. Cartwright, who, at the time of his last letter had been busy with his alcohol engine, and wrote to him as follows:

PARIS, 10*th March* 1802.

MY GOOD FRIEND,—Be so kind as to let me know how you have succeeded in your steam engine. To what state of perfection have you brought it? What will one of a six horse power making a three or four foot stroke, cost? How much will it weigh? How much space will it require when rendered as compact as possible? What weight and value of coals will it consume per hour? and how soon can it be made? I think you once mentioned to me your intention to use spirits of wine, and that you could obtain a power of at least 30 lbs to the square inch. Have you succeeded in these great objects? The object of these inquiries is to make part of an examination on the possibility of moving boats of about six or seven tons by steam engine, and your engine I conceive best calculated for such a work; particularly as the condenser may always have the advantage of cold water without adding much to the weight of the boat; and having the advantage of cold water may enable you to work with ardent spirits and produce the desired elasticity of steam with one half the heat,—hence in calculating the weight of the apparatus, the weight of the condensing water will be trifling, it is therefore the *weight of the engine and the fluid in the boiler which are to be calculated.* For this object I believe the engine should be double with the steam acting on the top and bottom of the piston, or in two cylinders, the one ascending while the other descends. For the particular case where such a boat is wanted, I believe it is of more importance to have a light and compact engine, than to have too much regard to the economy of fuel, unless the additional weight of the fuel to go twenty miles would be more than the additional weight of the engine to economize the heat. To gain power in a small space, how would it answer to make the boiler sufficiently strong to heat the steam to two atmospheres or 30 pounds to the square inch? then a cylinder of 6 inches would give a purchase of 300 lbs; that is 900 pounds' constant purchase which is about the sum of my demand—as for example three pounds will draw a piece of timber 20 feet long which presents a butt end of one foot square, at the speed of

	1 mile per hour
12 pounds	2 " "
48 "	4 " "
96 "	6 " "
120 "	7 " "

Now supposing my boat to be 40 feet long and five feet wide—boat, passengers, and engines weighing 6 tons—it will present a front of about 6 feet resistance or 720 pounds purchase to run such a boat seven miles per hour.

Suppose the boat to weigh	2 tons
30 Passengers with their baggage	3 "
	5 tons

One ton is left for the engine and machinery. From this calculation you will be able to judge what can be done by your invention; and if by your means I can perfect my plan I have got a good opportunity of rendering your engine productive to you, and it will give me pleasure to do so. You will be so good as [to] write to me as soon as possible, answering in a particular manner the questions stated with any observations you think proper and will be so good as to make on my proposed attempt.

ROBT. FULTON.

This letter is interesting if only as showing the data possessed by Fulton, derived from Beaufoy's experiments on floating solids of uniform section, upon which he based his calculations of the power necessary to drive a boat. Of course this meant that the boat was treated as if it were a parallelopiped of uniform section and not shipshape. More noteworthy still is that Fulton, although he did not understand the principle of the alcohol engine, yet suggests the use of steam of much higher pressure than was then usual.

Cartwright, although he had really done nothing to reduce his ideas to practice, replied with a glowing account of his engine. Evidently Fulton saw through this, for his reply was as follows:

PARIS, 28*th March* 1802.

MY DEAR SIR,—It is with great pleasure I have received your flattering account of your steam engine; and although attachment to you makes me believe everything you say, yet such belief is merely a work of faith, for I cannot see the reason why you have 13½ pounds purchase to the square inch. Is this in consequence of the friction taken off by your circles [*i.e.* the metallic packing, Patent No. 2202 (1797), of which Cartwright was the original inventor]. How have you found that mode to answer? Is it that by your mode of condensing the water becomes deprived of its air and that the steam may be heated four, five or more pounds per inch above the atmosphere? If the engine can be made so light as you mention, and give only ten pounds to the square inch, it will answer my purpose; but it must be a double engine, making thirty double strokes, or sixty single strokes per minute of three feet each; that is to say three feet per second. As I can afford to give five feet by six for the engine, it will not be necessary to place the cylinder in the boiler. If it stands outside of the boiler, repairs can be made with more ease; but when we have decided on the engine, I will give a sketch of the mode in which I propose it should stand, to give movement to the machinery which is to drive the boat. If for my case, you propose to condense without injection, the condensing vessel may be a long cylinder or tube, with another tube through its centre, through which a current of water will pass with a velocity equal to the speed of the boat and thus carry off the *caloric* very quick. I do not see how the engine, water in the boiler and fly included can weigh so little as a ton and say a half. What will be the weight and diameter of the fly? Another important consideration—is it permitted to send such engines out of the country? the design is to America. The smoke jack flyers will not answer for a quick movement. Reduced to 2 arms thus,

it answers admirably for my plunging boat, where the velocity is not more than two miles per hour between two waters, and where oars cannot be used. I was so pleased with it in that experiment, that I last summer built a pinish (*i.e.* pinnace) thirty six feet long and five feet wide extremely light and of the best workmanship. I placed in her quadruple cranks, from bow to stern thus,

to each of which were six men, total twenty-four of the best seamen of the fleet. The multiplication from the crank to the flyers was at first fourteen to one; the flyers, four feet diameter, angle, thirty degrees. We could not make more than four miles per hour. I reduced the multiplication to seven to one. We went about four miles but with less fatigue to the men. I changed the diameter of the flyers from four down to two feet and the angle from forty down gradually five degrees at a time to fifteen degrees. Still our speed was never more than about four

ROBERT FULTON
ÆTATIS SUÆ 39

miles per hour. When the boat gains a certain velocity, the water running quick past the flyers they lose their purchase; and multiplying them to a velocity so as to overtake the boat, or strike the water sufficiently quick, causes a friction which consumes much of the power. However, I have found an excellent mode of taking my purchase on the water in all possible velocities, and where the whole power will be applied to advantage. The question now is only to find the best steam engine to put it in movement; and I sincerely hope it will be yours. For political reasons, I have never yet confided to *but one person* the combination of my plunging boat and committed the whole to drawing and explanation, in case of any accident happening to me; however it will be satisfactory to you to know that the experiments have been very successful. I was very fortunate in surmounting some great difficulties; and navigating under water is now easy to be performed and without risk.

The incredulity evinced by Fulton in this letter may well be pardoned, and Cartwright, having before him an inquiry for an engine of definite horse-power which was not to occupy more than a certain space, must have been driven to confess that he was unable to supply what was wanted, and Fulton was therefore thrown once more on his own resources.

Just about this time Mrs. Barlow was ordered to the famous medicinal springs of Plombières for the benefit of her health. Fulton was her escort. They left Paris on April 26, 1802, and remained at the spa the whole of the summer. From the letters which passed between Barlow and his wife we are able to glean interesting glimpses of Fulton's doings there. On the 15th Floréal (May 5th) he says:[1]

"Toot: the little rascal Cala[2] has not yet sent off the

[1] C. B. Todd, *Life of Barlow*, p. 184.

[2] Etienne Calla (b. 1760, d. 1835), pupil of Vaucanson, was the most celebrated mechanician of his day and an inventor of some merit.

boat; he says he has had to get made a *barrelier*, and to get the boat painted several times."

Again on the 17th Floréal (May 7) he writes:

"Toot: I believe little Cala has sent the model but am not sure. I have run and scolded and arranged with the diligence and given him the address, and he has promised time after time; but he is a shuffler."

With this model, which was 3 feet long by 8 inch beam provided with "strong clock springs," Fulton made a series of experiments; these are fully detailed in a note book which has been preserved,[1] entitled on the first page:

"EXPERIMENTS AND CALCULATIONS ON PROPELING BOATS WITH STEAM ENGINES.

PLOMBIERS THE 5TH OF JUNE 1802.
ROBT. FULTON."

Below this is a sketch of a steamboat with endless chain of float boards running over two wheels and entitled:

"THE STEAM BOAT FROM NEW YORK TO ALBANY IN 12 HOURS."

The way in which the tests were carried out is also given:

"The model being arranged, a small rivulet was stopped so as to form a stagnant pond 66 feet long, 9 or 10 feet wide and from 3 to 2 feet deep at the upper end; thus prepared and with a good watch which beat the seconds, the experiments commenced." They were directed to finding whether "paddles, skulls, endless chains, or water wheels" were the best "mode of taking the purchase" on the water.

It will at once strike the naval architect when reading of the above-mentioned experiments that we have here the

[1] Sutcliffe, *Robert Fult n and the "Clermont,"* p. 141.

first crude idea of the model tanks now so extensively used at Haslar, Dumbarton, and elsewhere for predicting, from the behaviour of scale models under varying conditions, the performances of the actual vessels to be constructed from them.

From the experiments and the sketch already mentioned it is quite clear that Fulton at this moment was in favour of the endless chain of float boards for propulsion. The calculations that follow all relate definitely to a steamboat service between New York and Albany. Fulton expected to be able to realise a speed of 16 miles per hour, but he also saw clearly that it could not be done unless he had sufficient displacement.

To return now to the correspondence; on the 30 Floréal (May 20) Barlow wrote [1] to his wife:

"Toot is calling for funds. Besides the [$]3,000 which I must pay for him to-morrow and [$]3,000 more at the end of the month, he wants [$]3,000 more still to build another new boat at Brest. I see no end to it; he is plunging deeper all the time, and if he don't succeed I don't know what will become of him. I will do all I can for him, but the best way I can serve him is to keep a sheet anchor for him at home that he might be sure to ride out a gale there if he can't keep the sea nor get into port. St. Aubin says it's a grand damage that he is not here now; Roderer is so enthusiased with his small canals that he would certainly be employed to make one. French froth!!"

The new submarine was never built, although it has been asserted repeatedly that it was.

On the 1st Prairial (May 21) Barlow mentions having seen in the *Morning Chronicle* a report of the speech made in the House of Lords by the Earl Stanhope relative to submarine navigation, in the course of which he stated that it had been brought to such perfection by a person in France as to render the destruction of ships absolutely sure.

This statement created considerable stir, and a certain

[1] C. B. Todd, *Life of Barlow*, p. 186.

amount of uneasiness that led British Ministers eventually to enter into negotiations with the object of withdrawing Fulton from France, the result of which will be seen later.

Fulton was also devoting some time to artistic pursuits, for in a succeeding letter there is a mention of his painting the portrait of Charlotte Villette; later Barlow expresses pleasure that he is getting on so well with the drawings for the *Columbiad.* This was an epic poem based upon and amplified from an earlier work of his—the *Vision of Columbus*—that Barlow had written describing the rise and progress of the United States. We shall hear more of this, for it was not published till 1807.

On the 25th Prairial (June 14) Barlow wrote to Fulton:

"DEAR TOOT—To-day I went to the National Depot of Machines with Parker to show it him and there I met Montgolfier and there I saw a strange thing; it was no less than your very steamboat in all its parts and principles in a very elegant model. It contains your wheel-oars precisely as you have placed them, except that it has four wheels on each side to guide round the endless chain instead of two.

"The two upper wheels seem to be only to support the chain; perhaps it is an improvement."

Barlow proceeds to give details of the company who were going to exploit the invention on the river Rhône. He says further that Montgolfier disbelieves in the whole thing, and adds: "I shall say nothing to Livingston about the model."

This steamboat was patented April 7, 1802, by Desblanc et Cie. of Trévoux.[1]

There cannot be much doubt that this news upset Fulton somewhat, but not for long, as his active mind soon reverted to his earlier idea of paddle wheels. On his

[1] *Description des machines*, vol. xxii. p. 329.

return to Paris in October he inspected the model and effectually disposed of Desblanc, in some notes which have been preserved, because the latter gives neither the proportions of the boat nor the size of the engines to obtain any given speed, and therefore "cannot be said to have made any clear and distinct discovery or useful invention." As a matter of fact Desblanc never did achieve any success.

The reader will be interested to learn that the model is still in existence, and is preserved in the Conservatoire National des Arts et Métiers, the Institution which Barlow calls the "National Depôt of Machines."

Barlow now seems to have paid a flying visit to England —the countries were still at peace—and incidentally he called upon William Chapman[1] to inquire about engines. The interview is referred to on 12 Messidor (July 1st) in a letter from Dover as follows:

"He says that a 26-inch cylinder in what he calls a double engine gives the force of 50 horses; he says to move a boat of 6 feet wide, one foot deep in water and 80 feet long 8 miles an hour, will not require a cylinder more than 14 inches."

On the 14th Messidor (July 3) Barlow dined with Livingston and says:

"TOOT . . . There I met Count Rumford and he and I were friends in a moment. He told me a great many things new and good, and all the particulars about the Royal Institution. I complimented him liberally and handsomely. He talked a great deal about the plunging boat of Fulton's. He and Sir Charles [*i.e.* Blagden, Secretary of the Royal Society of London] agreed that its effects could not be doubted but that it would never be brought into use, because no civilized nation would consent to use it: that men, governments and nations would fight and that it was better for morals and general happiness of all people that the fighting should be done on land. Here Livingston

[1] See p. 38.

interposed with dignity and energy, and observed that the greater part of modern wars were commercial wars, and that these were occasioned by navies, and that the system ought to be overturned; that as to the humanity of the use of the plunging boat, he was so convinced of it that he had written to the American Government recommending those experiments to be made which should prove its efficacy, and then to adopt it as a general mode of defence for our harbours and coasts. Volney joined in enforcing with his usual strength of expression these ideas. Schimmelpennick sat by and said not a word."

On the 21st Messidor (July 10) Barlow mentions having studied Fulton's "memoir of experiments and calculations pretty well."

Barlow's next reference to the steamboat is under date 29th Messidor (July 18).

"Toot, I had a great talk with Livingston. He says he is perfectly satisfied with your experiments and calculations, but is always suspicious that the engine beating up and down will break the boat to pieces. He seems to be for trying the horizontal cylinder or for returning to his mercurial engine. I see his mind is not settled, and he promises now to write you. . . . He thinks the scale you talk of going on is much too large, and especially that part which respects the money. You converted him as to the preference of the wheels above all other modes, but he says they cannot be patented in America because a man (I forget his name)[1] has proposed the same thing there. . . . Parker is highly gratified with your experiments; he wishes, however, something further to remove his doubts—about keeping the proportions and as to the loss of power in different velocities. He wishes to have another *barrelier* made four times as strong as this or thereabouts to see whether the proportional velocity would be the same when moving by the paddles as when moving by the fixture on shore. . . ."

[1] It was Capt. Samuel Morey in 1794.

The last reference by Barlow is on the 7th Thermidor (July 26).

"My project would be that you should pass directly over to England, *silent and steady*, make Chapman construct an engine of 12 inches while you are building a boat of a proportionate size. Make the experiments on that scale *all quiet and quick*. If it answers, put the machinery on board a vessel and go directly to New York (ordering another engine as large as you please to follow you) then secure your patent and begin your operation first small and then large. I think I will find you the funds without any noise for the first operation in England, and if it promises well you may get as many funds and friends in America as you want."

It is fairly clear from these last two letters that there was considerable hesitation on the part of all except Barlow as to whether to back up Fulton with sufficient capital to make the necessary experiments on the large scale. Livingston was alarmed by the boldness of Fulton's proposals, and doubted the necessity for so large a size of boat as he suggested, whereas displacement had been the very thing lacking in nearly all previous experiments.

The letters to Plombières ceased on 27th Fructidor (September 14th), immediately after which Mrs. Barlow and her escort returned to Paris. The circle at 50 rue de Vaugirard was once more complete, and remained unbroken for the next twelve months with the exception of a short absence of Barlow in England, when he was instrumental in mediating between Benjamin West and Fulton; the former had been much offended by some proposition made by the latter, the nature of which has not transpired.

Considerable light is thrown on the conclusions to which Fulton had arrived as to the proper form of propeller for marine propulsion at this time by the following letter[1] addressed to the American Consul-General at Paris in

[1] Reproduced by permission of Mr. C. H. Hart, of Philadelphia, who possesses the original.

reply to an inquiry for information and advice about a proposal of a client:

PARIS, *the 20th September* 1802.

TO MR. FULNER SKIPWITH.

SIR,—The expense of a patent in France is 300 livres (*i.e.* £12) for three years, 800 ditto for ten years, and 1500 ditto for fifteen years; there can be no difficulty in obtaining a patent for the mode of propelling a boat which you have shown me; but if the author of the model wishes to be assured of the merits of his invention before he goes to the expense of a patent, I advise him to make a model of a boat, in which he can place a clock spring which will give about eight revolutions; he can then combine the movements so as to try oars, paddles, and the leaves which he proposes; if he finds that the leaves drive the boat a greater distance in the same time than either oars or paddles they consequently are a better application of power. About eight years ago the Earl of Stanhope tried an experiment on similar leaves in Greenland Dock, London, but without success. I have also tried experiments on similar leaves, wheel-oars, paddles, and flyers similar to those of a smoke jack, and found oars to be the best. The velocity with which a boat moves is in proportion as the sum of the surfaces of the oars, paddles, leaves or other machine is to the bow of the boat presented to the water, and in proportion to the power with which such machinery is put in motion; hence if the sum of the surfaces of the oars is equal to the sum of the surfaces of the leaves, and they pass through similar curves in the same time, the effect must be the same; but oars have their advantage, they return through air to make a second stroke, and hence create very little resistance; whereas the leaves return through water and add considerably to the resistance, which resistance is increased as the velocity of the boat is augmented; no kind of machinery can create power; all that can be done is to apply the manual or other power to the best advantage. If the author of the model is fond of mechanics he will be much amused, and not lose his time, by trying the experiments in the manner I propose, and this perhaps is the most prudent measure, before a patent is taken.

I am, Sir, with much respect, Yours,

ROBT FULTON.

We might remark that the "leaves" referred to are expanding and contracting surfaces like the foot of an aquatic bird; "wheel-oars" mean paddle wheels as we know them; "paddles" mean a chain of float boards passing over two wheels, or the paddles used by Fitch; "flyers" mean screw propellers. In this letter Fulton is very generously giving away a good deal of the information gained by his experiments.

Fulton's presence in Paris and his own confidence seems to have quickly reassured his friends and critics, for we find him almost immediately thereafter entering into partnership with Livingston. The deed of partnership that was executed by them has been preserved,[1] and opens thus:

"Memorandum of an Agreement entered into this tenth day of October in the Year One Thousand Eight hundred and two between Robert R. Livingston, Esq. of the State of New York and Robert Fulton of the State of Pennsylvania.

"Whereas the said Livingston and Fulton have for several years past separately tried various mechanical Combinations for the purpose of propelling boats and vessels by the power of Steam Engines, and conceiving that their experiments have demonstrated the possibility of success, they hereby agree to make an attempt to carry their invention into useful operation, and for that purpose enter into partnership on the following conditions."

[1] In the possession of Mr. J. H. Livingston, of Clermont, who kindly furnished the author with a copy.

These conditions are too long to be given *in extenso*, but the following is a brief summary:

First. A boat 120 feet long, 8 feet wide and 15 inches draught is to be constructed to carry sixty passengers, and to run between New York and Albany at the rate of eight miles per hour in still water.

Second. A United States patent is to be taken out by Fulton, and the property in it is to be divided into 100 shares, fifty of which are to be held by each. All the profits are to be shared equally.

Third. Fulton is to go to England to construct an experimental boat, the estimated cost of which, £500, is to be advanced by Livingston. If unsuccessful, Fulton agrees to repay half that sum within two years. If successful, Fulton is to take out the U.S. patent and superintend the work of establishing the steamboat.

Fourth. When the work is complete, either party may dispose of any number, not exceeding forty, of their shares, but these shareholders are to have no voice in the management. All extensions are to be made out of revenue, and the surplus profits are to be divided twice a year.

Fifth. The duration of the partnership is to be coterminous with the duration of the patent—fourteen years—or whatever extension may be granted, after which each share to have a voice in the disposal of the property.

Sixth. In the case of the death of either partner within the period of partnership his heir or heirs holding twenty shares are jointly to have an equal voice with the primitive partner.

Seventh. Livingston may withdraw at any time after the £500 has been expended on the first experiment, on giving notice in writing to Fulton.

The document is signed by Livingston and Fulton, and witnessed by Robert L. Livingston.

The winter appears to have been spent in further ex-

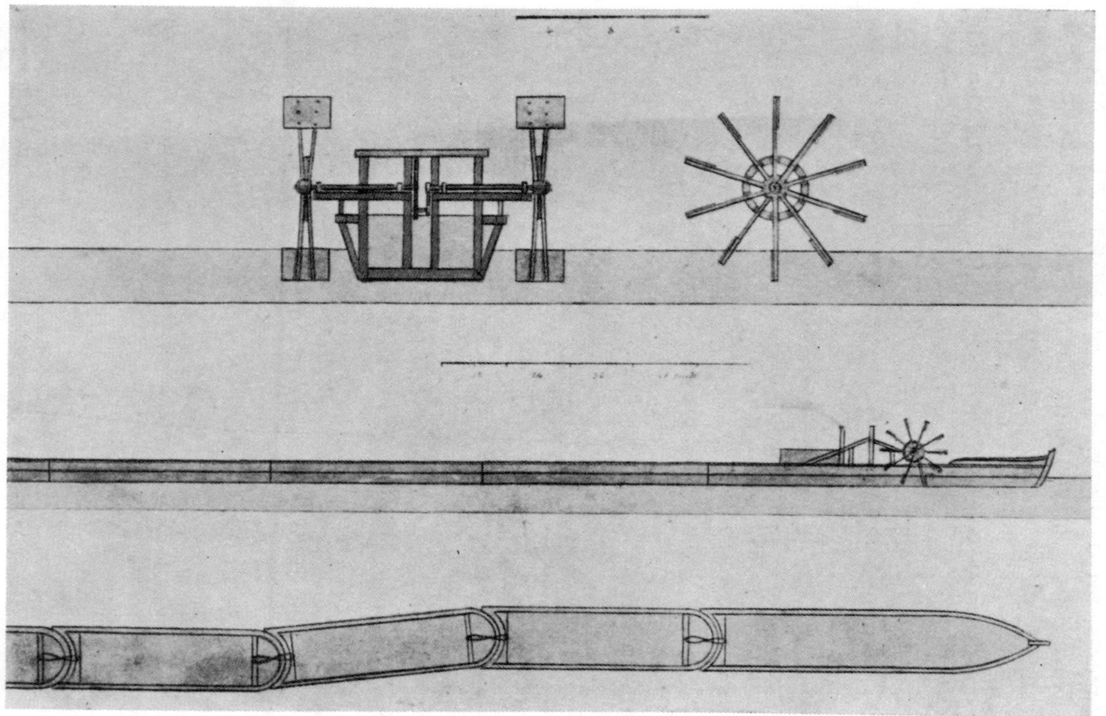

FULTON'S DRAWING FOR HIS FIRST STEAMBOAT, 1803

periments, for a MS. is still preserved dated "Paris the 19 Nevose Anno 11, January the 9th 1803," entitled "Experiments on the model of a boat to be moved by a steam engine," in which six experiments are carefully detailed.

On January 24th Fulton forwarded a plan that he had prepared with the following description to the Demonstrators of the Conservatoire des Arts et Métiers, where the document is still preserved.

(*Translation.*)

PARIS, 4 *Pluviose, An XI.*

Robert Fulton to the Citizens Molar,[1] Bardell, and Montgolfier,[2] Friends of the Arts.

I send you herewith sketch designs of a machine that I am about to construct with which I propose soon to make experiments on the towing of boats upon rivers by the help of fire engines. My first aim in busying myself with this was to put it in practice upon the long rivers of America where there are no roads suitable for haulage or they are scarcely practicable, and where in consequence the expense of navigation by the aid of steam will be put in comparison with the labour of men and not with that of horses as in France.

You will easily see that such a discovery, if it succeeds, would be of infinitely greater importance to America than to France where there exist everywhere roads suitable for haulage and companies who concern themselves with

[1] P. C. Molard (b. 1758, d. 1827) was appointed in 1794 member of a Commission of Arts charged with the preservation of the objects of art and science existing in the country. On the 10th October, when the Conservatoire des Arts et Métiers was definitely established, Molard was appointed one of three Demonstrators. In 1801, the sole administration was confided to him, and this pôst he retained till his retirement in 1816. He was a prolific inventor, and was a member of the Academie des Sciences.

[2] J. M. de Montgolfier (b. 1740, d. 1810) is best known for his inventions, in conjunction with his brother Jacques Etienne (b. 1745, d. 1799) of the hydraulic ram and of the fire balloon. He was appointed Demonstrator of the Conservatoire in 1800, and he held the post till his death.

the transport of merchandize at such moderate charges that I doubt very much if a steam boat however perfect it might be, can gain anything over horses for merchandize. But for passengers it is possible to gain something on the score of speed.

In these plans you will find nothing new since they are only water wheels, a means which has often been tried but always abandoned because it was believed that they give a disadvantageous purchase on the water. But after the experiments which I have already made I am convinced that the fault has not been in the wheel but in the ignorance of proportions, speeds, powers, and probably mechanical combinations.

I have proved by exact experiments that water wheels are much to be preferred to the chain of floats: consequently although the wheels are not a new application yet if I combine them in such a way that a large proportion of the power of the engine acts to propel the boat in the same way as if the purchase was upon the ground the combination will be better than anything that has been done up to the present and it is in fact a new discovery.

For the transport of merchandize I propose to use an engine boat intended for towing one or several freight boats each of which shall be so close to the preceding that the water does not flow between to create resistance. I have already done this in my patent for small canals and it is indispensable for the freight boats moved by fire engines.

For example:

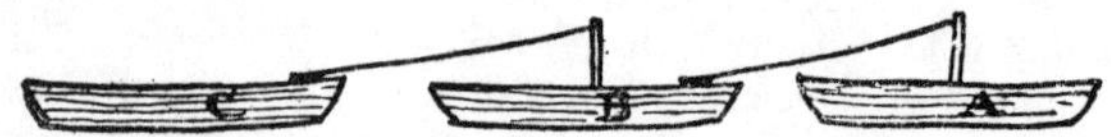

Suppose the boat A with the engine presents to the water a face of 20 [square] feet but inclined at an angle of 50 degrees it will be necessary for it to have an engine of 420 lb. power making 3 feet per second in order to move

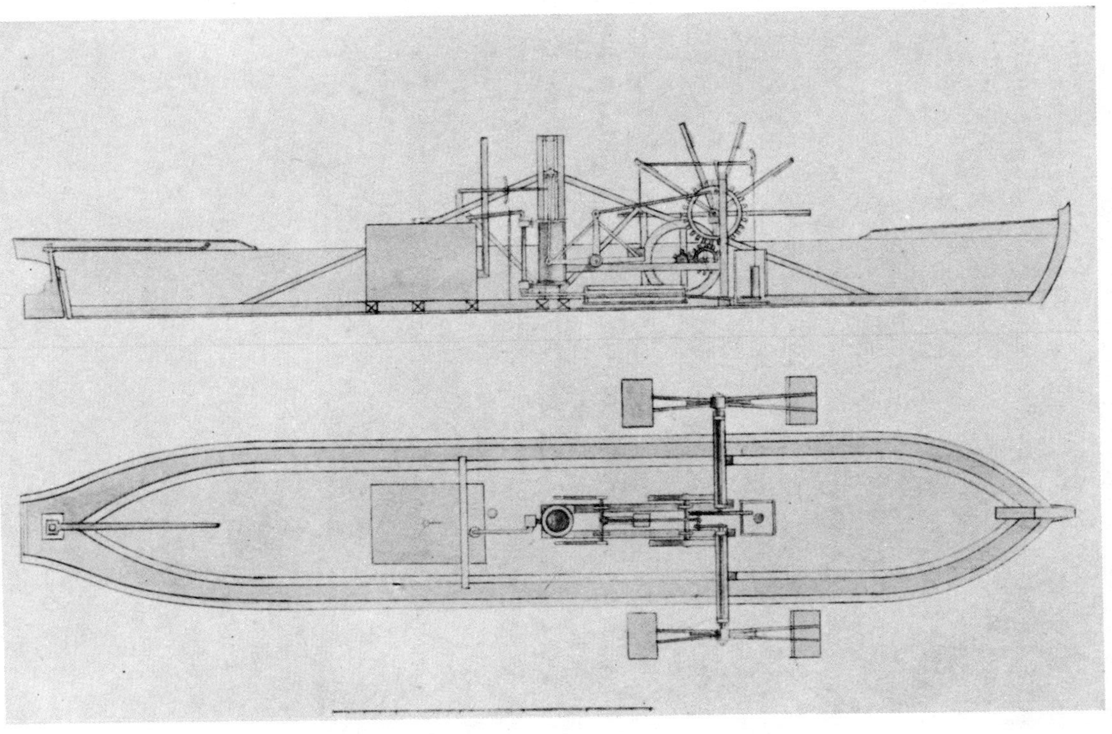

FULTON'S DRAWINGS FOR HIS FIRST STEAMBOAT, 1803

it one league per hour in still water. If the boats B. and C. have similar faces to A. each will require a like power of 420 pounds that is to say 1260 pounds for the three, whilst if they are tied together in the way that I have indicated the force of 420 will suffice for all. This great economy in power is too important to be neglected in such an enterprise.

Citizens:

When my experiments are ready, I shall have the pleasure of inviting you to see them and if they succeed I reserve to myself the right of making a present of my labours to the Republic or to reap from them the advantage which the law allows. Actually, I place these notes in your hands in order that if a similar project comes before you before my experiments are finished it may not have the preference over mine.

Health and Respect,
ROBERT FULTON.

NO. 50 RUE VAUGIRARD.

We must conclude from this letter that Fulton had decided that he might as well reap what benefit, if any, there was to be had in France, as the result of his experiments, and also that he would build the trial boat there. He had been forestalled once by Desblanc, and he did not want the same thing to happen again, and therefore thought it best to secure himself from further anticipation. He freely admits that there is nothing new in his plans—everything depends on the proper proportions of the hull combined with well-known mechanisms. His attitude throughout is totally different from that which he displayed with respect to his submarine.

Fulton with Livingston's financial aid[1] now set to work in earnest to construct the steamboat. Apparently

[1] A receipt signed by him 17 Ventose an 11 (8th March 1803) shows that he had by then received the sum agreed upon, *i.e.* 11,000 francs in nine instalments. *The Livingstons of Callendar*, vol. v. p. 594.

the design submitted to the Conservatoire was only adhered to in its general arrangement; anything in fact that came to hand was used. The engine is stated by Fulton to have been borrowed from M. Perrier and to have been of about eight horse-power. The boiler and the other parts of the machinery seem to have been constructed by M. Etienne Calla, rue du Faubourg St. Denis No. 9. The paddle wheels were 12 feet diameter.

The boiler originally designed by Fulton was remarkable; in fact it was of the "flash" type, in which water is injected into a red-hot chamber in just sufficient quantities to make the steam as required—a system that in these days has been made a success by the labours of M. Serpollet. Fulton's boiler is thus described by a French engineer[1] who had a copy of the original drawing, scale 1 : 3, from Calla:

(*Translation.*)

The steam chamber placed in the middle of the fire-box (foyer) is a copper cylinder 4 inches diameter by the same in height. The piston cylinder is in brass 2 inches diameter by about 24 inches long and is screwed into the steam chamber. A little above this junction it is crossed by two inclined tubes whose internal diameter is about $\frac{1}{8}$ inch. Water from the reservoir falls through one of these tubes into the steam chamber which communicates with the air by the other tube. This double communication being controlled by cocks which the piston rod of the motive cylinder opens and shuts at the proper intervals, steam is formed in the red-hot chamber and exerts its pressure on the underside of the piston. When at the top of its stroke it opens the cocks to the steam chamber and atmosphere while the piston descends under the action of a counterweight.

Fulton intended to employ steam at 32 atmospheres! but

[1] Hachette, *Traité des Machines*, 1828.

after some experiments with M. Calla the steam chambers so deteriorated under the action of the fuel that the apparatus was abandoned; and no wonder, for the idea was far in advance of the constructive resources of the time. Apparently a simple externally-fired boiler was eventually used.

It would appear that the boat was ready early in the spring, and that Livingston already anticipated its success, for he wrote to his friends in the States, and by their interest an Act was passed on April 5, 1803, by which the rights and privileges of the lapsed Act of 1798 were extended to himself and Fulton jointly for twenty years from the date of the new Act on condition of proof being produced within two years; this time of proof was extended by a subsequent Act till April 1807.

One night when the boat was lying moored in the Seine ready for her trial trip an untoward accident happened. A violent storm arose, with the consequence that the boat, never intended to resist the weight of heavy machinery in such circumstances, proved unequal to the strain; the engine went through the bottom and the whole sank in the bed of the river. This misfortune was announced to Fulton while still in bed; he rushed at once to the spot, and laboured all day in the river without rest or food, getting up the machinery. Never at any time strong in the lungs, this imprudence left behind it a weakness which he felt to the end of his life.

Nothing daunted by the mishap, he set to work to build a boat of somewhat larger size and heavier proportions. His own statement is that it was 70 French feet long, 8 French feet wide, 3 French feet deep (*i.e.* 74.6 feet by 8.2 feet by 3.2 feet). The engine was uninjured and was again used, and the boat was ready towards the end of July, as is shown by a playful letter of invitation,[1] dated July 24, 1803, which he sent to his friend Skipwith. To understand it,

[1] Reproduced by permission of Mr. C. H. Hart, of Philadelphia, who possesses the original.

it should be premised that the latter's first child had not long been born.

PARIS, *the 5th Thermidor Anno* II.

MY DEAR FRIEND,—You have experienced all the anxiety of a fond father on a child's coming into the world. So have I. The little cherub, now plump as a partridge, advances to the perfection of her nature and each day presents some new charm. I wish mine may do the same. Some weeks hence, when you will be sitting in one corner of the room and Mrs. Skipwith in the other, learning the little creature to walk, the first unsteady step will scarcely balance the tottering frame; but you will have the pleasing perspective of seeing it grow to a steady walk and then to dancing. I wish mine may do the same. My boy, who is all bones and corners just like his daddy, and whose birth has given me much uneasiness, or rather anxiety,—is just learning to walk and I hope in time he will be an active runner. I therefore have the honour to invite you and the ladies to see his first movements on Monday next from 6 till 9 in the evening between the Barrière des Bons Hommes and the steam engine. May our children, my friend, be an honour to their country and a comfort to the grey hairs of their doting parents. Yours,

R. FULTON.

As the 24th was a Sunday, this private trial must have been on July 25th or August 1st—probably the former, because Fulton's doings appear to have been reported before that date to Napoleon, who learnt everything that was going on among the intellectuals of Paris. On July 21st he wrote to M. Champagny, Councillor of State in the department of Marine, a letter showing keen insight into the real meaning of the invention.

(*Translation.*)

I have just read the project of Citizen Fulton which you have sent to me much too late *in that it may change the face of the world.* However that may be, I desire you immediately to confide its examination to a commission of members chosen by you from among the different classes of the Institute. It is there that learned Europe would seek for judges to solve the question under consideration. As soon as the report is made it will be sent to you and you will forward it to me. Try and let the whole matter be determined within a week as I am impatient.[1]

Whether in consequence of this or not, the project was certainly referred to the Institut National des Sciences et des Arts, for in their order book is an entry dated 20 Thermidor (8th Aug.) of an invitation from Robert Fulton "to see the experiment of a boat ascending the stream by means of a steam engine" to which he adds reflections relative to the project. Citizens Bossut, Bougainville, and Carnot are ordered to be present and make a report. Strangely enough, beyond the entry there is no trace either of the letter of invitation, of the memoir, or of the report. Equally curious to relate, search among the National Archives reveals no trace of the report either. It has been suggested that as the Minister of the Interior was absent from 21st June to 8th August the matter may have been dealt with outside the office, but the more reasonable explanation is that Fulton left Paris very soon after, and that the matter was dropped for that reason.

We are therefore forced to rely, for an account of this public trial, upon one of the newspapers of the day.[2] It runs as follows:

(*Translation.*)

On the 21st Thermidor (9th Aug. 1803) a trial was made of a new invention, of which the complete and brilliant success should have important consequences for the commerce and internal navigation of France. During

[1] *Desbrière*, vol. iii. p. 331.
[2] *Journal des Debats*, 23 Thermidor.

the past two or three months there has been seen at the end of the quay Chaillot a boat of curious appearance, equipped with two large wheels mounted on an axle like a cart, while behind these wheels was a kind of large stove with a pipe, as if there was some kind of a small fire engine intended to operate the wheels of the boat. Several weeks ago some evil-minded persons threw the structure down. The builder, having repaired the damage, received the day before yesterday a most flattering reward for his labours and talent.

At six o'clock in the evening, assisted by three persons only, he put his boat in motion with two other boats in tow behind it, and for an hour and a half he afforded the curious spectacle of a boat moved by wheels like a cart, these wheels being provided with paddles or flat plates and being moved by a fire engine.

In following it along the quay the speed against the current of the Seine appeared to us about that of a rapid pedestrian, that is about 2400 toises (*i.e.* 2.9 miles) per hour; while in going down stream it was more rapid: it ascended and descended four times from Les Bons-Hommes as far as the engine of Chaillot; it was manœuvred with facility, turned to the right and left, came to anchor, started again, and passed by the swimming school.

One of the boats took to the quay a number of savants and representatives of the Institute, among whom were Citizens Bossut, Carnot, Prony, Perrier, Volney, &c. Doubtless they will make a report which will give to this discovery all the *éclat* which it deserves; for this mechanism applied to our rivers, the Seine, the Loire, and the Rhône, would be fraught with the most advantageous consequences to our internal navigation. The tows of barges which now require four months to come from Nantes to Paris would arrive promptly in from 10 to 15 days. The author of this brilliant invention is M. Fulton, an American and a celebrated mechanician.

The Pompe de Chaillot—the steam pumping plant that had supplied Paris with water since about 1780—stood close to what is now the Pont de l'Alma. How few of the thousands who to-day travel, whether for business or for pleasure, by the comfortable steamers that ply on the Seine ever know or think of the little steamboat that preceded them more than a century ago.

It was not, however, with any view of submitting his work for approval to the National Institute or to the French Government that Fulton had taken up this steamboat project. He was too disgusted with the way in which he had been treated already officially, nor did he want to encounter possible opposition from Desblanc. He and Livingston, although destined to be drawn aside from it for awhile, had in view a definite scheme, and that was simply to apply the knowledge thus acquired in a place where they were certain of reaping a substantial reward. All along Fulton had never claimed any invention in the constituent parts of the steamboat, and he probably realised that a patent merely for arrangement and proportion of parts would be of little value, whereas a monopoly by legislative act was quite different. This latter was what awaited him in America on the Hudson River.

Before the public trial had taken place he wrote, enclosing a sketch of his requirements, to Boulton, Watt and Co., the most famous firm of engine builders in the world at that time, in the following terms:

PARIS, *the 6th August* 1803.

MESSRS. BOLTON AND WATT, BIRMINGHAM.[1]

GENTLEMEN,—If there is not a law which prohibits the exportation of Steam engines to the United States of America or if you can get a permit to export parts of an engine, will you be so good as to make me a Cylinder of

[1] Boulton & Watt MSS.

a 24 horse-power double effect, the piston making a 4 foot stroke;

Also the piston and piston rod.

The Valves and movements for opening and shutting them.

The air pump, piston and rod.

The condensor with its communication to the cylinder and air pump.

The bottom of the cylinder cast in form as on the drawing and the disposition of the parts as near as possible as they stand in the drawing. The other parts can be made at New York, and as it will save the expense of transport and they require a particular arrangement which must be done while I am present, I prefer having them done there. Therefore if it is permitted to export the above parts, you will confer on me a great obligation by favouring me with them and placing me the next on your list. When finished please to pack them in such a manner as not to receive injury, and send them to the nearest port, which, I suppose, is Liverpool, to be shiped to New York to the address of Brockhurst Livingston Esqre. the Amount of the expenses will be placed to your order in the hands of George Wm. Erving,[1] American Consul, Nicholas Lane, Lombard Street, No. 10, London.

The situation for which the engine is designed and the Machinery which is to be combined with it will not admit of placing the Condensor under the cylinder as usual, but I hope the communicating tube to the condensor will not render the condensation less perfect or Injure the working of the engine.

Should you find a difficulty in getting a permit to export the parts above mentioned, I hope to be able to obtain it through our Minister, Mr. Monroe. And as there

[1] George W. Erving (b. 1771, d. 1850), diplomatist—educated at Oxford Made Consul in London by President Jefferson. From there in 1804 he went as Secretary of Legation to Spain and remained there till 1810; in the following year he was special Minister to Denmark, and from 1814 to 1819 he was U.S. Minister to Spain.

is some difficulty in passing letters to and from Paris and Birmingham, which may loose much time You will be so good as to furnish me the above parts as soon as possible without waiting to hear further from me.

Please to write as soon as possible under cover to Mr. Erving as before mentioned. In which I beg you to Answer the following questions :

What must be the size of the boiler for such an engine, how much space for the water and how much for the steam? What is the most improved method of making the Boiler, and economic mode of setting it? How many pounds of coal will such an engine require per hour, and what is the expence at Birmingham?

Can you inform me what is the difference in heating with coals or wood, as in most cases wood must be used in America, and must not the furnace be made different when wood is to be used?

What will be the consequence of condencing with water a little salt As in the place where the engine is to work the water is brackish? What will be the Interior and exterior diameter of the cylinder and its length and what will be the Velocity of the piston per second? This information will enable me to combine the other parts of the machinery.

When can the engine be finished and how much will be the expence? Your favouring me with the execution of this order, and answering the above questions will very much oblige

Your most obedient,
ROBERT FULTON.

RUE VAUGIRARD, NO. 50 à PARIS.

Can the position of this Cylinder Condensor and air pump be adhered to as in the drawing without Injuring the working of the engine?

The drawing referred to is executed on a sheet of

writing paper and served as the enclosure of the above letter. The MS. notes upon it are as follows:

It is desired to have a cylinder of a 24 horse power with a Stroke of four feet as the particular use for which the engine is intended will not admit of the condensor standing under the cylinder. I hope there is no objection to placing it and the air pump as in this Sketch. The Square which is formed on the bottom of the cylinder, and which is to be its support to be preserved as near the dimentions he(re) delineated as possible. The distance from the Centre of the cylinder to the centre of the condensor 30 Inches and the distance from the centre of the condensor to the centre of the air pump 37 Inches also the 46 Inches from the bottom of the cylinder to the bottom of the condensor to be observed and not if not attended with any inconvenience or detriment to the working of the engine; this drawing is made by the scale of one inch to a foot. The air pump has a stroke of 2 feet; this quantity of movement and these proportions are fitted to the composition of the other parts of the machinery.

I submit them to your better judgement: begging only that they may be preserved as near as possible without diminishing the power of the machine.

August the 6th, 1803.

ROBERT FULTON.

The firm's London agent replied to this on August 22nd by a letter which has not been preserved, but its nature may be inferred from Fulton's next letter, which was written in triplicate on the 1st, 8th, and 11th, in case of any miscarriage—a very frequent occurrence in those days. It runs as follows:

PARIS, *the 1st September* 1803.

MESSRS. BOLTON AND WATT.

GENTLEMEN,—I have received your letter of the 22 of August by Mr. Barlow. I had previously calculated that some additional time and expence would be necessary to make models for disposing of the condensor and Air pump as in my drawing; however, if you have models for an engine of a 24 horse power with a 4 foot stroke, I presume very little alteration will be necessary, the air pump will be as usual; and the condensor with its communication to the steam box will be the only variation; but what I am most anxious to know is whether there is any objection to the manner in which I have disposed of the condensor, if not that you will be so good as to execute my order as soon as possible, and forward it to New York as before desired without hearing further from me. This I mention as the communication between this country and England is daily growing more difficult and not to lose time on that account.

At the same time I beg of you an answer to the questions in my former letter which you will much oblige me by sending as soon as possible by the circuitous but certain route which the post office in London has adopted for passing letters on to the continent.

My address

RUE VAUGIRARD, NO. 50
FB ST GERMAINS
à PARIS.

Mr. Barlow refered you to Mr. Thomas Willson Bucklersbury, London for the amount of the charges.

I am with much respect your most obedient

ROBERT FULTON.

May I beg the favour of your sending a duplicate of your answer by a second post fearing the first may not arrive?

The letter is addressed to Boulton, Watt & Co., London Street, London. It came via Hamburg to the Foreign Office, which is evidently the "circuitous route" referred to. All three letters came safely to hand, but immediately on receipt of the first the firm replied as follows:

SOHO, *4th October* 1803.

ROBERT FULTON, ESQ. PARIS.

Your favour of the 1st Ult^o. is just come to hand from which we notice the receipt of our Agent's letter to Mr. Barlow of 22 August.

We have since that time made application to the proper officer of Government for permission to export the Articles ordered in your former favour, but as no answer has been returned, we should be compromising ourselves by proceeding farther without authority. We must beg leave therefore to decline the order and shall deliver your drawing to any person you may please to appoint to receive it.[1]

We remain, Sir,
Your obt. Servts,
BOULTON, WATT & CO.

P.S.—We are not aware of any detrimental consequences that will accrue to the operation of the Engine, from the condenser being placed in the position you have drawn it.

Fulton did not, however, take this refusal quietly, for on November 3rd he wrote from Amsterdam to his Excellency James Monroe, American Minister at the Court of St. James, asking him to use his influence to get the permit.

One extract reads: [2]

"It will be well to ask the permission for yourself without mentioning my name as I have reason to believe

[1] The drawing was never claimed, however, and is still preserved in the Boulton and Watt MSS. These and succeeding letters from Boulton, Watt & Co. are taken from the firm's press copy letter books, the invention of the great James Watt himself, and at that time still an innovation in business circles.

[2] Sutcliffe, *Robert Fulton and the "Clermont,"* p. 155.

Government will not be much disposed to favour any wish of mine."

Mr. Monroe did not reply, so that Fulton wrote again [1] on November 17, from Paris, strongly urging him to take action, but again without effect.

Thus were Fulton's hopes, for the time being, dashed to the ground, and he was therefore probably more open to the negotiations which had led to his presence in Amsterdam. He had been there to meet an agent of the British Government sent at the instigation of Earl Stanhope by Lord Sidmouth, who was trying to withdraw Fulton from France and from any scheme inimical to Britain's naval supremacy.

Fulton writes of this incident in his notebook: [2]

"I agreed on certain conditions and Mr. Smith set off for London to give in my terms. I then met him in Amsterdam in December with the reply, which, not being satisfactory, he returned to London with other proposals and I went on to Paris."

A portfolio of sketches of the Dutch people and their surroundings, executed in the happiest vein, remain to testify of his employment during this time.[3]

In March "Mr. Smith" arrived in Paris with a letter from Lord Hawkesbury, which was more satisfactory, and this induced Fulton to proceed to London and transfer his services to the British Government.

It is this conduct which merits, in the opinion of many persons, the accusation of treachery. Had the countries been at war there might be something in the charge, but they were still at peace, nor did the rupture occur till May 12, 1804, when the British Ambassador, Lord Whitworth, demanded his passports. The fact of the matter is that, as the citizen of a friendly state, Fulton had offered warlike inventions to the French Government. More than a year

[1] *Loc. cit.*, p. 158.

[2] *Century Magazine*, vol. lxxvi. p. 945, by permission of Mrs. Sutcliffe.

[3] Colden's *Life*, p. 51.

had elapsed since those proposals had finally been declined, and although he had been reimbursed part of the expense that he had incurred in his experiments, he had never been in the pay of, nor was he under the slightest obligation to, the French Government. He was therefore at liberty to transfer his services whithersoever he pleased. In any case he would have had to have crossed over to England in order to get the engine he wanted, for in no other way did that seem feasible.

It might be remarked, in passing, that, to a republican like Fulton, the form that the government in France was now assuming under Napoleon, who declared himself Emperor on May 18 following, was utterly repugnant to, and a sad falling away from the ideals that had inspired the leaders of the French Revolution. That this was Fulton's opinion is conclusively shown in several of his letters.

Before leaving France he despatched his MSS. to the United States. The vessel was wrecked, and when the case containing them was recovered the contents were found to be much injured.

CHAPTER VIII

RETURNS TO ENGLAND — ORDERS A STEAMBOAT ENGINE — EXPERIMENTS WITH THE TORPEDO AGAINST THE BOULOGNE FLOTILLA—LEAVES FOR THE UNITED STATES

FULTON at length left Paris on April 29, and set foot once more on English soil, reaching London on May 19, 1804. For diplomatic reasons, he passed under the assumed name of Francis—a somewhat thin disguise, but one that was sufficient, in one instance as we shall see later, to hide his true identity.

It would naturally be imagined that he would at once report himself at the Foreign Office, or to the Prime Minister. Probably he did so, only we have no record of the fact. At any rate we do know that he plunged at once into the engine business, for we find him writing on May 30 from "Story Gate Coffee House," asking Mr. Hammond for a passport for Mr. and Mrs. Barlow to proceed through London to the United States. He also says:

"I also beg permission to ship one of Mr. Watt's Steam Engines to New York for the purpose of carrying into effect an experiment in which I have fortunately succeeded—that of navigating boats against currents of not more than four miles an hour, hence calculated for most of our rivers."[1]

He concludes his letter with remarks as to the prospective advantages to England.

The first request at any rate was granted, for Barlow passed through London and sailed from Falmouth about August, while Fulton went off to Birmingham to pay a visit to the Soho Works for the purpose of ordering

[1] Sutcliffe, *Robert Fulton and the "Clermont,"* p. 163.

his engine. In his notebook under date July 5, 1804, there is the entry: "Travelling from London to Birmingham and back again to order the Steam engine £8, 0*s*. 0*d*."

With his usual ease of manner, he seems to have made himself at home with the members of the firm, including Matthew Boulton, but apparently he did not meet the celebrated James Watt, for the latter had retired from the business in 1800, and was now living at Heathfield Hall some distance away.

The correspondence that ensued[1] is almost self-explanatory, and is so interesting that we give it in full.

SOHO, 4*th July* 1804.

ROBT. FULTON.

SIR,—In compliance with your request we have prepared an Estimate of the Materials undermentioned, which fitted up in our usual manner, will amount to Three Hundred and Eighty Pounds delivered here, and payable by our Draft upon a banker or merchant in London upon such delivery.

We remain, Sir, Your obt. Servts.

BOULTON, WATT & CO.

Schedule of material above referred to

1. A Steam Cylinder 24 Inches Diameter, 4 feet stroke, with its top and plate to bottom, gland and brasses compleat.
2. Piston, its Cover, Bottom Plate and spanners.
3. Piston rod, its cap and cutters.
4. Nozzles compleat with Valves and Levers.
5. Working Gear compleat with Brackets.
6. Perpendicular Steam Pipe & Eduction Pipe.
7. Condenser Vessel with Blow pipe & Blowing Valve.
8. Injection Cock, Rod, Handle and Index.

[1] Boulton & Watt MSS. in the possession of Mr. George Tangye, and now published for the first time with his permission.

9. Air pump its bucket and top and bottom valves compleat.
10. Air pump bucket rod with cap and bracket.
11. Eduction Pipe to Condenser.
12. Two boxes of Cement.

BOULTON, WATT & CO.

SOHO, *4th July* 1804.

LONDON, *July the 13th*, 1804.

MESSRS. BOULTON WATT & CO.

GENTLEMEN,—Inclosed I Send you a guarantee for the 380£, but as it is possible altering models or making same to fit the engine to my particular case, may raise your demand to a greater amount any further Sum shall be paid.

On writing to Mr. Hammond it may be that you do not receive an Answer for some time. Ministers are now so occupied with their own affairs, the[y] often forget or neglect what they consider trifles, however I hope that will not stop the work, the permit given to me, will I hope quiet you, particularly as the engine is to be delivered to my order at Soho and I take the shiping myself for which I must have another permit when the Vessel is named.

Since having the pleasure of seeing you and your Works, I have disposed the condenser horizontal as In the inclosed drawing. if there is no objection to this it will make the work more compact and well Suited to the boat, it also avoids the risque of water rising into the cylinder as in the first drawing. The Air pump I have made to descend between the floor timbers so as to be lower than the condenser with a view to keep it always clear of water and have as much space within as possible.

If you approve of this mode of composing, the bottom of the Cylinder must be square so as to rest on the condensing Vat. As I never can have more than one boiler I have sketched a design for the steam to enter the centre of the upper nozel, and the condensation to pass from the bottom of the lower one, this arrangement will keep everything trim in the middle line of the boat, and not interrupt the other movements. If you will have the goodness to indulge me in those alterations you will oblige me, provided, *however*, they do not injure the working of the engine.

I forgot to ask you if there are instances of Engines working with Salt water, and what is the effect on the boiler, condensation and working of the engine.

Have the goodness to write me and when time will permit please to give me your thoughts on my boiler, excuse the trouble I give you. I hope at some future day to acquire sufficient merit to be admitted among the [circle] of your friends *when* solicitations to promote useful improvements will give more pleasure than pain.

Yours with sincere respect

ROBT. FULTON.

Please to direct for R. Francis Storeys gate Coffeehouse[1] George Street Westminster.

The enclosed Brochure is for Mr. Boulton Senior please to present it him with my thanks for his civilities.

The guarantees were in the following terms:

MESSRS BOULTON & WATT,
BIRMINGHAM.

LONDON, 10 *July* 1804.

GENTN.,—Mr. Robert Fulton having informed me that you have agreed to make a Steam Engine for him, the cost of which will be about £380 sterling, & having desired me to guarantee the payment of this Sum to you:

I do hereby accordingly promise to pay you whatever sum shall be agreed upon between you and Mr. Fulton on the account aforementioned, on your complying with the

[1] This coffeehouse was much resorted to by members of Parliament. It existed as Storey's Gate Tavern till 1912, when it was absorbed by extensions of the buildings of the Institution of Mechanical Engineers.

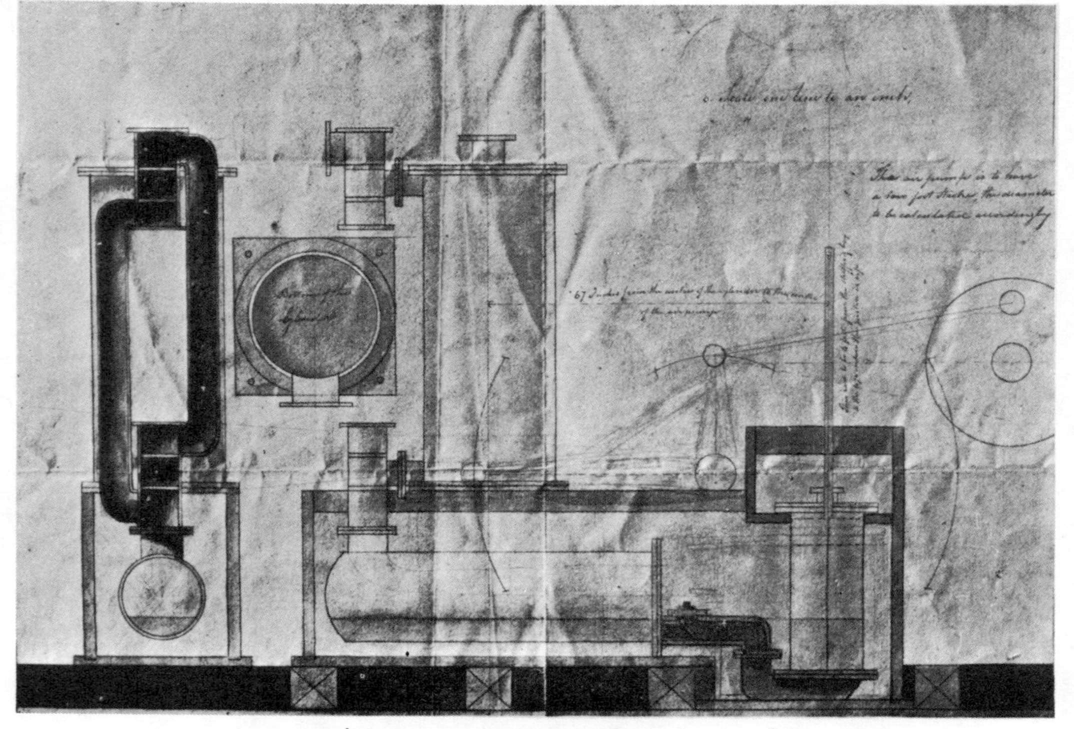

FULTON'S SKETCH FOR THE STEAMBOAT ENGINE, 1804

terms settled, or to be settled between you and that Gentleman. I am, Gen^{n}. Your very ob^{t}. Ser^{t}.

GEORGE W. ERVING.

Our friend George Wm. Erving Esqr. having informed us that you require a farther security than his for the payment of the above £380, we hereby guarantee to give the due payment of the sum on the terms above stated and remain, Gent^{n}. Your most hble. Servts,

LEES, SATTERTHWAITE & BRASSEY.

MESSRS. BOLTON & WATT.

The drawing which was enclosed with the letter is dated "July 8th, 1804," and has been preserved; it is to a "Scale one line to an inch," and is coloured. Besides the condenser in the horizontal position, the centre lines of the proposed connections, by means of a bell-crank lever, between the cylinder and the paddle wheels are also shown. This therefore is the origin of the bell-crank engine.

It is obvious from this and subsequent letters that Fulton made no secret of the purpose for which he wanted the engine, notwithstanding statements to the contrary. Indeed why should he have done so? It was not the first engine that the firm had made for a boat, as witness the one[1] for Lord Stanhope.

The firm's reply of July 18 has not been preserved, but Fulton's next letter is:

LONDON, *July the 20th*, 1804.

MESSRS. BOULTON WATT AND CO.

GENTLEMEN,—I this morning received yours. You will be so good as to place the steam pipe on the side of the Nozle as usual, And as I wish to guard against all events —least I should have to act in salt water, you will be so good as to make the air pump of Brass. As to the Condensor I presume it must be a considerable time cor-

[1] See p. 26.

roding so as to be useless. In this work I do not take expence into consideration honour me with your confidence your demand whatever it may be shall be as honorably paid.

Does not salt rapidly form in the boiler when salt water is used ?

I lament the state of Mr. Gregory Watt's health, and am flattered by his remembrance of me ; his Virtues will render his memory dear to his friends.

Yours with much respect,

ROBERT FULTON.

Gregory Watt, who is here referred to, was the talented and promising son of James Watt by his second wife. He died of consumption at the early age of twenty-four in October of this same year, to the intense grief of his father and mother.

The firm in their reply to Fulton's instructions and queries asked for further sanction for the condenser.

SOHO, 25*th July* 1804.

ROBERT FULTON, ESQ. LONDON.

SIR,—We have your favour of the 20th and shall accordingly make the Air pump its bucket and clack of brass and its rod of Copper. The condenser will do very well of Iron and we should propose to execute it in the manner represented in the annexed sketch which is sent for your approbation previous to our commencing the execution. The Air pump you will see is placed in the Condenser, which is a construction we have sometimes practised ; the mouth through which the water and air are discharged, is drawn towards one side but it may be placed in any direction you wish it to have. We recommend that the Cylinder should be placed on a solid block of stone or wood rather than on the edge of this Casting which may be of less dimensions than you had sketched.

The Boiler should be about 16 feet long to supply the Engine with steam at 20 strokes Per minute full load; and in proportion for a less supply, if you should wish to make it capable of working the Engine at a slower rate. It is supposed to have no flues at the sides or ends. The Chimney flue should have an Area of 400 or 500 inches.

We have not had the opportunity of making any direct observations upon the rapidity with which salt would be formed in the Boiler from Sea Water, but we conceive you will have no difficulty in carrying with you a sufficient quantity of fresh water for its supply; if not the evil must be guarded against by frequent emptying and cleaning. We shall be glad to have your sentiments when you have given the sketch the necessary consideration and remain,

Sir, Your obt. Servts,
BOULTON, WATT & CO.

This sketch referred to has been preserved also; it shows the air pump and condenser vertical and the cylinder on a block of stone 16 in. thick. There is also a sketch of a wagon boiler.

To this Fulton replied as follows:

MESSRS. BOULTON, WATT & CO.

GENTLEMEN,—I like your mode of placing the air pump in the condensor but as my measurements confine me to 3 feet in width the condensing vat ought not to exceed that *width*. Could not the condensor be made like a box about 4 feet long 20 inches wide and two feet deep as in this sketch? If so I shall be completely accommodated; if not you must use your particular composition of the parts. I must beg of you however to fit me in this respect if possible. Perhaps a hole at A may be convenient for a man to pass his arm and draw away Chips which might get into the [space] under the valve of the air pump the hole to be covered with a plate. In a former letter I mentioned that the air pump will have a stroke of two feet. I see by your drawing you have it 16 inched diameter in the Interior. I presume this width is calculated accordingly.

On tuesday I go out of town for 6 weeks or two months I shall not trouble you further about the construction. You will have the goodness to proceed immediately to the construction in the manner you deem best suited to my purpose. I am with much respect, Yours,

R. FULTON.

LONDON *the* 28*th July* 1804.

As we shall see shortly, Fulton had just come to terms with the Admiralty as to the use of his torpedo; the business that called him out of town was to superintend the work of making these torpedoes at Portsmouth Dockyard and the use of them against the French fleet. But before giving a relation of these doings it will be as well to finish the account of the engine business. Boulton, Watt & Co. now seem to have put the engine in hand. Two drawings of it as actually made have been preserved. The drawing of the cylinder, &c. (*see* illustration) is marked "R. Fulton, Esq. Inch to the foot Sept. 13, 1804." The instructions on the drawing show that the patterns were taken as far as could be done from the firm's "20 H(orse) engine." The other drawing (*see* illustration) shows the "Working and Injection Gears, Inch to the foot, R. Fulton, Esqre. 6 Nov. 1804." Murdock's socket valves are shown.

These drawings, representing as they do the engine that inaugurated steam navigation on a commercial scale, are invaluable documents of the highest possible interest.

Instead of two months, nearly four elapsed before

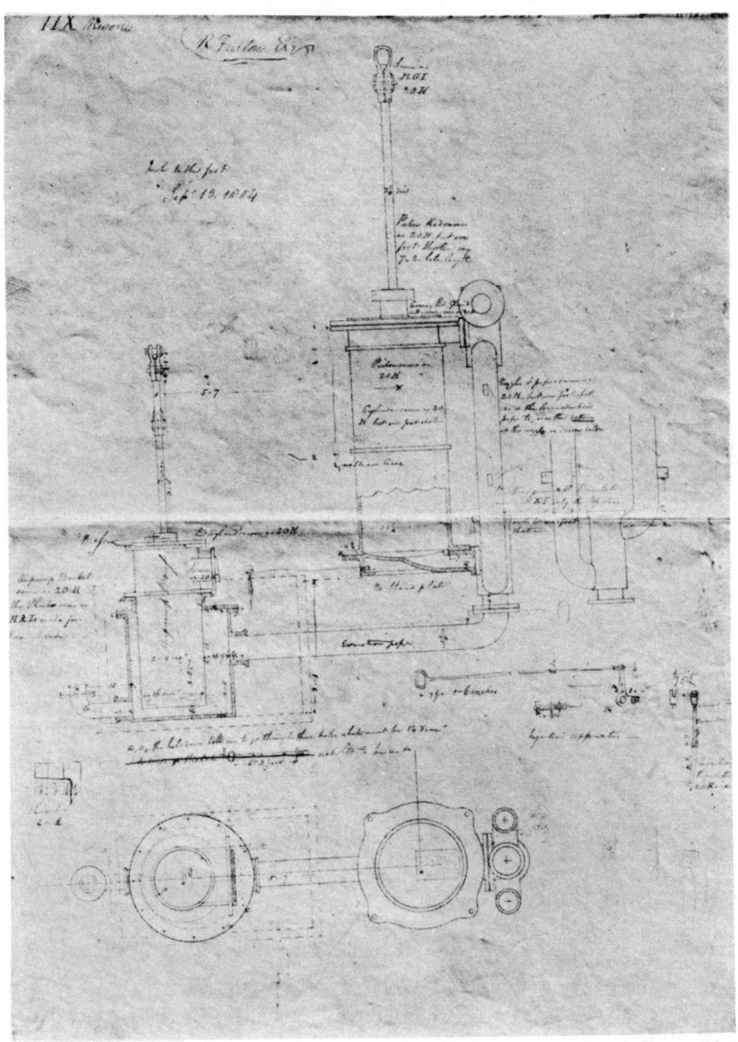

CYLINDER AND CONDENSER OF THE ENGINE FOR THE "CLERMONT," 1804

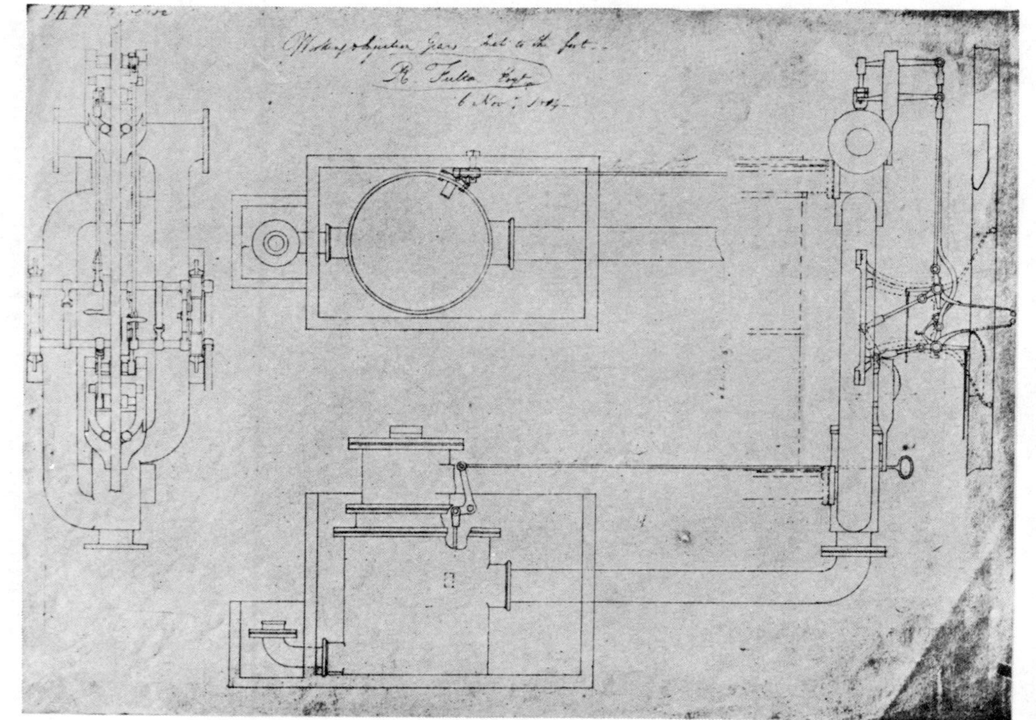

VALVE GEAR OF THE ENGINE FOR THE "CLERMONT," 1804

Fulton was back in town, when he wrote to inquire about the engine as follows:

LONDON, DECEMBRE *the* 19*th*, 1804.
BEDFORD STREET, BEDFORD SQUARE, NO. 9.

MESSRS. BOULTON WATT AND CO.

GENTLEMEN,—Have the goodness to let me know the state of my engine; when finished and put together I shall be tempted to go and see it.

Some time ago I Saw an engine working at Portsmouth with an Iron boiler and Salt water a Boiler is good for about 2 years it requires cleening once in 15 or 20 days—which fortunately is much less than I apprehended.

Can you undertake to make a copper boiler for me or do you advise my getting it made here? With much respect your most

obedient ROBT. FULTON.

Please to direct as formerly
R. FRANCIS.

To this the firm at once replied:

SOHO, *Dec.* 22*nd*, 1804.

R. FULTON, ESQ.

SIR,—In reply to your favour of the 19th inst. we have the pleasure to inform you that the materials of your Engine are compleated. All the different parts have been tried together and we were preparing to pack them up when we received your letter.

It will be attended with some little trouble and delay to put the whole together again, but if you are desirous of seeing it in that state we should make a point of complying with your wish and put them together for your inspection at the commencement of the week after the Christmas holidays, say on the 30th inst. We shall send through the hands of our house in town a detailed drawing of the nozzles working etc. which you may probably find sufficiently explicit to supersede seeing the parts put together. Upon this point we shall await your further instructions. You will oblige us also by saying to what part you wish the articles to be forwarded and the address of the house to whom they are to be consigned. We presume of course it is your intention to have them forwarded by Canal.

You will get the copper boiler made in London full as well as elsewhere, and we can recommend Wm. Shears, Coppersmith, Fleet Market, as a good workman in that line.

We are very respectfully,
Sir, Your Obed[t]. Serv[ts].,
BOULTON, WATT & CO.

Fulton's reply was as follows:

LONDON, *December the 26th*, 1804.

MESSRS. BOULTON, WATT & CO.

GENTLEMEN,—I thank you for the dispatch in executing my engine, had it not been packed up curiosity would have urged me to visit you, but being ready for transport I hope it will not be disturbed till it arrives in New York.

If there is water carriage to London I wish it to be forwarded to my Address as soon as the canals are open. In such case I can forward it in the same Vessel with the Boiler which I propose to get made here.

Have the goodness to send me an elevation and ground plan as it stood when put together drawn by an exact scale of one inch to a foot. Also a schedule of the parts that I may know if all arrives safe in America.

You will please to forward me your account
and believe me, Your much obliged
ROBT. FULTON.

BEDFORD STREET, BEDFORD
SQUARE, NO. 9.

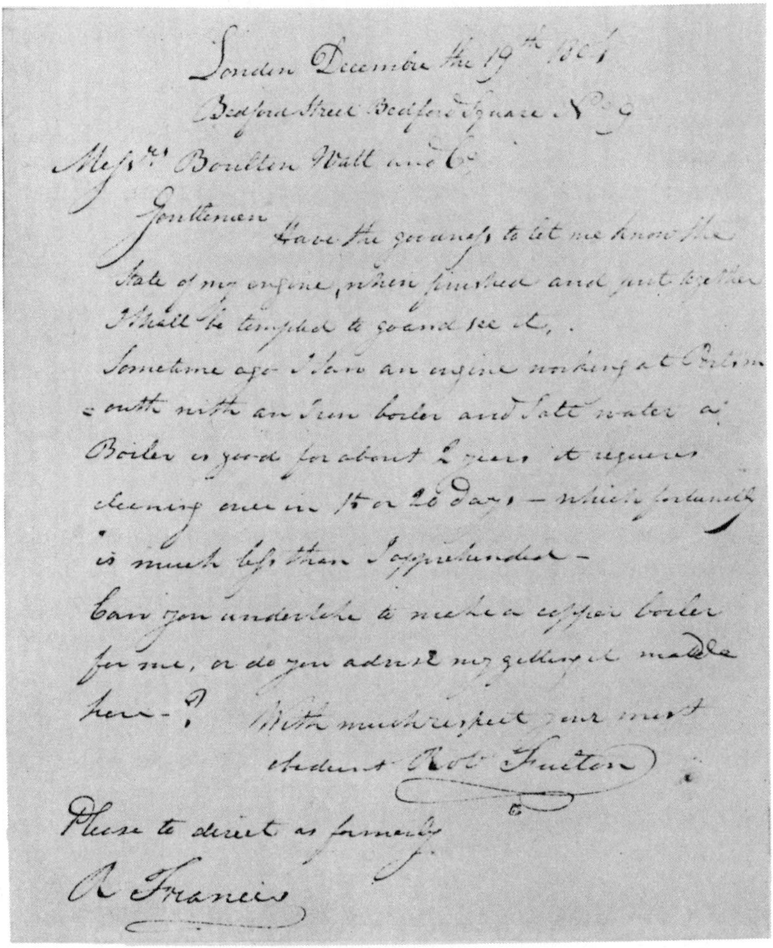

London December the 19th 1804
Bedford Street Bedford Square No 9

Messrs Boulton Watt and Co

Gentlemen
Have the goodness to let me know the state of my engine, when finished and put together I shall be tempted to go and see it.
Sometime ago I saw an engine working at Portsm-outh with an Iron boiler and salt water a Boiler is good for about 2 years it requires cleaning once in 15 or 20 days — which fortunately is much less than I apprehended —
Can you undertake to make a copper boiler for me, or do you advise my getting it made here —?

With much respect your most obedient Robt Fulton

Please to direct as formerly
R Francis

HOLOGRAPH LETTER OF FULTON ABOUT THE ENGINE, 1804

The account was as under :

ROBERT FULTON Esqr. D^r^.

TO BOULTON WATT & CO.

1805		£	s.	d.
17th Jan^y^.	To sundry materials of an Engine with a 24 Inch Cyl^r^. 4 feet Stroke as per agreement in their letters of 4th June & 18th July 1804, delivered at Soho	400	0	0
"	For difference of cost between an Iron & Brass air pump ordered per Mr. F's letter of 20 July . . .	148	0	0
		£548	0	0

SOHO, *17th January* 1805.

ROBT. FULTON, ESQR. LONDON.

SIR,—We forwarded on the 24 Ult^o^. a drawing of the working Gear of your Engine, through the medium of our house in London St., which we hope has been received and fully understood.

We now inclose a list of the Materials, which are compleatly ready and packed up, but cannot be sent off by water until the canals are thawed. We shall thank you to say to what address we are to send them in London.

Above you have a statement of our Account the amount of which you will please to settle with our Agent Mr. Woodward.

We have paid very particular attention to the fitting of every part so that you may have as little trouble as possible in putting them together. The Brass Air pump has come very high owing to the advanced price of copper, but we hope this will be compensated for by its superior durability.

If you should wish for any farther explanation or instructions, they will be furnished with much pleasure by

Sir, Your obt. Servts,

BOULTON, WATT & CO.

P.S.—If more convenient to you, we shall draw upon any house you may appoint.

In this account the extra £20 in the first item must be for the cost of altering patterns—fully explained no doubt in the letter of July 18, which has not been preserved. The date "4th June" must be a clerical error for 4th July. The item £148 for a brass air pump instead of an iron one is enormous, and shows the profits that were to be made at that time by engineering firms. "The advanced price of copper" is a happy phrase which has served its turn many times since. Fulton paid the account, as an entry in his notebook shows, on January 21, 1805.

On the 17th of the month following "R. Francis" wrote to Mr. Woodward, the firm's London agent, to inquire whether the engine was on the way, and if so when he expected its arrival. This note was forwarded to Soho, inquiry was made of the carriers there, and the following reply sent:

SOHO, *21st Feby* 1805.

R. FULTON, ESQr LONDON.

SIR,—In reply to your enquiry to Mr. Woodward we have the pleasure to inform you that the Goods for your Engine were forwarded on the 6th Instt. by Skey & Bird's boats with orders to deliver them to you (same address as this letter) and you will of course be apprized by them as soon as they reach London.

The carriers inform us in answer to a message to them this morning that they expect they will reach town in 8 or 10 days. We are respectfully,

Sir, Your obt. Servts.

BOULTON, WATT & CO.

P.S.—On the other sides you have the weights of the sundry packages, &c.

On the 23rd February 1805, Fulton wrote to the firm asking for the return of Mr. Erving's guarantee: on the 26th this was done, and with that letter the transaction was completed. It only remains to add that according to an entry in his notebook[1] in March Fulton paid £2. 14s. 6d. as "Fee at the Treasury on receiving permission to ship the Engine for America." A further entry on March 18 is "To Messrs. Cave & Son, for Copper boiler weighing 4,399 lbs. at 2/2 the lb. . . . £476. 11s. 2d.," showing that the boiler also was made in England as he had intended.

It will be proper at this juncture, while we are still on the subject of the steam engine, to refer to a visit which Fulton admittedly paid to William Symington to see the steam tug *Charlotte Dundas,* which had been engined by him and tried on the Forth and Clyde Canal between 1802 and 1804. As we have already seen,[2] Symington was no novice in such matters, for he had engaged in successful trials with pleasure steamboats as far back as 1788–9, and now with funds supplied by Thomas, Lord Dundas of Kerse, was experimenting with a steam engine for canal haulage on a plan patented by him in 1801 [No. 2544].

These experiments were carried out to the complete satisfaction of his Lordship and other gentlemen, but the majority of their co-proprietors in the canal declined to sanction the use of the tug on the ground that the wash of the paddles would be destructive to the canal banks.

No documentary evidence of the date when Fulton went to inspect this most interesting steamboat appears to have been preserved. Symington in a statement drawn up in 1829 and attested to by a number of affidavits says: [3]

"In July 1801 . . . a stranger came to the banks of the canal and requested to see me. He very politely

[1] Sutcliffe, *Robert Fulton and the "Clermont,"* p. 185.

[2] See p. 133.

[3] Symington, *A Brief History of Steam Navigation*, 1829 (reprinted 1863), p. 9.

announced himself as Mr. Fulton, a native of North America, and told me that he intended to return to his native country in a few months, but having heard of the steamboat experiment he could not think of leaving the country without waiting upon me in the hope of seeing the boat and machinery and procuring some information as to the principles upon which it was moved. He remarked that, however beneficial such an invention might be to Great Britain, it would certainly be of much more importance to North America."[1]

Symington very generously gave him all the information he wanted, caused the boiler fire to be lit, and the engine to be set in motion, and along with others carried Fulton from Lock No. 18, a distance of four miles to the westward and back, in 1 hour 20 minutes, "to the great astonishment of Mr. Fulton and the other gentlemen present."

A scrutiny of the dates of Fulton's movements from 1801 till his arrival in England, taken in conjunction with the general nature of his occupations, will show the impossibility of his having taken a journey as far as Scotland before 1804. The simplest explanation is that Symington's statement, not having been drawn up till more than a quarter of a century after the event, is slightly inaccurate in point of date.

There have not been lacking detractors who have declared that Fulton borrowed from Symington all his ideas, even down to the stroke and diameter of his cylinder; but the difference between the plans of the two engineers was fundamental, and connotes an independent origin such as we have endeavoured to establish. Symington had a horizontal engine, with a cylinder 22 in. diam. by 4 ft. stroke, acting directly on a paddle wheel in a recess in the stern, while Fulton had a vertical beam engine 24 in.

[1] Bowie, *A Brief Narrative Proving . . . Symington to be . . . an Inventor of . . . Steam Navigation*, 1833, gives an account of this incident in almost the same words, but gives the date as 1802.

diam. by 4 ft. stroke connected by gearing through a fly wheel to drive side paddle wheels. Any impartial person, even if not an engineer, must see that there was no plagiarism here. It is an occasion for surprise rather that Fulton did not take some hints from Symington. We can only suppose that Fulton was already too deeply committed to, or enamoured of, his own plan, to change it, although without doubt Symington's was the better arrangement, yet strangely enough it was about half a century later before marine engineers, after trying almost every conceivable arrangement, came back to Symington's simple direct-acting plan. Fulton's engine was of the bell-crank type,[1] which has often been thought to have originated with William Murdock of the Soho Foundry, Birmingham, but the credit, such as it is, must now be assigned to Fulton.

It is somewhat humbling to our insular pride to have to acknowledge that Symington's experiments had no permanent abiding result, else should we have been the first in this as in so many other technical developments. The *Charlotte Dundas* was eventually laid up at Bainsford near Carron Ironworks, where she lay till 1861, when she was broken up.

We must now return to the negotiations which were going on between Fulton and the British Cabinet. It must be remembered that one of the great objects at this moment in the minds of Ministers was to repel Napoleon's threatened invasion of our shores. A flotilla was in Boulogne Harbour, and only waited for an opportunity, by eluding the vigilance of the British ships, to descend upon the South Coast. What a reality this scare was, how the country responded to the call of duty, and what were the schemes of defence proposed and adopted, are very fully detailed in a recent work[2] of great value.

[1] A bell-crank engine was in use in the machine shop at the Soho Works till 1896; many others were made.

[2] Wheeler and Broadley, *Napoleon and the Invasion of England—The Story of a Great Terror*, 1908.

Among the proposals for counteracting the invasion was that of Fulton, and the two reasons that seemed to have influenced Pitt to employ him were the stir made in the House of Lords by his relative, Lord Stanhope, and the desire to have Fulton, if really dangerous, on the side of rather than opposed to Great Britain. By July preliminaries had been settled, and the following agreement[1] had been entered into:

Articles of Agreement between the Right Honourable William Pitt, first Lord Commissioner of his Majesty's treasury and Chancelor of the Exchequer, and the Right Honourable Lord Viscount Melville, first Lord of the Admiralty, in behalf of his Majesty's government on the one part, and Robert Fulton, citizen of the United States of America and inventor of a plan of attacking fleets by submarine Bombs, on the other part.

The said Robert Fulton agrees to disclose the principles of his scheme to Sir Home Popham and to superintend the execution of it on the following conditions:

First.—To be paid Two hundred pounds a month while he is employed on this Service for his personal trouble and Expences.

Second.—To have a credit lodged from time to time for the payment of his Mechanical preparation, not to exceed Seven thousand pounds.

Third.—That in his Majesty's dockyards and Arsenals shall be made or furnished all such articles as may be required which are applicable to this purpose.

Fourth.—If any circumstance should arise to prevent government carrying this plan into execution then the parties are each to name two commissioners for the purpose of examining the principles; and trying such experiments as they may think proper, and if it should appear to the Majority of the members that the plan is practicable and offers a more effectual mode of destroying

[1] Public Record Office, Admiralty Secretary, in-letters 5121.

the enemies fleet at Boulogne, Brest, or elsewhere, than any now in practise and with less risk, then government is to pay the said Robert Fulton the sum of Forty Thousand Pounds as a compensation for demonstrating the principles, and making over the entire possession of his submarine mode of attack.

Fifth.—When the said Robert Fulton has destroyed by his submarine carcasses or Bombs one of the enemies decked Vessels, then Government is to pay him the sum of Forty Thousand pounds, provided Commissioners appointed As in the previous article shall be of opinion that the same Scheme can be practically applied to the destruction of the enemies fleets.

Sixth.—If the Arbitrators differ in opinion then they are to draw lots for the choice of an Umpire and the majority of the Voices to decide all points of reference within the construction of this agreement and that decision to be final.

Seventh.—One half the supposed value of all vessels destroyed by Mr. Fulton's Submarine mode of attack to be paid him by government as long as he superintends the execution of his plan; but when government has no further occasion for his services; or that he wishes to retire then he is only to be paid one quarter of the supposed value of such vessels as may be destroyed by his scheme, and this remuneration to continue for the space of fourteen years from the date hereof.

Eighth.—In case the Vessels destroyed by this scheme should exceed in amount Forty thousand pounds, then the Forty Thousand pounds first stipulated to be paid, shall be considered as part payment of the whole sum which may become due to the said Robert Fulton.

Ninth.—If in the course of practice any improvements Should be Suggested that can only be esteemed as a collateral Aid to the general principles of Mr. Fulton's mode of attack, then such improvements are not to demenesh or set aside his claims on government.

Tenth.—All monies which may become due to Mr. Fulton to be paid within six months from the time when they shall be so adjudged according to the tenor of this agreement.

Eleventh.—This agreement to be considered by both parties as a liberal covenant with a View to protect the Rights of the individual, and to prevent any unproper advantage being taken of his Majesty's Government.

Mr. Fulton having deposited the drawings and plans of his submarine scheme of attack; in the hands of a confidential friend with a view to their being delivered to the American government in case of his death, does hereby bind himself to withdraw all such plans and drawings and not divulge them or any part of his principles to any person whatever for the space of fourteen years; which is the term during which he is to derive all the advantages of their operation from the British Government.

The benefit of the foregoing agreement shall be extended to the heir and executors of the said Robert Fulton.

Signed this Twentieth day of July One thousand eight hundred and four.

ROBERT FULTON.

Witness, HOME POPHAM

There is a note by Sir Home Popham in the margin:

"Exchanged with a counterpart signed by the Right Honble. William Pitt and the Right Honble. Lord Melville.

H. P."

The whole is in Fulton's handwriting; the attesting clause is in different ink to the rest and the writing is hurried. The seal is missing and it is interesting as showing the secrecy observed that this document was retained by Viscount Castlereagh among his private papers till his death in 1819.

It must be confessed that Fulton's terms were somewhat grasping. He had never been able to extract anything from the French, but then their finances were at a low ebb; now that he had to deal with a wealthy country he seems to have determined to make as much as possible out of his opportunity. It may not be inappropriate to remark that there have been similar cases in more recent times.

No time was lost it seems in appointing the commissioners, who were: Sir Joseph Banks, K.C.B., President of the Royal Society; the Hon. H. Cavendish, the celebrated chemist; Major William Congreve, himself an inventor of military projectiles; John Rennie, the civil engineer; and Captain Sir Home Popham.[1]

Possibly the first two were nominated by Fulton and the second two by the Admiralty, whilst Captain Popham was there to act as intermediary and umpire.

"A packet of sealed papers and drawings were sent to them as coming from a person of the name of *Francis*, and on these documents alone they delivered as they were desired to do . . . a sound and honest opinion."[2]

Evidently the balance of opinion was on the whole unfavourable to the submarine for we hear no more about it. The torpedo, however, was not altogether condemned and steps were taken to give Fulton an opportunity of showing what he could do. Immediately he set to work to prepare his engines for an attack on the Boulogne flotilla, an attack known at the time as the "Catamaran expedition." The submarine "carcasses," "bombs," or "coffers" employed by Fulton were similar to those experimented with by him in France. An officer who took part in the operations describes them as being made square in section with wedge-shaped ends "of thick plank lined with lead. A plank is left out for filling it. When

[1] According to his daughter's statement, the Rev. Edmund Cartwright, D.D., was on the Commission, but this must be a mistake as his friendship with Fulton would have been a sufficient bar.

[2] *Quarterly Review*, vol. xix. p. 351, in a review of Colden's *Life of Fulton* written, as internal evidence shows, by John Rennie himself.

filled the plank is put in, nailed and caulked, paid all over with tar, covered with canvas, and paid with hot pitch."[1]

Clockwork, set to run a certain time before releasing a hammer, was affixed to the carcass. The clockwork was set going by the removal of a pin, and a reward depended upon bringing this away. The coffers, some of which were 18 feet long and weighed 2 tons, were weighted with shot so as to float just awash and so escape observation. To each coffer were attached two lines, floated with pieces of cork, one a tow line and the other a grapnel. The latter was intended to be hooked on the cable by which a ship was riding at anchor, when the coffer would swing round by the tide and lay alongside. The coffer was taken in tow by a "catamaran" consisting of "two pieces of timber about 9 feet long and 9 inches square placed parallel to one another at such a distance as to receive a man to sit between them on a bar which admitted of his sinking nearly flush with the water and occasionally immersing himself so as to prevent his being seen in the dark or by moonlight." This seaman was clad in black guernsey, waistcoat, and trousers, with a black cap which covered his face; he had a paddle, and the idea was that he should drop down with the tide towards the enemy's vessel, attach the coffer to the cable and then paddle back to safety.

At last all was ready and on October 2, 1804, at 9.15 P.M.—Lord Keith, Admiral of the Blue, in command on board his flagship, H.M.S. *Monarch*—the catamarans with coffers in tow, accompanied by five explosion vessels, were despatched into Boulogne Harbour. The attempt was, however, almost a complete failure: only one torpedo took effect, destroying a pinnace and her crew of twenty-one men. The French avoided the explosion vessels, which went ashore and there blew up without doing any serious damage. The attack ceased at 4.15 A.M. without any

[1] *Naval Chronicle*, vol. xii. p. 313.

casualties on the British side. The destruction of the pinnace was not noticed by the English officers, but is reported in the French account of the affair.

It is a significant fact that Admiral Keith's despatches giving an account of the occurrences[1] make no mention whatever of Fulton's share in the transaction, although we know from his own book that he was present with the blockading fleet on this as well as on a subsequent occasion in 1805. Captain Sir Home Popham, however, who had charge of all the necessary preparations up to the eve of the attack, is highly commended. A fact that shows that the occasion was deemed to be one of some little importance is the presence on board the flagship of Viscount Melville himself.

The news of the attack was received in England with indignation, not so much on account of its failure, but rather because it was considered to be an unfair method of fighting and against the laws of war.

The event was lampooned very cleverly in the press[2] in "The Catamarans, an excellent new ballad," in which the Right Hon. William Dundas, Secretary for War, is supposed to be speaking:

"See here my casks and coffers
With triggers pulled by clocks!
But to the Frenchmen's rigging
Who first will lash these blocks?

Catamarans are ready
(*Jack* turns his quid and grins)
Where snugly you may paddle
In water to your chins.

Then who my blocks will fasten,
My casks and coffers lay?
My pendulums set ticking
And bring the pins away?

---

[1] Admiralty Secretary, in letters. 544.

[2] Cobbett's *Weekly Political Register*, Oct. 27, 1804, p. 640.

Your project new? Jack mutters
Avast! 'tis very stale:
'Tis catching birds, land-lubbers!
By salt upon the tail."

. . . .

Considering the secrecy that appears to have been observed, it is remarkable that such knowledge of details as is shown in these lines should have leaked out to the general public.

Another expedition was made on the night of December 8, when Captain Sir Home Popham sent in an explosion vessel and two carcasses against Fort Rouge in Calais Harbour. The explosion vessel was moored against the piles and exploded. One carcass did not explode for some reason and the other had to be brought back.[1]

There is no doubt whatever that naval officers were averse to the mode of attack: Lord Keith in a despatch during August, when the expedition was in contemplation, said that he considered the method costly and likely to meet with little success.

Apparently no further attempts were made to carry out Fulton's plans till, wearied by the delay, he wrote to the Right Hon. William Pitt the following letter:[2]

August 9, 1805.

SIR,—As the circumstances which led to my engagements with this Government, and my particular situation, may not be known to Lord Barham, the heads of them may aid in his decision with you on my business.

[1] *Naval Chronicle*, vol. xii. p. 488.

[2] *Correspondence . . . of Viscount Castlereagh . . .* edited by his brother, vol. v., 1851, p. 86, dealing with various operations undertaken by the British against the Boulogne flotilla.

The author conjectures that Mr. Francis was an American, but quite fails to pierce through his somewhat thin disguise!!

First.—My experiments on submarine navigation in France having excited some curiosity in this country, Ministers thought it prudent to know the real merits of the invention, and sent an agent to me in Paris, inviting me to this country; which agent made three voyages with various proposals, the purport of which on my part were that, on my arrival here, I would exhibit the principles of my engines to Government, and should they conceive the introduction of them into practice in France, America, or elsewhere, to be injurious to the interests of Great Britain, I proposed to take the value of one ship of the line of £100,000 to let the discovery lie dormant. Letters to this effect are in possession of Mr. Addington, or Lord Hawkesbury.

Second.—Being a neutral, and having flattering prospects at home, it was not my intention to take part in European wars; and when I agreed to act against the French fleets, I hoped my system would be so well understood and established by this time, that I might return to America this autumn. But unforeseen events having occupied Ministers for the last four months, prevented giving effect to my mode of attack, yet I hope there will now be time for the following considerations:

If I am to act, it is necessary means should be adopted which shall give every possible effect to my system, with the least loss of time and risk of persons. For this purpose a small squadron of three frigates, and one or two cutters to carry boats, catamarans, carcasses, and implements, should be put under the command of an active, enterprising officer, who should have an independent cruising commission to run along the whole line of the enemy's coast, and attack any vessel or vessels of the enemy, wherever he found it practicable with his means. As such might be calculated an experimental cruise, I conceive the inventor of a new mode of warfare ought to be considered the best judge of the mode of using his own engines to advantage; and I ought not to have more than one commander to consult, who should be a man of resource of mind and some enthusiasm. If this measure is not adopted, and men exercised to the engines, I despair of doing any good for Government or honour to myself. Hence if Ministers cannot adopt this plan the next consideration is:

Is this invention, if carried to its full extent and generally known, a thing which may tend to reduce the British power by sea, or give strength to minor powers? And is it the best policy of the British Government to make it my interest to let it rest in its present state?

If the invention is insignificant, I do not expect anything for it. If it is an invention which is capable of working a total revolution in marine war *and which I believe,* I of course must have a high idea of its value to myself and country. But of this his Majesty's Ministers will judge.

These considerations lead to the following conclusions: Will Ministers form it into a system, as before mentioned, so as to give it full effect? If not will they agree with me to let it lie dormant? If not, I am willing to retire. I have so equally balanced each of those cases in my own mind that either of them will be equally agreeable to me.

I beg you, sir, to believe that in thus expressing my sentiments I am nowise displeased with the treatment I have received; on the contrary, I am fully satisfied with your open and liberal mode of acting; but to prevent fruitless negotiations and loss of time, and clearly exhibit my turn of mind on this subject, also to reduce the points for consideration to as few as possible, I have thought this short explanation necessary.

I have the honour, etc.,

R. FRANCIS.

Whether in consequence of this appeal or not, greater activity now seems to have been displayed. Lord Castlereagh, writing to Lord Barham, First Lord of the Admiralty, on 10th September 1805, says:[1]

"The Ordnance Stores connected with Mr. Francis's mode of warfare were some time since landed from the *Sceptre* and *Diadem* armed defence ships, and placed for safety in ordnance stores at Portsmouth." He asks for these stores to be put on board some vessels and sent round to Dover.

Again writing to Sir Sidney Smith on the 19th September he mentions having seen Mr. Francis and encloses a memorandum of the latter which suggests the provision of 9 row galleys with 12 men to each including 1 officer = 108 men and 10 catamarans with 2 men to each = 20 men. It also suggests a scale of rewards for the vessels to be captured.

Mr. Cooke, Lord Castlereagh's private secretary, writing to Mr. Robert Francis on September 25, 1805, says:[2]

"I am directed by Lord Castlereagh to acknowledge your letter of the 23rd instant, stating that you have made a contract with Messrs. Caverton for one hundred carcasses of copper at 2*s.* 6*d.* per pound, equal to £550 sterling. Also that you had received an estimate for making one hundred clockwork locks at £14 each, amounting to £1400 sterling, and I am commanded by his Lordship to express his approbation of the contract you have entered into for the carcasses, and to desire that you will lose no time in contracting for the clockwork locks above mentioned."

On September 27th Lord Castlereagh signifies to Lord Barham the King's command to execute a secret service of importance with Captain Sir Sidney Smith, to whom the Controller of the Navy is directed to imprest £30,000. Later we learn that of this sum about £3000 had already

[1] *Loc. cit.* p. 90. [2] *Loc. cit.* p. 98.

been advanced to Mr. Francis, not inclusive of the £1400 for the locks.

At length all was ready for another attack on the Boulogne flotilla. Captain E. W. C. R. Owen, an intelligent and enterprising officer under the command of Lord Keith, was chosen to superintend the operations. The wind, weather and tide favouring, an attack was made with two carcasses on the night of September 30, lasting till 2 A.M., the next morning under the charge of Captain Seccombe and Lieut. Payne. The carcasses blew up without doing any damage: no casualties, except one wounded, were sustained.

In the French account of the affair,[1] given with great detail, it is mentioned that the next morning there was found on the shore "a lock like that of the fire machines which the English used last year with so much ridicule and with so little success."

It was probably the ill-success of this expedition that made Fulton realise that something must be done to restore confidence and show that it was the plan of the attack and not the torpedo that was at fault.

A Norwegian or Danish brig, the *Dorothea*, 100 tons, which had been captured on the 19th April previous by H.M.S. *Furious*, happened to be laid up in Deal Harbour almost under the windows of Walmer Castle, Pitt's official residence. On October 15 Fulton placed a torpedo across the bows of the brig, and, after a predetermined interval, she was blown in two, completely destroyed and sunk[2] in the presence of a distinguished company of naval and military officers and a large concourse of spectators. As showing how little belief there was in Fulton's torpedoes, it may be mentioned that one of the naval officers, only ten minutes before the explosion, said that he would be quite unconcerned if sitting at dinner at that moment in the cabin of the *Dorothea*.

[1] Translated in Cobbett's *Annual Political Register*, 1805, p. 557.

[2] Fulton, *Torpedo War and Submarine Explosions*, 1810.

A contemporary account[1] is as follows:

DEAL, *October* 16.—"On Monday morning (*i.e.* the 14th October) Mr. Francis, who last year contrived the Expedition and constructed the machines which Sir Home Popham ran among the Enemy's Flotilla at Boulogne arrived here from Dover; and a rumour was soon spread that he was going to make an experiment to blow up a brig of 300 tons with one of his new invented Catamarans. Curiosity was soon alive, and about 4 P.M. great crowds of People assembled on the Beach, from Deal to Walmer Castle, opposite which the brig lay."

We continue the account in Fulton's own words:[2]

"Two boats, each with eight men, commanded by lieutenant Robinson, were put under my direction. I prepared two empty Torpedoes in such a manner, that each was only from two to three pounds specifically heavier than salt water; and I so suspended them, that they hung fifteen feet under water. They were then tied one to each end of a small rope eighty feet long; thus arranged, and the brig drawing twelve feet of water, the 14th day of October was spent in practice. Each boat having a Torpedo in the stern, they started from the shore about a mile above the brig, and rowed down towards her; the uniting line of the Torpedoes being stretched to its full extent, the two boats were distant from each other seventy feet; thus they approached in such a manner, that one boat kept the larboard, the other the starboard side of the brig in view. So soon as the connecting line of the Torpedoes passed the buoy of the brig, they were thrown into the water and carried on by the tide, until the connecting line touched the brig's cable; the tide then drove them under her bottom. The experiment being repeated several times taught the men how to act, and proved to my satisfaction that, when properly

[1] *Naval Chronicle*, vol. xiv. p. 341.

[2] *Torpedo War and Submarine Explosions*, 1810, p. 5.

placed on the tide, the Torpedoes would invariably go under the bottom of the vessel. I then filled one of the Torpedoes with one hundred and eighty pounds of powder and set its clockwork to eighteen minutes. Everything being ready, the experiment was announced for the next day, the 15th, at five o'clock in the afternoon. Urgent business had called Mr. Pitt and Lord Melville to London. Admiral Holloway, Sir Sidney Smith, Captain Owen, Captain Kingston, Colonel Congreve, and the major part of the officers of the fleet under the command of Lord Keith were present; at forty minutes past four the boats rowed towards the brig, and the Torpedoes were thrown into the water; the tide carried them, as before described, under the bottom of the brig, where, at the expiration of eighteen minutes, the explosion seemed to raise her bodily about six feet; she separated in the middle, and the two ends went down; in twenty seconds nothing was to be seen of her except floating fragments; the pumps and foremast were blown out of her; the fore-topsail-yard was thrown up to the crosstrees; the fore chain plates, with their bolts, were torn from her sides; the mizen-chain-plates and shrouds being stronger than those of the foremast, or the shock being more forward than aft, the mizenmast was broke off in two places; these discoveries were made by means of the pieces which were found afloat."

Subsequent to this Fulton had an interview with Earl St. Vincent, to whom he explained the torpedo and the experiment with it in blowing up the *Dorothea;* the Earl said:

"Pitt was the greatest fool that ever existed, to encourage a mode of war which they who commanded the seas did not want, and which if successful would deprive them of it."

On the other hand, as showing how different were the views held by Ministers, Lord Castlereagh, on October 21, commenting on Sir Sidney Smith's report upon the blowing up of the brig, says[1] that "the success of Mr. Francis's experiment gives me great confidence in our means of annoying the enemy in their own ports with little comparative risk to ourselves."

On October 27, influenced probably by this success, another attempt was made upon the flotilla in Boulogne Harbour. Lieutenant Charles F. Payne, on board H.M.S. *Bloodhound*, with boats reached the centre of the enemy's line, rowed in at 9.30 P.M. and placed a carcass across the second vessel's cable. They were discovered and fired upon, so withdrew for a short time. When the firing had abated they rowed in to see the effect: The torpedo "exploded and made a similar crash as the Brig lately blown up in the Downes," without, however, the same destructive effect.

Shortly after this the news of Nelson's great victory off Trafalgar on October 21, 1805, completely annihilating the naval power of France and Spain, reached England, and, as Napoleon was faced by the coalition of Russia and Austria, he was compelled to withdraw the troops from the camp at Boulogne to take part in the campaigns of Ulm and Austerlitz. The danger of invasion was at an end, the tension was relieved, and the necessity for any further torpedo attempts was obviated.

Fulton, however, did not abandon his project, for it was not confined to a single form of attack, such as that on the Boulogne flotilla, but was generally applicable at any harbour where the enemy's vessels could be found at anchor. Nevertheless the fact remained that the immediate purpose for which Fulton's services had been secured had been gained and there was but little need to continue the engagement. With his usual pertinacity he kept on importuning Ministers. On November 25, 1805, Mr. Francis wrote from Dover to Lord Castlereagh enclosing a copy of a long letter to Sir Sidney Smith :

"From the day I found Mr. Pitt determined to practice

[1] *Castlereagh*, p. 121.

my invention on the French fleets, I urged that it might be arranged into a system by itself. After thirteen months' essay and argument I have still to plead that it may be systematized, and I do believing it the best interest of Government; for as to myself, having shown how to construct the carcasses and apply them with simplicity and certainty, little more can be required of me; it must be for regular bred seamen to use them and seek opportunities to destroy the enemy."

On November 26 Mr. Francis sent to Lord Castlereagh a long letter suggesting an attack on the fleet in the inner Roads of Brest. On the 28th Francis sent a memorandum to Sir Sidney Smith suggesting the abandonment for the present of the large wooden coffers and using small copper carcasses instead.

On December 13, 1805, from Ibbotson's Hotel, Vere Street, Oxford Road, Francis sent proposals for a final settlement with Government. On January 6, 1806, from the same address he wrote to the Right Hon. William Pitt enclosing a copy of his proposal to Lord Castlereagh: [1]

"Now, in this business, I will not disguise that I have full confidence in the power which I possess, which is no less than to be the means, *should I think proper*, of giving to the world a system which must of necessity sweep all military marines from the ocean, by giving to the weaker maritime powers advantages over the stronger, which the stronger cannot prevent. . . .

"In the following proposal I have not raised the sum first mentioned to Lord Hawkesbury; and it must be observed, I did not come here so much with a view to do you any material good as to show that I have the power, and might in the exercise of my plan to acquire fortune, do you an infinite injury, which Ministers, if they think proper, may prevent by an arrangement with me."

[1] *Correspondence of Lord Castlereagh*, vol. v. p. 149.

It can hardly be denied that, considering Fulton's ill-success with his carcasses against the enemy, this letter was a piece of bluff.

All along it would appear that it was the Cabinet who had supported Fulton's schemes and, as William Pitt died in January 1806 and Lord Melville was impeached for his irregular conduct in not keeping his private accounts separate from his public ones, these schemes naturally fell to the ground with the advent of Lords Grenville and Howick, their successors, who were opposed to such methods of warfare.

The closing scenes of Fulton's connection with the British Government are outlined in the correspondence[1] relative to the final disposition of the carcasses.

Lieutenant William Robinson of the Marine Artillery, who, it will be recalled, was in charge of the boats when the *Dorothea* was blown up at Deal, writes to Robert Francis on May 2, 1806, from Dover:

"I am very sorry that Government have not yet disided on useing the carcasses, for they are now so well arranged that I think them sure of success—I have got them all on b^d the *Atalanta* Cutter—with everything necessary to compleat them at a moment's notice."

This letter Fulton encloses to the Secretary of the Admiralty with the following observations:

MY LORDS,—I beg leave to Submit to your Lordship's consideration a letter from Lieutenant Robinson. You will have the goodness to decide on the manner the *Atalanta* and carcasses are to be disposed of, the removal of such engines from ship to ship and store to store is the cause of much injury to the clockwork in consequence of their falling into the hands of curious and inexperienced persons. My Lords If it be thought proper to take every

[1] Admiralty Secretary, In-letters, 4578.

advantage of the Enemy which the carcasses can give, a systematic plan must be pursued; if it be thought improper or impolitic to use them, at present it will be well to collect everything belonging to them in one warehouse, where they can be under the care of one person.

I took the liberty to write to your Lordships on the 28th April relative to my account. I beg to be honoured with an answer.—I am, My Lords,

your Lordships' most

obedient and very humble servant,

ROBT FULTON.

May the 3rd, 1806.

IBBOTSON'S HOTEL, VERE STREET.

This letter is docketed "6 May. Directions for putting them into Store at Deal. Commodore Owen to be acquainted."

On May 18 Lieutenant Robinson writes, evidently with a tinge of regret, to say that he has handed over all his stores marked, numbered, and lettered, and that he has explained everything as to the method of using the carcasses. He finishes by asking to be allowed to draw upon Fulton for the balance of his account. Fulton encloses this letter to the Secretary, merely suggesting that the financial part should be arranged with Lieutenant Robinson direct.

The Cabinet, however, dealt very fairly with Fulton, for although he did not get the original sum that he had demanded, yet considering the ill-success that had attended all the expeditions made with his warlike engines, one fourth of that sum, which he did actually receive, must be said to have been very liberal indeed, especially considering that he was released from the term of his contract as to time and secrecy. This sum did not include the cost of the experiments; that had been defrayed out of the secret service imprest placed in the hands of Sir Sidney Smith.

A letter, written to Barlow from London, in September

1806, *i.e.* when Fulton was on the eve of his final departure from England, explains the whole situation:[1]

"My arbitration is finished and I have been allowed the £10,000 which I had received with 5,000£ salary total £15,000, though £1600 which I have received on settling account will just square all old debts and expenses in London, and leave me about £200. My situation now is, my hands are free to burn, sink, and destroy whom I please, and I shall now seriously set about giving liberty to the seas by publishing my system of attack. I have or will have when Mr. Parker sends my two thousand pounds 500 sterling a year with a steam engine and pictures worth two thousand pounds. Therefore I am not in a state to be pitied. I am now busy winding up everything and will leave London about the 23rd inst. for Falmouth from whence I shall sail in the packet the first week in October and be with you, I hope, in November, perhaps about the 14th, my birthday, so you must have a roast goose ready. Do not write me again after receiving this. The packet, being well manned and provided will be more commodious and safe for an autumn passage, and I think their will be little or no risk; at least I prefer taking all the risk there is to idling here a winter. But although there is not much risk, yet accidents may happen, and that the produce of my studies and experience may not be lost to my country, I have made out a complete set of drawings and descriptions of my whole system of submarine attack, and another set of drawings with description af the steamboat. These with my *will*, I shall put in a tin cylinder, sealed and leave them in the care of General Lyman,[2] not to be opened unless I am lost. Should such an event happen, I have

[1] C. B. Todd, *Barlow's Life and Letters*, p. 209.

[2] General William Lyman (b. 1753, d. 1811), graduate of Yale, member of Massachusetts Senate, member of Congress 1793–97, was appointed in 1805 to succeed Mr. Erving as Consul-General, an office which he retained till his death.

left you the means to publish these works, with engravings, in a handsome manner, and to which you will add your own ideas—showing how the liberty of the seas may be gained by such means; and with such liberty, the immense advantages to America and civilization: you will also show the necessity of perfecting and establishing the steamboat and canals on the inclined plane principle. I have sent you three hundred complete sets of prints from the Columbiad by the Orb, directed to Mr. Tolman, New York, value £30. As the transport by land to Philadelphia will not be much, I have sent them by this opportunity, that they may arrive before the law for prohibiting such things is in force, and that the shipment and risk may not approach too near to winter. All my pictures, prints, and other things, I mean to leave here, to be shipped in spring vessels about April next, when the risk will be inconsiderable. How shall we manage this winter, as you must be in Philadelphia for the printing and I want to be at New York to build my boat? I am in excellent health—never better and in good spirits. You know I cannot exist without a project or projects and I have two or three of the first order of sublimity. . . . Mr. West has been retouching my pictures; they are charming."

The balance of the sum received by Fulton from the British Government "in satisfaction of all claims" was £1653, 18*s*. 8*d*. Apparently after deducting his living and travelling expenses, the cost of the engine and the pictures, the remainder of the £15,000 had been invested in order to be bringing in the income stated.

The pictures referred to were Benjamin West's "Ophelia" and "King Lear," that Fulton had bought for 125 and 205 guineas respectively on May 19 and 20, 1805, at the sale of the contents of Boydell's[1] Shakespeare

[1] John Boydell (*b*. 1719, *d*. 1804), Lord Mayor of London, celebrated engraver and print publisher, in his latter days owing to Continental wars found his business much curtailed and eventually he got into financial difficulties. One of the energies of his life had been the formation of a Gallery to contain

ROBERT FULTON

Gallery. This purchase created some little excitement, as it was an open secret that the pictures were intended to form the nucleus of a Gallery of Fine Arts to be established in Philadelphia.[1] This was probably the first instance on record of the practice, since so common, of the purchase of original works of art for America. This sale is referred to in the following letter[2] addressed to Richard Phillips, the proprietor of the *Monthly Magazine*. The "observations" were not, however, published, although a letter by him on another topic appeared at a later date.

DEAR SIR,—I gave Mr. Stephens some observations on Mr. Jefferson's speech to present to you and if no objections arose, to be printed in your magazine, this I still wish to have done also the inclosed paper on the Sale of the Shakspeare Gallery, and prospect of encouragement for fine arts in America, please to let me know by a note if they can both appear in the magazine for July. Your obedient servant,

ROBT. FULTON.

June 4, 1804.
NO. 13 SACKVILLE STREET,
PICCADILLY.

West's "King Lear" is now in the possession of the Athenæum, Boston, Massachusetts, but the whereabouts of the other picture is not known.

Another interesting sidelight upon Fulton's less important preoccupations during this period is afforded by

pictures to illustrate scenes in Shakespeare's plays, and to this end he had commissioned most of the eminent artists of the day. He was now obliged to realise this property and applied to Parliament to do so by lottery, as the fashion then was, but died before the application was granted. The drawing of the lottery took place on January 28, 1805, when the Gallery and its contents were won by William Tassie. The pictures were disposed of by auction at Christie's on May 18, 19, and 20, realising £6181, 18*s*. 6*d*.

[1] The Gallery was established eventually in 1807 under the title Pennsylvania Academy of Fine Arts, and thither Fulton sent these and other pictures. He tried some years later to induce the citizens to purchase a collection of West's pictures for £15,000.

[2] By kind permission of Mr. A. M. Broadley, from his MS. collection.

the following letter to Lord Stanhope on the subject of stereotype printing; it may perhaps explain the allusion to "projects" in Fulton's letter to Barlow previously quoted. No doubt he was brought into contact with the printing fraternity by the printing of the plates that Smirke had engraved for the *Columbiad.*

BRIDGE STREET,
Oct. 4, 1806.

MY LORD,—I wright to beg pardon for not calling in Stratford Place in my way from Hampstead to Bridge St. I have been anxious to do so, but various circumstances have conspired to prevent me. I should be happy to have an opportunity of conversing with your Lordship on the subject of Stereotype Printing and of explaining the motives which influenced the Booksellers in their rejection of the *Project* submitted to them by Mr. Wilson.

In the first Place it would have been impracticable to raise within a year the sum of 14,000£ which we were called upon to pay for Buildings, past expences, loss of time, &c., &c. A few, among whom I was one, would have advanced 500£ *apiece*, but the major part of the 12 or 20 persons concerned in Literary Property have little to spare and they would not be unanimous in their opinion of this or any new invention.

Secondly: As the Booksellers are of opinion that Stereotype Printing could only be advantageously applied to about 30 or 40 works, that sum of 14,000£ added to the expences of Stereotyping those works would not be inferior to the expence of setting up and keeping the whole standing in Movable Types while at the same time those Types would always be worth half their cost in the event of the works being broken up or rendered obsolete.

To account for the indisposition of the Booksellers generally, I shall observe that it has always been stipulated in every proposal of Mr. Wilson that the plates should be worked at his office *only*, that he should acquire an Interest in the work stereotyped, and should have it in his power to take a set of plates for America, [They demur to] all of these points which seriously infringe on literary Property, militate with the independence of the possessors of such property, and are most especially alien to those feelings of which an Englishman is most proud, and which he ought, my Lord, to cherish above all petty calculations of profit and loss in matters of business.

If Stereotype Printing can ever succeed in this country, it must be placed on the liberal footing of all other manufactures. If thrown open on a broad basis to all who choose to employ it, free from restrictions, and the spirit of monopoly, it will succeed, and those who have embarked their property in it will reimburse themselves with profit. Any other system, a spirit of opposition to the trade, and an invasion of the property of the Booksellers, will end in the discomfiture and ruin of the parties even though they were worth a million. Honesty and Liberality are ever the best Policy. In this business, my Lord, an attempt is making to *rob* the Booksellers of their established copy rights because they will not submit to illiberal restrictions.

You are, my Lord, the last man in the world who can lend your countenance to so foolish a course. No body of men ever suffered themselves to be dictated to and the Booksellers would indeed be deserving of contempt if under such circumstances they did not stand aloof and permit the present attempt at Stereotype Printing to sink under its own weight. I have nothing to object to Mr. Wilson but to his wrong estimate of human Nature. He possesses the intelligence, the integrity and the spirit of enterprize adequate to the undertaking which your Lordship has sanctioned with your patronage, but he has taken too high ground and has raised the Jealousies instead of cultivating the confidence and the co-operation of the Booksellers. At present I foresee nothing but mischief in a business from which only benefits ought to have resulted.

I write this letter confidentially to your Lordship, and am, my Lord,

your obdt. and obliged servt.,

RT. FULTON.

It may be remarked that stereotypy, although invented as early as 1725 by William Ged of Edinburgh, and re-introduced in 1784 by Alexander Tilloch, who brought it to considerable perfection, had by the end of the eighteenth century practically been abandoned for reasons that are not far to seek. The hand-press, which was then in use, was quite unequal to printing, nor was there a sufficient public to warrant, the large editions which alone could make stereotypy more economical than printing direct from movable types. But Earl Stanhope, having in 1798 considerably improved the hand-press by the introduction of the Stanhope levers and by making the whole in iron, had turned his attention to stereotypy. "After many expensive and tedious experiments Lord Stanhope, aided by Mr. Walker, an ingenious mechanist, succeeded in this important invention to the full extent of his highest expectations."[1] Lord Stanhope had the advantage of the instruction of Tilloch, who had removed to London, and of Andrew Wilson, a practical printer.

In 1804 the invention was with his Lordship's approbation offered to the University of Cambridge, but the negotiations fell through. In the letter before us we have evidence of another attempt by Wilson to get the London booksellers to take up the subject, but under very onerous conditions. Wilson's attempt also fell through and stereotyping died out for more than twenty years. The letter we have quoted is an important contribution to the history of the subject.

We might mention that before bidding final adieu to

[1] Hansard, *Typographia*, p. 638.

England Fulton had contemplated union in marriage with an English widow of considerable fortune. The only mention of it is in a very fatherly letter from Barlow, dated 3rd March 1806, wherein he tries all he knows to dissuade Fulton from his purpose, apparently with success, for he returned to the United States unmarried.

CHAPTER IX

ARRIVAL IN AMERICA — TORPEDO EXPERIMENTS — LAUNCH AND TRIAL TRIP OF THE STEAMBOAT — STEAM FERRY BOATS

FULTON left Falmouth at the end of October and arrived in New York by way of Halifax, N.S., on December 13, 1806, after an absence of nineteen years from his native country. He found himself eagerly awaited by his friends, prominent among whom were Barlow, who had settled down in a house which he had built for himself at Kalorama on the outskirts of Washington, and Chancellor Livingston, whose country-seat was at Clermont, near Albany, on the shores of the Hudson.

Fulton was acclaimed by his countrymen as a prominent citizen, and what honours a republic can bestow were showered upon him. He was elected a Director of the American Academy of Fine Arts, a Fellow of the American Philosophical Society and of the New York Historical Society, and assisted in the foundation of the Literary and Philosophical Society of New York.

The period that now ensued was one of greater activity than any that he had previously known. As he was engaged concurrently on several different enterprises it may be as well to depart from strict chronological order and treat each one consecutively, leaving the greatest, *i.e.* the steamboat enterprise, till the last.

Fulton had hardly been in the States a month before he had proposed to the executive government a series of experiments with torpedoes, undeterred by the fact that two foreign powers had already rejected them. A demonstration was held in January at Kalorama, at which

James Madison, Secretary of State, and Robert Smith, Secretary to the Navy, were present. Both were favourably impressed and permission to make the experiments was readily granted. Although already fully engaged with the preparation of plans for the machinery and with the superintendence of the building of his steamboat, he found time to arrange for a demonstration of blowing up a vessel by his torpedo in New York Harbour. This took place on July 20, 1807, but established nothing new, being merely a repetition, except that it was less successful, of that in Walmer Roads.

Fulton thus describes the experiment:

"The brig was anchored, the Torpedoes prepared and put into the water . . . ; the tide then drove them under the brig near her keel, but in consequence of the locks turning downwards the powder fell out of the pans and they both missed fire. This discovery of an error in the manner of fixing the locks to a Torpedo has been corrected. On the second attempt the Torpedo missed the brig; the explosion took place about one hundred yards from her and threw up a column of water 10 feet diameter, sixty or seventy feet high. On the third attempt she was blown up."[1]

On the day following this experiment Fulton addressed a letter to the Governor and Magistrates of the city of New York, of which the following is an extract:

"Having now clearly demonstrated the great effect of explosion under water, it is very easy to conceive that by organization and practice the application of the torpedoes will, like every other art, progress in perfection. Little difficulties and errors will occur in the commencement, as has been the case in all new inventions: but where there is little expense, so little risk, and so much to be gained, it is worthy of consideration whether this system should not have a fair trial. Gunpowder within the last three hundred years has totally changed the art of war, and all

[1] *Torpedo War*, p. 7.

my reflections have led me to believe that this application of it will in a few years put a stop to maritime wars, give that liberty on the seas which has been long and anxiously desired by every good man, and secure to America that liberty of commerce, tranquillity, and independence which will enable her citizens to apply their mental and corporeal faculties to useful and humane pursuits, to the improvement of our country and the happiness of the whole people."

Fulton's operations attracted some little attention on this side of the water and led to means being devised tc counteract them. Lord Stanhope, on 16th February 1807, in a patent (No. 3007) including some improvements in shipbuilding provided means for "counteracting or diminishing the danger of that most mischievous invention for destroying ships and vessels known by the name or appellation of Submarine Bombs, Carcasses, or Explosions." This can only have referred to Fulton's torpedoes.

Not only so, but Commodore (subsequently Admiral) Sir E. W. C. R. Owen, whose share in the operations against the Boulogne flotilla has already been mentioned, thought it his duty to submit to the Lords of the Admiralty a very detailed report, dated September 6, 1807, on the construction, operation, and means of defence against Fulton's torpedoes. The covering letter is interesting and the memorandum itself so lucid that we give them in full in an Appendix.[1]

The document gives from an unbiassed source a full description of Fulton's engines, and may therefore be relied upon. Commodore Owen's suggestions for withstanding torpedo attack contain the germ of the present generally adopted system of boom defence. The docket on the letter shows that the information was duly transmitted to Admiral Berkeley in command on the American station. Even had Fulton persuaded the U.S. Naval authorities to adopt his plans he would have found the British ready for

[1] See p. 284.

him and able to outmanœuvre him. No wonder that Britain remained Mistress of the Seas while her navy was commanded by such officers as Owen!

Fulton, in ignorance of this, continued his efforts to get his torpedo adopted. He also made public, as he had long before promised, some of the details of his torpedoes in his brochure, *Torpedo War and Submarine Explosions*, from which we have already quoted at some length; this was published in January 1810, and bears evidence, as he himself confesses, of having been hastily written, for it was meant more for the purpose of influencing Congress than to redeem a promise. He gives a number of different designs of torpedoes, but only one, *i.e.* that described by Commodore Owen, was actually successful. This was the method adopted at Brest, Dover, Boulogne, and New York.

Congress were so favourably impressed that in March 1810 they made an appropriation, for the purpose of carrying out experiments, of a sum of $5000 to be expended under the direction of the Secretary of the Navy, who at once appointed Commodores Rogers and Chauncey to superintend the operations.

In September Fulton exhibited to them his models and plans as described in his brochure, as well as a new apparatus for cutting the cables of vessels at anchor. This was a very crude affair—just a curved knife, the haft of which was in the barrel of a gun. The whole was to be floated by a buoy against the cable to be cut till the knife caught it, when it was to be discharged by a gun lock!! A model, incomplete, however, is in possession of the grandson of the inventor.

By the following month these officers were ready for the trials in the Navy Yard at Brooklyn. Commodore Rogers must have been a sly old sea-dog, for he had unknown to Fulton prepared the *Argus* sloop of war, Captain Lawrence, to resist attack by chains lashed to the cable and booms supporting netting extending down to the sea bottom. This is the first instance of the actual employment of this now widely adopted means of defence. Fulton was completely nonplussed and acknowledged defeat, although confident he would find means to overcome the obstacle. He had to content himself with trying his harpoon torpedo and cable cutter, neither of which answered his expectations, although he did actually succeed later in cutting a cable.

The report, together with a letter from Fulton, was forwarded to the Treasury. In the latter he observes, pertinently, that "an invention which will oblige every hostile vessel that enters our parts to guard herself by such means (*i.e.* torpedo netting) cannot but be of great importance in a system of defence," and also that he had now discovered a means to render "all such kinds of operations (*i.e.* protective means) totally useless."

Fulton, however, does not appear to have carried the matter further, and this is the last we hear of his torpedoes. Strictly speaking, they were floating mines and not torpedoes at all; we can therefore hardly call them the predecessors of the destructive weapon of to-day, but there was in them the germ of the idea—that of launching against an enemy's ship a missile which would explode on reaching it and inflict injury—and we must confess that Fulton worked out his idea for all it was worth. It was reserved for a later period, when the advance of mechanical science had made it possible to accommodate its motive power within the body of the projectile itself, to develop the germ into something formidable.

A matter which occupied some small amount of Fulton's attention was the long-deferred publication in the spring of 1807 of his friend Barlow's poem, the *Columbiad* to which we have already referred. There is good reason to doubt whether, but for the good offices of Fulton, this epic would ever have emerged from the MS. state; but having decided to do it, he did it well. It was an édition de luxe in quarto form, embellished

JOEL BARLOW

with a portrait of Barlow by Fulton and ten plates. The drawings for the latter had been made by Robert Smirke, and Fulton had had them engraved and printed in London. He also bore the cost of the typographical part, amounting in all to $5000, and the work thus became his private property.

Long after the work had been issued to the public, he wrote on July 1, 1810, to Barlow drawing his attention to a belated review of the book:[1]

"Have you seen the *Edinburgh Review* of the *Columbiad?* Their first principle is that polished literature is not to be expected from America more than from Manchester or Birmingham. The second position is that the day for epic poetry is gone by; man cannot now take pleasure in poetic fiction; the mere didactic is too dry. . . . However they call you a giant compared to modern British bards, though not equal, they think, to Milton."

Another subject on which Fulton's services were in request was to advise on the question of canals as a means of transport, a question that was then uppermost in men's minds. Had it not been for the coming of the steamboat, and, shortly after, of the locomotive engine, it is very likely that a United States canal system not inferior to that established in Great Britain would have been the outcome of the inquiries which were now being set on foot. Fulton, however, was obliged to decline any offers in this direction: Replying on March 20, 1807, to a letter from General Dearborn, Secretary of War, he says:

"I am infinitely obliged by the proposal of the President (*i.e.* Thomas Jefferson) that I should examine the ground and report on a canal to unite the waters of the Mississippi and Lake Pontchartrain, and am sorry I cannot undertake a work so interesting and honourable. The reason is I now have Ship Builders, Blacksmiths, and Carpenters occupied at New York in building and executing the machinery of my Steam Boat, and I must return to that

[1] C. B. Todd, *Barlow's Life and Letters*, p. 221.

City in ten days to direct the work till finished, which will probably require 4 months. The enterprise is of much importance to me individually and I hope will be of great use in facilitating the navigation of some of our long rivers. Like every enthusiast, I have no doubt of success. I therefore work with ardor, and when adjusting the parts of the machine I cannot leave the men for a day. I am also preparing the engines for an experiment of blowing up a vessel in the harbour of New York this Spring. The machines for this purpose are in great forwardness and I hope to convince the rational part of the inhabitants of our cities that vessels of war shall never enter our harbours or approach our Coasts but by our consent."[1]

An inquiry was conducted by Mr. A. Gallatin, on behalf of the U.S. Treasury, upon the subject of canals, and his report[2] embodies an extremely lucid statement by Fulton, dated December 8, 1807, of the advantages to be derived from small canals. He refers to his *Treatise on Canal Navigation* and gives estimates to show that carriage on water by horse haulage would cost less than one-tenth of that on the best roads then available.

While on the subject of internal communication we ought to mention that early in 1811 Fulton was seriously entertaining the idea of steam locomotion on rails as a rival to canals. He had an idea of building a railway at Richmond, Virginia, for transporting coal. Chancellor Livingston, replying on March 1, 1811, to a letter of Fulton's of February 25 previous, says:[3]

"I had before read of your very ingenious propositions as to railway communication. I fear, however, on mature reflection, that they will be liable to serious objections, and ultimately more expensive than a canal." Evidently Fulton had suggested the use of wood for rails, a material

[1] Sutcliffe, *Robert Fulton and the "Clermont,"* p. 288.

[2] Report of the Secretary of the Treasury on the subject of Public Roads and Canals, 1808, p. 108.

[3] Sutcliffe, *Robert Fulton and the "Clermont,"* p. 266.

which the Chancellor said "would not last a week." He also said that "the carriage of condensing water would be very troublesome," showing that Fulton had not proposed to use the high-pressure engine, so that evidently he had merely touched the fringe of the subject. Still it is noteworthy, because the steam locomotive had not yet come into commercial use in England much less anywhere else.

We must now turn to the crowning achievement of Fulton's life—that of the successful solution, on a commercial scale, of the problem of transport on water by the power of steam. After many years of study, experiment, and observation, the time for action had arrived, and he now proceeded to reduce his ideas to practice in the construction of a practical steamboat.

As we have endeavoured to show, Fulton's qualifications for the task were of a high order. He had studied closely the failures and successes of previous inventors, and analysed them as far as he could to find to what their failure or partial success had been due ; he had, moreover, studied during the time he was staying in France, we can hardly doubt, the theoretical works on the subject of ship resistance written by Bossut and others ; he had, above all, availed himself of the results of Colonel Mark Beaufoy's *Nautical Experiments* on the resistance to propulsion through water of variously shaped solids, carried out in Greenland Dock, Rotherhithe, in 1793–8, under the direction of the Society for the Improvement of Naval Architecture. In short Fulton had done what every engineer would do in like circumstances—he had availed himself of all practical information that he could find bearing on the subject he was dealing with and had applied also to it the results of theoretical investigations. He was the first to treat the elementary factors in steamship design : dimensions, form, horse-power, and speed in a scientific spirit ; to him belongs the credit of having coupled the boat and the engine as a working unit.

We have already referred to the experiments of early

inventors and to Fulton's knowledge of them, and it only remains to give the deductions that Beaufoy had made from his experiments. He showed that the important factors in the total resistance of a solid were:

1. Skin friction, proportional to the wetted area and to the square of the velocity.

2. Bow and stern resistance, proportional to the square of the sine of the angle of obliquity of the bow and stern.

The first is substantially the result accepted to-day, as verified by Froude, while the second is a partial recognition of the resistances due to wave making and eddy making as we now know them—partial because the stream line theory connoting the importance of length of entrance and of run aft was not yet enunciated. As Beaufoy's experiments were made with solids of prismatic shape, towed under still water by means of a pendulum apparatus, they were for that reason not directly applicable to ship-shaped solids floating on the surface; although he brought them under the notice of naval architects, it was without much success. Fulton, however, saw their value, and to him belongs the credit of being the first to apply them practically; indeed it is hardly too much to say that he was the first to apply theoretical investigations to practical ship design, so entirely was the latter at that time a question of "rule of thumb."

Fulton, in applying Beaufoy's results to his own case, adopted a midship section as nearly as possible rectangular with bow and stern wedge-shaped subtending an angle of 60 degrees. He calculated a table of resistances for each speed from 1 to 6 miles an hour for (*a*) the skin friction, and (*b*) the bow and stern resistance. To the bow resistance he added what was called the "plus pressure," *i.e.* "the additional pressure against the bow while the boat moves forwards"; from the stern resistance he deducted the "minus pressure occasioned by the fluid not pressing so strongly against the stern when the boat moves forward as when at rest." From this table the total resistance of a boat of any dimensions could quickly be calculated. He then added "a like power for the propellers," and this he considered to be the total power felt at the paddle-wheels. Piston speed being practically constant, the gearing necessary between the engine and propeller could be calculated and this would give the power that it would be necessary to develop in the cylinder, whence a convenient diameter and stroke could be deduced. The weight of engine and boiler could then be calculated, and subtracting it from the displacement the tonnage the boat could carry would be known.

All this is explained at very great length in Fulton's own words in the specification which he enrolled in the United States Patent Office in 1809, and which is reproduced in an Appendix.[1]

Even the calculations for the actual boat herself are given. The shape of this boat was a decided departure from established practice, for she was rectangular in cross-section for the greater part of her length; no wonder therefore that her coefficient of fineness was nearly 0.9. Unfortunately no drawings of the boat have been preserved, although we may be certain that such were made, even if only an outline, for this was always Fulton's practice. A satisfactory reproduction and model have been made, however, from what little details were in existence.

The construction of the boat was entrusted to Charles Browne, a well-known shipbuilder, whose yard was at Corlear's Hook on the East River. She was pushed forward rapidly during the spring of 1807, as is shown by a letter to the Chancellor, dated March 16, in which Fulton says: "The boat is now building." When launched she was not christened, apparently, but was known simply as "the steam boat." It was distinctive enough, too, for she was the only one in the world. After launching she

[1] See p. 289.

was taken over to Paulus Hook Ferry (not Paulus Hook itself, now known as Jersey City), where Fulton had secured some land for a workshop and was building the framing and gearing for the Boulton & Watt engine. After arrival it had remained for some time in the New York Custom House, as it was not immediately wanted, but it was eventually cleared and taken to a Mr. Barker's warehouse, whence it was removed on April 23 to the boat.

The difficulties that were encountered in the construction of the gearing and paddle-wheels at a time when smiths and carpenters were the only mechanics available were overcome, so that on the 4th of July Fulton was able to tell the Chancellor that "I have all my wheels up; they move admirably." But this was not the only hitch: the cost had already exceeded Fulton's estimate, and it was necessary to seek for assistance. John Stevens, as a politic stroke for he also had a steamboat project on hand, was invited to join the enterprise, but he declined. Many racy stories are told of the expedients that Fulton resorted to get money out of his incredulous friends, a number of whom did advance small amounts on bills.

At length all was ready; the preliminary trials took place on Sunday, August 9, just four years to a day since the trial trip on the Seine. Fulton wrote an account of it, dated August 10, 1807, to the Chancellor, and from it the following extract is taken:[1]

"Yesterday about 12 o'clock I put the steamboat in motion first with a paddle 8 inches broad 3 feet long with which I ran about one mile up the East River against a tide of about one mile an hour, it being nearly high water. I then anchored and put on another paddle 8 inches wide 3 feet long, started again and then, according to my best observations, I went 3 miles an hour, that is two against a tide of one: another board of 8 inches was wanting, which

[1] E. B. Livingston, *The Livingstons of Callendar*, privately printed, 1892, vol. v. p. 594.

"THE STEAMBOAT" AS SHE APPEARED IN 1807

had not been prepared; I therefore turned the boat and ran down with the tide . . . and turned her round neatly into the berth from which I parted. She answers the helm equal to anything that ever was built, and I turned her twice in three times her own length. Much has been proved by this experiment. *First*, that she will when in complete order run up to my full calculations; *Second* that my axles, I believe, will be sufficiently strong to run the engine to her full power; *Third*, that she steers well and can be turned with ease."

Fulton also mentions that "corrections, with the finishing of the cabins will take me the whole week, and I shall start on Monday next at 4 miles an hour."

The steamboat was not yet in a finished condition. The necessity for providing guards to protect the paddle-wheels from injury had not been realised, nor were they boxed in. The engine also was exposed to view. She was described, not without some point, as "an ungainly craft looking precisely like a backwoods' sawmill mounted on a scow and set on fire."

However, incomplete as she was, the trial trip took place on the day Fulton had appointed—Monday, August 17, 1807—a day to be kept in remembrance. At one o'clock the boat left her moorings at a dock on the North River near the State's Prison; on board were about forty guests, almost wholly relatives or intimate friends. So quietly had everything been done that only one paper, the *American Citizen*, announced the coming event; nevertheless a large number of spectators were present. The excitement was intense, the incredulity, scorn, and ridicule that had met him at every turn while "Fulton's Folly," for so the boat was nicknamed, was being built, gave way perforce to silence first and then to shouts of applause and congratulation.

We cannot do better than give an account of the voyage in Fulton's own words in a letter [1] to Joel Barlow.

[1] Todd, *Barlow's Life and Letters*, p. 233.

"My steamboat voyage to Albany and back has turned out rather more favourably than I had calculated. The distance from New York to Albany is one hundred and fifty miles. I ran it up in thirty-two hours and down in thirty. I had a light breeze against me the whole way both going and coming and the voyage has been performed wholly by the power of the steam-engine. I overtook many sloops and schooners beating to windward and parted with them as if they had been at anchor.

"The power of propelling boats by steam is now fully proved. The morning I left New York, there were not perhaps thirty persons in the city who believed that the boat would ever move one mile an hour, or be of the least utility, and while we were putting off from the wharf, which was crowded with spectators, I heard a number of sarcastic remarks. This is the way in which ignorant men compliment what they call philosophers and projectors.

"Having employed much time, money, and zeal in accomplishing this work, it gives me, as it will you, great pleasure to see it fully answer my expectations. It will give a cheap and quick conveyance to the merchants on the Mississippi, Missouri, and other great rivers which are now laying open their treasures to the enterprise of our countrymen; and although the prospect of personal emolument has been some inducement to me, yet I feel infinitely more pleasure in reflecting on the immense advantages that my country will draw from the invention. . . ."

The references to the Mississippi, Missouri, and "other great rivers which are now laying open their treasures" is of course to the recent purchase of Louisiana from France, and shows that Fulton had already directed his attention to this very wide field for enterprise; he embarked upon it shortly afterwards.

To correct erroneous impressions, Fulton, on his return to New York on Friday, August 21, wrote the following letter to the editor of the *American Citizen*, giving what might be called a log of the voyage.

"I arrived this afternoon at 4 o'clock in the steamboat from Albany. As the success of my experiment gives me great hopes that such boats may be rendered of much importance to my country, to prevent erroneous opinions and to give some satisfaction to the friends of useful improvements, you will have the goodness to publish the following statement of facts:

"I left New York on Monday at 1 o'clock and arrived at Clermont, the seat of Chancellor Livingston, at 1 o'clock on Tuesday; time 24 hours; distance 110 miles. On Wednesday I departed from the Chancellor's at 9 in the morning and arrived at Albany at 5 in the afternoon; distance 40 miles; time 8 hours; the sum of this is 150 miles in 32 hours—equal near 5 miles an hour.

"On Thursday, at 9 o'clock in the morning, I left Albany and arrived at the Chancellor's at 6 in the evening; I started from thence at 7 and arrived at New York at 4 in the afternoon; time 30 hours, space run through, 150 miles—equal to 5 miles an hour. Throughout my whole way, both going and returning, the wind was ahead; no advantage could be derived from my sail. The whole has therefore been performed by the power of the steam engine."

Another contemporary account which appeared in the English press is even more interesting than the foregoing:

"I have now the pleasure to state to you the particulars of a late excursion to Albany in the steam-boat, made and completed under the directions of the Hon. Robert R. Livingston and Mr. Fulton, together with my remarks thereon. On the morning of the 19th of August, Edward P. Livingston, Esq., and myself were honoured with an invitation from the chancellor and Mr. Fulton to proceed with them to Albany, in trying the first experiment up the river Hudson, in the steam-boat. She was then lying off Claremont (the seat of the chancellor), where she had arrived in twenty-four hours from New York, being 110 miles. Precisely at thirteen minutes past nine o'clock A.M. the engine was put in motion, when we made a head against the ebb-tide and head-wind, blowing a pleasant breeze. We continued our course for about eight miles, when we took the flood, the wind still a-head. We arrived at Albany about five o'clock P.M., being a distance from Claremont of forty-five miles (as agreed upon by those best acquainted with the river), which was performed in eight hours, without any accident or interruption whatever. This decidedly gave the boat upwards of five miles an hour, the tide sometimes against us, neither the sails nor any other implement but the steam used. The next morning we left Albany with several passengers on the return to New York, the tide in favour, but a head-wind. We left Albany at twenty-five minutes past nine A.M. and arrived at Claremont in nine hours precisely, which gave us five miles an hour. The current, on returning, was stronger than when going up. After landing us at Claremont, Mr. Fulton proceeded with the passengers to New York. The excursion to Albany was very pleasant, and represented a most interesting spectacle. As we passed the farms on the borders of the river, every eye was intent, and from village to village, the heights and conspicuous places were occupied by the sentinels of curiosity, not viewing a thing they could possibly anticipate any idea of, but conjecturing about the possibility of the motion. As we passed and repassed the towns of Athens and Hudson, we were politely saluted by the inhabitants and several vessels, and at Albany we were visited by his excellency, the governor, and many citizens. Boats must be very cautious how they attempt to board her when under way, as several accidents had nearly happened when boarding her: to board a-head will endanger a boat being crushed by the wheels, and no boat can board a-stern. . . . The boat is 146 feet in length and

12 in width (merely an experimental thing); draws to the depth of her wheels two feet of water; 100 feet deck for exercise, free of rigging or any encumbrances. She is unquestionably the most pleasant boat I ever went in. In her the mind is free from suspense. Perpetual motion authorises you to calculate on a certain time to land; her works move with all the facility of a clock; and the noise when on board is not greater than that of a vessel sailing with a good breeze."[1]

After her return from her first voyage the steamboat was laid up for more than a fortnight in order to complete her equipment and to carry out the improvements that had suggested themselves. These are detailed in a letter which Fulton wrote to the Chancellor from New York on August 29: from this we make the following extract:

"I have been making every effort to get off on Monday morning, but there has been much work to do—boarding all the sides, decking over the boiler and works, finishing each cabin with twelve berths to make them comfortable, and strengthening many parts of the ironwork. So much to do and the rain which delays the caulkers will, I fear, not let me off till Wednesday morning. Then, however, the boat will be as complete as she can be made—all strong and in good order and the men well-organized and I hope nothing to do but to run her for six weeks or two months. . . . I will have her registered[2] and everything done which I can recollect. Everything looks well and I have no doubt will be very productive."

In the postscript he says:

"I think it would be well to write to your brother Edward to get information on the velocity of the Mississippi, the size and form of the boats used, the number of hands

[1] *Naval Chronicle*, 1808, vol. xix. p. 188. The letter is dated September 8, 1807.

[2] *i.e.* In the New York Custom House. This was done on September 3, 1807; the record of her dimensions has not been preserved.

and quantity of tons in each boat, the number of miles they make against the current in the hour, and the quantity of tons which go up the river in a year."

The steamboat was not ready, however, to start till Friday, Sept. 4, as shown by advertisements in the *Albany Gazette* of Sept. 2—the first notice to the public of the inauguration of the new method of transport. This, which ran as follows, continued to appear for three weeks:

> "THE NORTH RIVER STEAM BOAT
>
> Will leave Pauler's Hook Ferry on Friday the 4th of September at 6 in the morning and Arrive at Albany at 6 in the afternoon. Provisions, good births and accommodations are provided."

The announcement proceeds to say that she would then leave Albany twice and New York once in the week following and vice versa in the succeeding week, after which date (*i.e.* September 16) further arrangements would be made.

True to promise the steamboat sailed on Friday morning from New York on her first voyage as a commercial venture. She left at 6.42 A.M. Fulton himself was a passenger as far as Clermont; besides him there were fourteen others, who, before arriving at Albany, drew up and signed a short account of the voyage. It was quite uneventful, the only thing to note being that it was done in better time than on the occasion of the trial trip, the whole distance to Albany having been accomplished in 28 hours 45 minutes. The account concludes:

"The subscribers, passengers on board of this boat on her first voyage as a packet, think it but justice to state that the accommodation and conveniences on board exceeded their most sanguine expectations." [1]

The boat did not adhere to her programme exactly on

[1] *Albany Register*, September 8, 1807, quoted in Munsell's *Annals of Albany*, vol. vi. p. 25.

account of a mishap. One of the sailing packets, whether by accident, or, as some people thought, by design, came into collision with the steamboat and carried away one of her paddle-wheels. The damage, however, was quickly repaired, and on September 23 the following advertisement as to her future sailings appeared:

"THE STEAM BOAT being thoroughly repaired, and precautions taken that injury shall not be done to her wheels in future, it is intended to run her as a PACKET for the remainder of the season. She will take her departure from New York and Albany at 9 o'clock in the morning, and always perform her voyage in from 30 to 36 hours."

Then follows the announcement of dates of sailing from September 25 till October 9.

Day by day the number of passengers who availed themselves of the new and speedy mode of travel increased. On October 1 the steamboat came from Albany in 28 hours with 60 passengers on board, and next day she left New York with 90 people on board,[1] showing what a favourite she was becoming. The newspaper which gives this information pertinently remarks:

"Would it not be well if she could contract with the Postmaster-General to carry the mail from this city to Albany?"

It is instructive, as illustrating how events fraught with the greatest import to the human race are ushered into the world almost without comment, to observe the little impression made upon the public by the new mode of transport judging by the notice taken of it in the press of the day. Although New York then boasted a population of 83,000 souls, and possessed at least twenty newspapers, half of them dailies, besides weekly papers and magazines, yet, excepting the letters written by Fulton and some of the passengers, there is only the barest mention of the steamboat outside the advertisement columns.

[1] *Evening Post*, October 2, 1807.

On October 9 Fulton wrote to Andrew Brink, the captain of the boat, giving him instructions, decidedly of a hustling character, as to the management of the boat and discipline to be observed on board, as follows:[1]

SIR,—Inclosed is the number of voyages which it is intended the Boat should run this season. You may have them published in the Albany papers.

As she is strongly man'd and every one except Jackson under your command, you must insist on each one doing his duty or turn him on shore and put another in his place. Everything must be kept in order, everything in its place, and all parts of the Boat scoured and clean. It is not sufficient to tell men to do a thing, but stand over them and make them do it. One pair of Quick and good eyes is worth six pair of hands in a commander. If the Boat is dirty and out of order the fault shall be yours. Let no man be Idle when there is the least thing to do, and make them move quick.

Run no risques of any kind when you meet or overtake vessels beating or crossing your way. Always run under their stern if there be the least doubt that you cannot clear their head by 50 yards or more. Give in the account of Receipts and expenses every week to the Chancellor.

Your most obedient,
ROBT. FULTON.

All went well with the steamboat till November 13, when, just as she was leaving New York, "one of the axletrees broke off short and she was obliged to return." These shafts, it should be remembered, were only of cast iron, so that the accident is not to be wondered at. Repairs were made in the course of the day and she was again on her station by the morrow.

By November 19, however, it was reported in the papers that the Hudson from Albany as far down as

[1] Sutcliffe, *Robert Fulton and the "Clermont,"* p. 253.

Coxsackie was frozen across entirely, but this did not interfere with the running of the boat, apparently, for in the *Evening Post* appeared a letter, dated the 19th November, giving an account of a very rough passage during which the boat had to ride at anchor for seven hours. The passengers on this occasion, however, expressed their approbation of the treatment they had received and their pleasure in being able to report that no accident had happened.

A few days later it was decided to lay up the boat for the winter, as is clear from the following most interesting letter[1] of Fulton to Livingston, dated November 20:

I have received your letter of the 12th inst. After all accidents and delays our boat has cleared 5 per cent. on the capital expended, and as the people are not discouraged, but continue to go in her at all risques and even increase in numbers, I think with you that one which should be complete would produce us from 8 to 10,000 dollars a year or perhaps more and that another boat which will cost 15,000 dollars will also produce us 10,000 dollars a year; therefore, as this is the only method which I know of gaining 50 or 75 per cent., I am, on my part, determined not to dispose of any portion of my interest on the North River; but I will sell so much of my funds as will pay my part of rendering this boat complete and for establishing another, so that one will depart from Albany and one from New York every other day and carry all the passengers. It is now necessary to consider how to put our first boat in a complete state for 8 or 10 years—and when I reflect that the present one is so weak that she must have additional knees and timbers, new side timbers, deck beams and deck, new windows and cabins altered, that she perhaps must be sheathed, her boiler taken out and a new one put in, her axels forged and Iron work strengthened. With all this

[1] Reproduced by permission of the New York Historical Society, who possess the original.

work the saving of the present hull is of little consequence particularly as many of her Knees Bolts timbers and planks could enter into the construction of a new boat. My present opinion therefore is that we should build a new hull her knees and floor timbers to be of oak her bottom planks of 2 Inch oak her side planks two Inch oak for 3 feet high. She to be 16 feet wide 150 feet long this will make her near twice as stiff as at present and enable us to carry a much greater quantity of sail, the 4 feet additional width will require 1146 lbs. additional purchase at the engine moving 2 feet a second or 15 double strokes a minute—this will be gained by raising the steam 5 lbs. to the inch as 24 Inches the diameter of the cylinder gives 570 round Inches at 3 lb. to the inch = 1710 lb. purchase gained to accomplish this with a good boiler and a commodious boat running our present speed, of a voyage in 30 hours, I think better and more productive to us than to gain one mile on the present boat.

The new boat, Cabins and all complete, including our materials will cost perhaps .	2000 dols.
Boiler	800 ,,
Iron work in the best manner and men's wages during the winter	1200 ,,
	4000 ,,

To meet this I find that our copper boiler weighs 3930 lbs. which at 40 cents all the price paid by Government will produce .	1570 dols.
Profits of this year	1000 ,,
	2570 ,,

So that we shall have to provide about 1500 dols. added to 3000 Bills against us in the Bank. With this arrangement we shall have one Boat in complete play, producing about 10,000 dollars a year to enable us to proceed with the second, to come out in the spring of 1809, and then our receipts will be about 20,000 dollars a year.

Please to think of this and if you like it to try and

contract with the carpenter at Hudson for the hull and let him immediately prepare his timbers, knees, and planks.

She should be almost wall-sided: if 16 feet at bottom she need not be more than 18 on deck. Streight sides will be strong; it fits the mill work and prevents motion in the waves. . . .

It is now time to lay her up for the winter.

Nothing should be risqued from bad weather—the gain will be trifling, the risque great.

I cannot be with you before the first week in January.

Compliments to all friends. Write me again.

Yours truly,

R. FULTON.

Do not risque the engine in the winds and waves of the season.

It appears from this letter that the steamboat had, from start to finish, cost 20,000 dollars, of which sum 3000 had been borrowed on bills, possibly the money that we have already mentioned as having been lent by friends. The capital that Fulton had sunk must, therefore, have been 8500 dollars—that is to say, it had not exhausted his resources; indeed, that is clear from his remark, "I will sell so much of my funds."

As usual Fulton is sanguine; the profit on the three months' working had been 1000 dollars. For the following year he was reckoning on eight times as much, although the period during which the boat could run would not be as much as four times as long!

Fulton's proposal about building a new hull of increased beam appears to have been carried out and this will explain the fact that, while in his patent specification[1] he gives the beam as 13 feet, in other places he gives it as 16 or 18 feet. In her rebuilt state the steamboat might be said to

[1] See p. 324.

be like the Irishman's knife in which everything had been renewed at different times, but it was still the same knife. In fact so great were the changes in the steamboat that under the Act of Congress regulating such matters a new registration at the Custom House became necessary. The enrolment[1] is dated May 14, 1808, and is as follows:

"Robert R. Livingston of Clermont, Columbia County, State of New York, having taken and subscribed to the Oath required by the said Act and having sworn that he, together with Robert Fulton of the City of New York, are citizens of the United States and sole owners of the ship or vessel called the North River Steamboat of Clermont, whereof Samuel Wiswall is at present master, and as he hath sworn he is a citizen of the United States and that the said ship or vessel was built in the City of New York in the year 1807 as per enrollment 973 issued at this port on the 3d day of September 1807 now given up, the vessel being enlarged. And Peter A. Schenck, Surveyor of the Port, having certified that the said ship or vessel has one deck and two masts and that her length is 149 ft.; breadth 17 ft. 11 in.; depth 7 ft., and that she measures $182\frac{48}{95}$ tons. That she is a square sterned boat, has square tuck; no quarter galleries and no figure head."

Known for short as the *North River*, she started running in May, and in June, Fulton in a letter to C. W. Peale says:

"My steamboat is now in complete operation and works much to my satisfaction, making the voyage from or to New York or Albany, 160 miles, on an average in 35 hours. She has three excellent Cabins or rather rooms, containing 54 births with kitchen, larder, pantry, Bar, and steward's room. Passengers have been encourageing. Last Saturday she started from New York with 70, which is doing very well for these times when trade has not its usual activity."[2]

A period of prosperity for the partners now began and

[1] Morrison, *History of American Steam Navigation*, p. 20.

[2] Sutcliffe, *Robert Fulton and the "Clermont,"* p. 269.

everything promised well. In the following year the *North River* made upwards of 50 trips of which complete passenger lists have been preserved.

The time during which Livingston and Fulton had to produce proof of their ability to propel a boat by the agency of steam had expired in April 1807, but in the session of 1808 the Legislature of New York passed a law to prolong the exclusive privilege of Livingston and Fulton for 5 years for each additional boat they should establish provided that the whole time should not exceed 30 years; their original privilege was, it will be remembered, for 20 years from 1803—*i.e.* to terminate in 1823. This therefore was a very valuable concession because the prejudice against the new mode of travel had disappeared and passengers attracted by its speed and punctuality crowded to take passage in the *North River.*

Naturally this success aroused the cupidity of those harpies who live by preying on other people's labour and inventions. Unwilling to aid Fulton the previous year when he was ready to part with one-third of his exclusive right to lessen the pressure on his finances, they now prepared to wrest from him the profits of his enterprise, with the result that will appear later. Nor was this all, for the flyboat and scow owners were already beginning to feel the effects of competition and began the short-sighted policy of endeavouring to do malicious injury to the boat by collisions and obstructions. So serious did this become that in 1811 the New York Legislature passed a supplementary Act giving summary remedies against those who should be guilty of these malpractices.

But success also spurred on the partners to further efforts, and a second steamboat, the *Car of Neptune,* was planned. She was practically a duplicate of the *North River,* being 175 feet long over all, 24 feet beam, 39 feet over the guards, and having the same draught of water. The whole of the machinery appears to have been designed and executed by Fulton himself. This boat was building during the summer of 1809, but was not ready till that autumn or the spring of the following year in time for the season. It appears to have cost about 25,000 dollars—*i.e.* about 50 per cent. more than he had estimated. With these two boats a service twice a week was run.

The necessity having now arisen to give the older boat a more distinctive name than she had had, it was at this juncture that she was called[1] the *Clermont*, undoubtedly after the residence of his associate and friend Livingston.

Apparently success completely justified the enterprise, for the partners now planned the construction of a third boat: not only so but they had already extended their sphere of operations to the Mississippi, where, in the autumn of 1810, having received an assurance of obtaining from the state of Louisiana an exclusive privilege which was duly accorded on April 19, 1811, the *New Orleans* was being built under the superintendence of Nicholas J. Roosevelt. This boat occasioned a reduction of 25 per cent. as the cost of freight between New Orleans and Natchez.[2] The work that was crowding in upon them must have decided Fulton that he could not do it all himself, and he was therefore led to apply once more to Boulton, Watt & Co. for another engine.

The letter is as follows:

NEW YORK, *September* 15, 1810.

MESSRS. BOULTON & WATT,

GENTLEMEN,—In 1804 you constructed for me a steam engine with a 24 Inch Cylinder and a four foot stroke, which engine has for four years past been driving a boat 166 feet long, 18 feet wide drawing 2½ feet of water at the speed of 5 miles an hour on the Hudson River; that is taking the tide for and against the boat her average velocity is 5 miles an hour; This application of your Invention to drive boats, has been, and will ever continue to to (*sic*) be

[1] *Hudson Bee*, May 13, 1810.

[2] Marestier, *Mémoire sur les Bateaux à vapeur*, 1824, p. 161.

of great public Utility in this State, by carrying passengers Between the Cities of New York and Albany distance 160 miles, the profits have also been such as to induce me to form similar establishments on some of our other rivers. I will therefore esteem it a favour if you will have the goodness to make for me another engine as soon as possible, the Cylinder to be 26 inches, the stroke as before 4 feet.

SCHEDULE OF MATERIALS WANTED

1st. A Steam Cylinder 26 inches diameter 4 feet stroke, with its top and plate, its bottom gland and brasses complete.
2d. Piston, its cover, bottom plate and spanners.
3d. Piston rod, its cap and cutters.
4. Nozzles complete with Valves and Levers.
5. Working gear Complete with brackets.
6. Perpendicular steam and eduction pipe.
7. Condenser Vessel with blow pipe and blowing Valve.
8. Injection cock and handle not wanted as I shall have to arrange them to a tube passing through the bottom of the boat.
9. Air pump its bucket and top and bottom Valves complete.
10. Air pump bucket rod with cap and brackets.
11. Eduction pipe to Condenser.
12. Two boxes of Cement.

This, gentlemen, has been copied from your original estimate and was to be made for 380£ delivered at Soho. I afterwards found it necessary to have a brass air pump in consequence of working in salt water, that with altering models, Packing cases, &c., &c., brought your final bill to 548£. In this engine the Air pump may be Iron, and all the work as usual where fresh water is used; The American Minister will obtain permission of the Government to ship the engine to America. I wish it to be sent to the most convenient port from Birmingham which I presume is Liverpool. I will write to my Correspondent in London to take charge of the shipment and to settle final accounts with you. Inclosed are the first Nos. of bills of exchange of 527£.[1] You will have the goodness to let me know by the first packet if they are accepted and if the engine will be ready to ship in February or March next.—In this, Gentlemen you will much oblige, your most obedient,

ROBERT FULTON.

P.S.—Should there be any improvement in the manner of constructing engines since I had the pleasure of seeing you, you will have the goodness to make for me that which you conceive most perfect.

A coloured sketch giving "the position and distances of a piston" must have been enclosed, for one of the above date has been preserved among the Boulton & Watt MSS.

This letter was despatched in triplicate; in the duplicate written on December 4 he alters the diameter of the cylinder from 26 inches to 28 inches "if not already cast." Speaking of the air pump he also says:

"In my letter of September I mentioned that it might be of Iron, but having changed the destination of the engine to a place where it must work in salt water it is necessary the air pump should be Brass and everything about the Buckets and Valves either Brass or copper, as the Iron screws, pins and nuts on your first engine rusted off in 6 months."

The working drawing of this engine has been preserved. It is entitled "Mr. R. Fulton, Inch to the foot, 23rd Febr. 1811"; the cylinder is marked "28 inside" and the stroke is 4 feet.

Evidently the parts were taken from the firm's 30 H.P. engine.

[1] A note shows that enclosed there were two bills, one for £300 and one for £275.

From a subsequent letter[1] it will be seen that the engine was not quite complete in January 1812: apparently, however, the engine must have been delivered soon after, for James Watt, writing[2] from Heathfield on April 13 of the same year to a correspondent who had inquired about engines for canal boats, explains that he had retired from business for many years, but that "It is a Mr. Fulton who has constructed the steamboats in America; two of the engines have been made by Boulton, Watt & Co., but the machinery has been made entirely in America under his own direction." He further mentions that the cylinders were 24-inch and 28-inch diameter respectively by 4-feet stroke. It is not certain in which of the boats this engine was fitted, the only one whose diameter and stroke agree with it was the *Washington*, 1813, which, however, was not built to ply in salt water. The next boat to be built after the *Car of Neptune* was the *Paragon*. With her, Fulton was able to inaugurate a service three times a week, as is shown by the following advertisement:[3]

"HUDSON RIVER STEAMBOATS

FOR THE INFORMATION OF THE PUBLIC

The *Paragon*, Capt. Wiswell, will leave New York every Saturday afternoon at five o'clock.

The *Car of Neptune*, Capt. Roorbach, d°. d°. every Tuesday afternoon at five o'clock.

The *North River*, Capt. Bartholomew, every Thursday afternoon at five o'clock.

The *Paragon* will leave Albany every Thursday morning at nine o'clock.

The *Car of Neptune* d°. every Saturday morning at nine o'clock.

The *North River* d°. every Tuesday morning at nine o'clock.

---

[1] P. 250.

[2] Muirhead, *Mechanical Inventions of James Watt*, vol. ii. p. 338.

[3] New York *Evening Post*, June 1813.

PRICES OF PASSAGE

From *New York* to Verplanck's Point $2; West Point $2.50; Newburgh $3; Wappinger's Creek $3.25; Poughkeepsie $3.50; Hyde Park $4; Esopus $4.25; Catskill $5; Hudson $5; Coxsachie $5.50; Kinderhook $5.75; Albany $7. From *Albany* to Kinderhook $1.50; Coxsachie $2; Hudson $2; Catskill $2.25; Red Hook $2.75; Esopus $3; Hyde Park $3.25; Poughkeepsie $3.50; Wappinger's Creek $4; Newburgh $4.25; West Point $4.75; Verplanck's Point $5.25; New York $7.

All other passengers to pay at the rate of 1 dollar for every twenty miles. No one can be taken on board and put on shore however short the distance for less than 1 dollar.

Young persons from two to ten years of age to pay half price; Children under two years one fourth price. Servants who use a berth, two thirds price; half price if none."

The boats are placed inversely in order of date of construction, being that of general convenience and comfort showing that the *North River* was now a "back number." The list of fares is interesting. The fare between New York and Albany had been 7 dollars from the very first, while fares to and from intermediate places had been reduced from time to time. The number of places of call had increased and yet in spite of that the journey had been gradually accelerated.

Meanwhile another application of the steamboat had been engaging Fulton's active brain—that of the possibility of improving the communication between New York and Jersey City, where the Hudson is 1¼ to 1½ miles across. Up to that moment the cities had been somewhat inefficiently served by Ferry rowboats; their slowness and uncertainty were experienced by Fulton every time he had occasion to go from his home in New York to Jersey City.

In 1809 a company was formed with a capital of $50,000. They acquired a lease for nineteen years from the Corporation of New York and from the proprietors of Jersey City of their respective rights, wharves, and boats at New York and Paulus Hook respectively. Fulton was applied to to construct a steam ferry-boat, the details being left entirely in his hands.[1]

His plans for this, the first one of its kind, embodied, as might have been expected from Fulton, novel features. With the idea of preventing injury to the propelling machinery and of minimising rolling, he constructed the boat with two ship-shaped hulls with a single paddle-wheel in the space between and the engine resting on the connecting beams. The fact that a similar arrangement had been adopted by Patrick Miller in his doubled-hulled boats of 1787, propelled by muscular power, may have been known to Fulton and suggested the idea to him. Each hull was 80 feet long by 10 feet beam and 5 feet deep in the hold—the space between the hulls was 10 feet. This gave a wide platform for carriage and passengers, and as the hulls were double-ended putting about was obviated. At each side of the river was moored the usual pontoon rising and falling with the tide. Fixed at its shore end and sliding over the pontoon was the bridge. There were floating timbers on either side of the pontoon to guide in the ferry-boat. To take up the shock of impact there was a fender or buffer in front, connected by chains over a pulley so as to raise buckets of water. These buckets had holes in to let out the water so as to bring the whole to rest gradually. A half-hourly service was instituted, the boat taking 15 to 20 minutes for each trip.

"She has had in her at one time 8 four-wheeled carriages 29 horses and 100 passengers, and could have

[1] *American Medical and Philosophical Register*, 1813, vol. iii. pp. 196–203, description by Fulton himself.

taken 300 more." So great was the success of this boat that in 1811 she was followed by another and in 1812 by a third over the East Hudson River.

When in 1816 a thoroughfare between these two ferries was opened it was named most appropriately in his honour Fulton Street.

Before leaving the subject of steamboats a few words are desirable as to the progress that was made during the remainder of Fulton's lifetime and under his direction.[1] With this end in view a table of dimensions of steamboats, whence many interesting comparisons emerge, has been compiled from all available sources and is given in an Appendix.[2]

All the early boats were built, like the *Clermont*, flat-bottomed and wall-sided. The *Fulton*, for navigating Long Island Sound, was the first made ship-shaped, and, proving successful, all subsequent boats were so built. Fulton yielded in this matter because of the increased strength given to the vessel by regular curves in the moulds rather than from a conviction that the shape diminished resistance. The ratio of length to breadth, which in the *Clermont* was about 10 : 1, was reduced gradually till in the *Chancellor Livingston* (1816), also a river steamer, the ratio was 4.7 : 1. In the case of the *Connecticut* (1816), which like the *Fulton* was for navigating Long Island Sound, really an arm of the sea, the ratio was 4.1 : 1. This no doubt resulted from an attempt to counteract the "hogging" and "sagging" which took place in the early boats. Fulton's own evidence[3] as to the *Clermont* on this point is conclusive, and Marestier in 1824 notes that the deck of the *Paragon* was sensibly undulating.

The position of the paddle-wheels in the *Clermont* was halfway between stem and stern; afterwards it was

[1] For much of this matter we are indebted to Marestier, *Mémoire sur les Bateaux à vapeur des Etats Unis d'Amerique*, 1824, 4to, p. 41 *et seq.* Marestier made an official visit to the States on behalf of the French Government to report as to the advisability of establishing steam navigation in France.

[2] See p. 326.

[3] See p. 317.

P.S. "CHANCELLOR LIVINGSTON," 1816

further forward, but there was never any consensus of opinion on this point.

The growth in tonnage and with it the increase of engine power due to the growth of traffic was inevitable. The design of the engine was still tentative. The unmechanical bell-crank engine of the *Clermont* was modified by a reduction in the number of working parts. The fly-wheel was not done away with till about 1815, although as early as 1810 Fulton had realised that the paddle wheels themselves gave a fly wheel effect. In the *Chancellor Livingston* the square crosshead or steeple engine due to Stevens was adopted.

No finality was reached in the type of boiler. It was generally of the internally-fired, return tube type, but the details differed in nearly every boat.

As the *Chancellor Livingston* was the last and finest of Fulton's vessels, a detailed description[1] and drawing will be of interest.

The paddle wheels were placed at the middle of the length of the boat with the engine forward of them and the boiler forward of that again. The paddle wheels were boxed in to obviate splashing. They were supported and protected by sponson beams, over which extended a deck used for the stowage of fuel and for latrines. Space around the engine was occupied by wood and coal bunkers, the galleys and a bar where refreshments were sold. The boiler and engine were covered by a casing open at the sides to allow free circulation of air. The *Chancellor Livingston* was the first vessel to employ coal as fuel.

The steering wheel was raised above the casing of the engine so that the pilot might have an uninterrupted view forward.

The accommodation for passengers was liberal. The after end of the boat was occupied by a large dining saloon, on each side of which were two tiers of berths separated by curtains, and lockers or couches below on

[1] Marestier, *loc. cit.*, p. 64 *et seq.*

which beds were placed when necessary. There was a side light to each of the upper berths. It is interesting, as showing the points from which development started, to note that this arrangement was adopted for the car for overland travel on the advent of the railway, while in England the sub-division of the railway coach by compartments was modelled upon stage coach practice.

On the maindeck above the saloon was a ladies' cabin similarly arranged, access to the saloon being by a companion way aft. Forward was a second class cabin with berths in two tiers as before and two similar rows back to back along a partition down the middle line. The crew were accommodated in the forecastle, while the captain's cabin, the purser's cabin, and the baggage room were on the main deck. Nothing was spared to make the boat superior in appointments to anything that had gone before. She cost over £25,000.

In 1823 the capital of the Hudson Steamboat Company invested in their fleet—*Car of Neptune*, *Paragon*, *Firefly*, *Richmond*, and *Chancellor Livingston*—including the value of the privilege was estimated[1] at £132,000, the gross annual receipts were £30,000, or £10,000 less working expenses, equal to a return of about 8 per cent on the capital. It is quite clear that after Fulton's death the policy of the Company was most unprogressive, and that their whole aim was to make as much money as possible while the privilege lasted.

It must not be imagined that other inventors had been idle while Fulton had been so busy. On the contrary, had he not appeared at all on the scene there is every probability that steam navigation would have arisen, not quite so quickly perhaps, nor yet possibly so successfully, at the hands of one of the most prolific American inventors—we refer to Colonel John C. Stevens of Hoboken. As early as 1803, although not versed in practical engineering, he had constructed a remarkable twin screw steam launch, with a

[1] Marestier, *loc. cit.*, p.153.

not less remarkable high pressure tubular boiler, which are now safely housed in the Smithsonian Institution at Washington. It was over this boiler that Stevens came to grief—he had in fact run up against a problem that, with the mechanical knowledge and materials of construction of those days, was not ripe for solution. Nothing daunted, however, Stevens tried along another line—that of Fulton himself—low pressure and paddle wheels, and built a vessel called appropriately enough the *Phœnix*, which was ready for its trials only a month after the *Clermont*. Colonel Stevens, finding himself debarred by Fulton's monopoly from navigating the Hudson, was compelled, in order to make pecuniary use of the vessel, to transfer its services to another quarter. In July 1809 the *Phœnix* was taken under her own steam under the command of Robert L. Stevens, son of the Colonel, coastwise to Philadelphia, whence she plied to Trenton on the Delaware River. Thus he was the first to navigate the open sea by steam.

CHAPTER X

UNITED STATES PATENTS—THE STEAMBOAT MONOPOLY AND LITIGATION TO WHICH IT GAVE RISE—STEAMBOAT ENTERPRISE IN EUROPE AND ASIA

IT is now necessary to record a fact of considerable significance. As we have already seen, Fulton had all along had in view a much wider field of enterprise than the Hudson River. No doubt it was with a view to securing to himself a monopoly over the whole of the United States territory that he now applied for his first patent. Possibly, too, he had some idea that it might be a "second string to his bow" in case his monopoly of the Hudson broke down, the gathering of a storm for that purpose being already apparent, as we shall see later. His application, which is for "Improvements in Steamboats," is dated January 1, 1809, and the patent was granted February 11th the same year.

Fulton's patent is not to be found in the archives of the U.S. Patent Office. It must have perished with many other records in the disastrous fire which occurred there in 1831.

The author, however, has been fortunate enough to meet with two MS. copies of the specification—one in the Patent Office Library, and the other in the Boulton and Watt MSS., which is of such interest as to be worthy of reproduction in full[1] on another page.

There are thirteen sheets of tables and drawings attached to it which appear to be based on actual practice. A definite reference is made to the *Clermont*, which is

[1] See Appendix E, p. 289.

selected as an example, and there can be little doubt that we have now actual drawings of the engine arrangements of that boat if not of the *Paragon* and *Car of Neptune* as well.

One of the sheets of drawings gives a "table of the resistance of bodies moved through water" "taken from experiments made in England by a Society for Improving Naval Architecture between the years 1793 and 1798." Incidentally this refutes one charge of plagiarism directed against Fulton. The charge need never have been made, for the information was common property, having been published by the Society in 1798.

Practically the whole claim in this patent is for the right proportioning of the engine to the boat and for the combination of the parts. Indeed no other valid claim was possible, as none of the parts in themselves were novel. To elucidate these points, we find a great deal of the text taken up by calculations showing how to obtain the proportions of a boat and of the engine suitable for it to go at 1, 2, 3, 4, 5 or 6 miles an hour with a given load. Fulton finds the total resistance of the boat to be the sum of—

i. The immersed cross section of the boat in square feet multiplied by the "plus and minus pressure" the co-efficient for which he obtains from a table, based on the aforementioned experiments, for each of the speeds named.

ii. The friction of the sum of the areas of the bow and stern together multiplied by a corresponding co-efficient.

iii. The friction of the sides and bottom of the boat similarly calculated.

To this total he adds a like power for the paddle-wheels. As these are always to go at twice the speed of the boat, and as he assumes the piston speed to be constant, he is able to decide the necessary ratio of gearing and a convenient diameter for a cylinder to give the power required.

Following upon his calculations for a boat to run at 6 miles per hour he remarks:

"As to 6 miles an hour, were it attempted and to succeed, I should consider it more a work of curiosity than utility, as I do not believe it possible to build a steam-boat with any engine which is now known to run 6 miles an hour in still water, and carry either passengers or cargo to pay the expenses."

He retained the same opinion even as late as 1811, for, writing on January 9 to Dr. S. Thornton, superintendent of the American Patent Office, he says:

"If you succeed to run 6 miles an hour in still water with One hundred tons of merchandise I will contract to reimburse the cost of the boat and give you one hundred and fifty thousand dollars for your patent, or if you can convince me of the success by drawings or demonstrations I will join you in the expenses and profits."

Such an attitude of mind in a man like Fulton seems hardly credible, especially seeing that in 1802 he had anticipated a speed of 16 miles per hour; with the steady advance that he was making, it was not more than a year or two later before one of his own boats was doing what he now considered impossible.

On October 2, 1810, Fulton applied for another patent[1] for "constructing boats or vessels which are to be navigated by the power of the steam-engine"; it was granted on February 9, 1811. It is supplementary to the first, and in it he claims, among other things, the coupling boxes, wheel guards, fender strakes, covering over the paddle wheels, placing the steering wheel forward, and hogging frames. Many of these details, while no doubt originating with him, had been public property for some years, so that the patent could hardly have been worth anything, and had the claims been successfully maintained it would have done more to retard than advance the progress of steam navigation.

[1] See Appendix F, p. 313.

The patent is interesting chiefly for the drawings which illustrate some advance in engine construction. One of the drawings foreshadows very clearly the side lever engine which remained for forty years the accepted type for steam navigation.

We have already alluded at some length to the monopoly of the waters of New York State enjoyed by Fulton and Livingston, and it is now necessary to explain why it was that it conferred such enormous powers and privileges, and why such a protracted and bitter legal fight was instituted to compass its overthrow.

The basis upon which the monopoly rested was that the State of New York claimed jurisdiction over all the waters of the Bay and of the Hudson River up to low water mark on the mainland or Jersey shore. As it was for the navigation of these waters that the State of New York had granted a monopoly to Livingston and Fulton, and as no steamboat could approach New York and enjoy trade with the City without traversing this stretch of water, we can see how it was that these two monopolists were able to keep out all such men as Colonel John Stevens with his steamer the *Phœnix*.

This claim on the part of the State of New York was founded neither on reason nor on common sense. A river or lake suggests itself naturally as a boundary between adjacent territories, and, when it is accepted as such, common law assumes that the boundary is in mid-channel or in the deepest part.

Now the State of New Jersey had always repudiated the claim of the State of New York; indeed in 1806 New York had consented to the appointment of a joint commission to try and come to an agreement but without result. It seems to us that it would have been an obvious course for New Jersey to have appealed to the United States Supreme Court for a settlement of this dispute, but possibly the temper of the people was too independent for such a course. Now that steam navigation had been introduced and the financial considerations involved were considerable, the question assumed very great importance. Livingston and Fulton's monopoly is so inextricably bound up with it that one can hardly be discussed without the other.

The first attack upon their vested interest appears to have been made in 1810 or at the beginning of 1811, when a company was formed at Albany to run in opposition to the Fulton line. Their first boat, the *Hope*, Captain Bunker, was launched March 19, 1811, and their second, the *Perseverance*, Captain Sherman, somewhat later. Soon after they were placed on the station. The rivalry between them and the Fulton line culminated in a steamboat race—the first in history and the forerunner of a kind of sport much indulged in subsequently. Both boats left Albany at 9 o'clock on the morning of July 27, the *Hope* leading. This position was maintained until the boats were within two miles of Hudson, when the *Clermont* by reason of her lighter draught took advantage of the shallows and tried to pass the *Hope*, which perforce kept to the channel. A collision resulted which, while not injuring either boat, put a stop to the race. Captain Bartholomew of the *Clermont* at once challenged the doughty Bunker to compete for a stake of 2000 dollars aside over any distance, but the latter declined.[1]

In order to counteract the designs of the opposition steamboat company Fulton and Livingston sought the advice of Thomas Addis Emmet, brother of Robert Emmet the Irish patriot and a famous advocate, who gave a long opinion,[2] dated January 19, 1811, in which he first recites the essential substance of the grants and the acts upon which their monopoly was based, substantially as has been given already. He then sets out the questions to be answered as being:

"1st. What is the effect and validity of the State Laws

[1] *Jour. Amer. Hist.*, 1907, p. 422.

[2] *New York Public Library Bulletin*, vol. xiii. p. 573.

in conferring any and what exclusive right on Messrs. Livingston and Fulton.

2nd. By what process can they carry into effect their right under the State Laws to the boat and to the Penalty."

After discussing the powers that the several States delegated to the Federal Constitution when the latter was formed, particularly with reference to useful inventions, he gives it as his opinion that:

"after the adoption of the Federal Constitution no State Legislature had any authority to grant an exclusive right of making, constructing, or employing any machine or invention."

This opinion of course covered both questions, but assuming the State law to be valid, he gives it as his further opinion that the forfeiture of the boat, &c., could be enforced, and also that Livingston and Fulton might:

"take and hold possession of the forfeited property without any preceding process of law, if they can accomplish that object without a breach of the Peace."

There are marginal notes on the document signifying disagreement with the opinion expressed which cannot have been otherwise than unpalatable. There was, however, no need to let the opinion be known, and Fulton and Livingston evidently decided to rely still on their original Act of Legislature. That Emmet's opinion was a true one the decisions of the courts subsequently showed.

The danger that threatened them only deepened when on January 25, 1811, the Legislature of New Jersey passed an Act[1] declaring that:

"the citizens of New Jersey have a full and equal right to navigate and have and use vessels and boats upon all

[1] For a number of facts relating to this case, the writer is indebted to a *Souvenir of the Hudson-Fulton Celebration*, prepared and published by the Free Library of Jersey City.

the waters lying between the States of New Jersey and New York, in all cases whatever not prohibited by the constitution, or any law of the United States."

The Act further provided that any person whose boat might be seized under the law of New York should have a right to retaliate upon any steamboat belonging to citizens of that State which might come into New Jersey waters. The provisions of this Act were much less defensible than were the claims of New York. It carried matters from bad to worse, and was in fact a direct encouragement to piracy.

The New York Legislature quickly responded in April 1811 by a law authorising Livingston and his associates to seize any steamboat infringing their monopoly, but providing that such steamboat should be held till the settlement of the case.

The only course now open was to attack the opposition steamboat company in the law courts. Fulton must have felt shaky about the validity of Livingston's original Act if submitted to searching attack in the courts, and he seems to have thought it best to prepare evidence by affidavit or deposition as to his actual priority in successful steam navigation. For this purpose he wrote to all his friends to secure their interest. One letter[1] to Earl Stanhope is so interesting that we give it in full:

"NEW YORK, *April* 10, 1811.

"MY LORD,—In my former letters I gave you an account of the success of my steam boats, which has been so great that, like every other useful and profitable invention, attempts are now making to evade my patent rights, and deprive me of my mental property. I am therefore under the necessity of collecting all possible evidence of the orginality and priority of my invention, *In which water wheels of right proportions and Velocities are of the first im-*

[1] Stanhope MSS.

portance. Your Lordship will recollect that, while was in Devonshire in 1793, I wrote you a letter on Using perpendicular oars or wheels to propell steam Vessels, of which the inclosed is an exact Copy; it was accompanied with other mechanical speculation which you may yet find among your papers; if so or your Lordship can distinctly recollect it, it will be of infinate service to me, and my cause, and I shall esteem it a particular favour if you will certify on the inclosed letter and drawing before the American consul or a notary public that the inclosed is a true copy of a letter written to you by me on steamships in 1793: such testimony will be important on the tryal which will commence in September next, in this City, and on which I have at least 7000£ sterling a year at stake. No one feels more sensibly than your Lordship the sacred right of mental property, no one knows better the difficulties which interposed to rendering steam Boats useful, and my clear right to my specific combinations; which have rendered them useful, *In which the wheel in my opinion is indispensible.* Your Lordship will therefore in so important a suit not hesitate to give evidence for an old friend and have the goodness to certify on the inclosed letter the time you received the original from me, after which certificate have the goodness to deliver it to the American Consul general in London, who will forward it to me. I will also thank your Lordship to let me know if there be any steam boat In operation In England or Ireland, if so, when built, by whom and how is she constructed; this information will be esteemed a favour in a private letter. I have seen the specification of your Lordship's Stanhope Weatherers with a plan for defending them against torpedoes, the ship is Very ingeneous, but the Torpedoes are now so far improved that any plan I have yet seen cannot defend a ship against a Vigorous attack with them. Our friend Barlow is going Ambassador to St. Cloud at which place I hope his talents will be of use to our country, which is rapidly improving and every day gaining strength although our exterior commerce is much embarrassed. The Edict of Nantz gave manufactures to England which she never lost but improved and multiplied to the sapping of the resources of France, the British orders in Council, the Berlin decrees, the war in Spain and Portugal, which has sent 8000 Mireno Sheep to this country in which they thrive and Improve, has given to us manufacture in Cotton, in Wood and Iron for which we now have the raw material in abundance, which manufactures we shall never loose but improve and multiply and which must tend to diminish or at least to produce the effect of not increasing in so rapid a degree the resources of England and France.

Have the goodness to remember me kindly to Mrs. Falkner; may success attend your Lordship's useful pursuits and happiness be your companion, is the sincere wish of

Your most obedient

ROBT. FULTON.

THE RIGHT HONBLE.
THE EARL OF STANHOPE.

P.S.—When I left London in 1806 there was no such thing as a steam boat anywhere in use in Europe; if any thing of the kind has since been established in England or Ireland, I will thank your Lordship for the particulars of her size and Velocity, to what purposes applied; by whom made and at what time and how propelled?

In a letter to Barlow, dated June 28, 1811, he gives further details with reference to this opposition steamboat company:

"My time is now occupied in building North River and Steam ferry boats, and in an interesting lawsuit to crush 22 Pirates who have clubbed their purses and copied my boats and have actually started my own Inventions in opposition to me by running one trip to Albany: her machinery however gave way in the first voyage and she is now repairing, which will detain her I presume until we obtain an Injunction to stop her. A more infamous and outrageous attack upon mental property has not disgraced America. Thornton has been one of the great causes of it. In this interesting suit which places a great fortune at stake I want you to go or send Lee to Thornton's office and demand a certified copy of my transfer of one half of my United States patents to Robert R. Livingston and let the certificate state that such transfer is legally registered in the patent office."

The transfer of one half of Fulton's interest in his patents to Livingston was in accordance with their original agreement.

Fulton also sends with the letter a deposition as to what his achievements in steam navigation had been; this he asks Barlow to persuade Thornton to sign, as if it were his own production. Thornton did not do so, by the way, but the deposition, giving as it does Fulton's side of the case, may be taken as correct where it gives credit to another than himself, as he does in one sentence:

"John Stevens Esq. of Broadway, in the City of New York, is the first . . . who has communicated the power from the piston rod to the water wheels by means of crank wheels and shackle bars which work on each side of the Cylender."

This was the return connecting-rod or steeple engine.

The lawsuit dragged on wearily, as only lawsuits can; and Fulton, evidently thinking he must get further evidence, wrote to Boulton, Watt & Co., asking for an affidavit from the great James Watt himself. As Watt had retired from business twelve years before, it is unlikely that he would want to be worried with such a matter; the firm may have sent a reply; if so, we have no record of it.

Fulton's letter is as follows:

New York, *January 4th*, 1812

Messrs Boulton & Watt

Gentlemen,—In consequence of the non-intercourse and the impossibility of getting the original to this country at present I have delayed for a long time to answer your letter, But you will please to finish the engine in the usual way with perpendicular Valves, as the wheels must have the power of turning Backwards and forwards and I will remit you the remainder of the Cost. In a conversation with Mr. Watt Senior in Paris I think in 1803 or 2 I believe he gave it to me as his opinion that it was impracticable to make a useful steamboat or Vessel, I have however succeeded to make a Vessel[1] 176 feet long 23 feet beam drawing 2 feet 6 inches of Water run 6 miles an hour in Still water, which Useful invention like your useful steam engine is already copied without my consent and my patent right Violated I am involved in a very expensive and important lawsuit, the Enemy cannot deny that they have copied, But they hope to succeed in proving that I am not the Inventor, for which purpose all abortive projects to navigate boats or Vessels by steam wheels [that] have been made within the last 30 years will be collected, in evidence against me, some of which however bear the least resemblance to the combinations or principles of my boats: But as such high authority as Mr. Watt would be of great importance to me on the tryal, I should esteem it as a great favour if he would State whether there was to the best of his knowledge a steam boat of any kind or what kind anywhere in permanent and efficient operation anywhere in the three kingdoms in 1803 or to the best of his knowledge anywhere in Europe. And what was his opinion and appeared to him to be the prevaily (*sic*) opinion of the practicability of making good steam boats, such for example as should run 5 miles an hour in still water and carry 100

[1] This was almost certainly the *Car of Neptune*. See Appendix G, p. 326.

tons; was it his opinion in 93 that such a project was practicable or was the mode of effecting it know[n] to him at that time or, to the best of his knowledge known to any other person, A Certificate of these facts as they appeared to him in 93 And affirmed to before the mayor of Birmingham And In presence of any American who may be at Birmingham and witnessed by by (*sic*) him, and particularly if he should be a person resident in New York, Boston or Phil^a. would be exceedingly useful to me. Or should any respectable gentleman of Birmingham see Mr. Watt affirm to the certificate and such person be going to London could swear before Mr. *Jonathan Russel American Charge des affairs that he knew it to be Mr. Watts handwriting* It would render the evidence on the science of steam boats in 93 Legal in our courts—and Mr. Russel would transmit the certificate sealed with his official seal to me; Gentlemen, you have known so much of the unblushing piracy of your own Inventions and the importance of evidance to defend such rights, That I shall hope for this most repectable and friendly evidence on the opinion and state of the science of steamboats in 93 which is the year I built my first boat, on the Seine near Paris and established all the powers proportions and velocities of parts which have given complete success to all the boats since built on these principles.

hoping for an answer to this letter as soon as possible believe me gentlemen with the greatest esteem and respect your most

obedient ROBT. FULTON.

The conversation that he mentions as having had with Watt in Paris in 1802 or 1803 cannot have taken place, as Watt was not there in those years. Besides, from the tone of Watt's reference to Fulton in a letter to a third party about this time, it would appear that they had never met.

The case was tried at Trenton, N.J. Fulton's party

was represented by their friend Thomas A. Emmet; lawyers of equal eminence being on the other side. Great stress was laid on the letter [1] written from Torquay to Lord Stanhope in 1793, and capital was made out of the fact that the letter put in by Fulton was a recent copy of it. No one seems to have thought of Fulton's book on Canals, where this correspondence is referred to; that would surely have substantiated his statement.

In the end, an injunction against the opposition steamboat company was obtained, and their boats, of which two had been built, were confiscated and destroyed.

Hardly had this case been disposed of than opposition arose in another quarter. It appears that Colonel Aaron Ogden,[2] an eminent citizen of New Jersey, in conjunction with Daniel Dod,[3] a well-known engine-builder, had constructed a steamboat called the *Sea Horse*, with which they intended to establish a ferry service between Elizabethtown, N.J., and New York. The engine of this vessel, by the way, was the first of the walking-beam type, which afterwards became so common, and Dod is usually credited with its introduction.

Finding that the Fulton monopoly prevented him carrying out his plan, Colonel Ogden petitioned the New York Legislature to rescind the monopoly. The resolution, to effect this, was lost by one vote only.

However, Colonel Ogden, who had been chosen by the Legislature of New Jersey on 29th October 1812 to succeed

[1] See p. 24.

[2] Aaron Ogden (b. 1756; d. 1839) took an active part in the War of Independence under Lafayette, and attained to the rank of Quartermaster-General. After the war he took up law, and practised with success. In 1801 he was made a U.S. senator, and held office for two years. In 1806 he was a commissioner in the Boundary Dispute between New York and New Jersey. Trustee of Princeton University from 1803–12, and from 1817 till his death; LL.D. in 1816.

[3] Daniel Dod (b. 1788; d. 1823) devoted himself to steam-engine construction, then in its infancy, with great success. Engined the *Savannah*, the first vessel to cross the Atlantic by the aid of steam. Killed in a boiler explosion.

Joseph Bloomfield, as Governor, managed to get a law passed by that body on November 3, 1813, granting to himself and Dod the exclusive right to run steamboats on the waters of New Jersey. The Livingston party were at once up in arms, and appealed to the next Legislature in 1814, to repeal the Act. Again the Livingston party were represented by Thomas A. Emmet; while the other party had two equally famous lawyers. The result was that the New Jersey grant was repealed on February 4, 1815.

Unfortunately, while this struggle was going on, Chancellor Livingston had died at Clermont, on February 26, 1813, at the age of sixty-seven; and just in the hour of victory Fulton contracted the chill which cut short his career.

We must, however, briefly pursue the vicissitudes of the steamboat monopoly. The matter was settled for a time by Colonel Ogden buying from the executors of Livingston and of Fulton the exclusive right to run ferry-boats for ten years on the route between Elizabethtown and New York.

He did not enjoy the privilege long before another storm began to gather on the horizon. Thomas Gibbons, a wealthy Southerner, who passed the summers at Elizabethtown, saw the desirability of running steamboats, and started an opposition line with the *Bellona* and the *Stoudinger*. By a strange vicissitude of fortune, it was the turn of Colonel Ogden, who had been the bitterest opponent of the steamboat monopoly, now to defend it against Gibbons. The latter was a lawyer and a man of means; as neither party would give way, the suit dragged on till it reached the U.S. Supreme Court, which in 1821 dismissed Gibbons's case on technical grounds. Beaten, but not crushed, he instituted a fresh trial. He engaged as his counsel Daniel Webster, the famous jurist, who argued that the monopoly infringed the prerogative of the Federal Government to regulate commerce, and that therefore it was unconstitutional. The result of it was that in March 1825 the United States Court of Errors, sitting at Albany, decided by a majority of 22 to 9 that no State could grant a monopoly of navigation. The Senate Chamber and gallery were crowded with people anxious to hear the decision of the Court on this momentous case. Thus ended a most oppressive monopoly, at the cost of ruining one at least of the parties.

The Boundary dispute, however, still flourished, and it is interesting to note the sequel. In 1829, at the instance of the State of New Jersey, the Supreme Court appointed a Commission, with representatives drawn from both States, to settle the question. They arrived at an agreement whereby New York so far abandoned their previous claims as to fix as the boundary the middle of the Hudson River, of New York Bay, and of the waters between Staten Island and New Jersey, subject to certain claims of jurisdiction over the Bay and the Hudson south of Spuyten Duyvel Creek. This agreement was ratified by both States in 1834.

As the meaning of the term "middle" was not clearly defined, it was not long before renewed controversy arose. This was brought to an acute stage when about 1870 the Central Railroad reclaimed land from the Hudson at Communipaw, by filling in. Under their agreement of 1834, New York State claimed jurisdiction over the reclaimed land. The case was taken to the New York Court of Appeal, who decided that the jurisdiction given to New York under that agreement was only for sanitary and police purposes. Finally, in 1888, Commissioners from the two States exactly located the boundary-line in the middle of the channel of the river and bay. Thus was settled a controversy which had lasted for over a hundred years.

We must now cast our minds back a little way to the year 1810, which may perhaps be said to have been the heyday of Fulton's mental and commercial activities; for besides the large number of steamboats[1] built or projected for various parts of the Union, Fulton meditated nothing less than the introduction of steam navigation throughout

[1] See Appendix G, p. 326.

the civilised world, so great was his belief in its commercial future.

To this end he enlisted in his interest, for exploiting English territory, the services of Mr. J. C. Dyer, a man already favourably known as an inventor. Many years later, after he had settled down to end his days in this country, he, when an octogenarian, told the story of his voyages on the *Clermont*, and his connection with this enterprise:[1]

"I undertook, in 1811, the task of inducing some of the leading engineers and capitalists of London to engage in the construction of steamboats, on Fulton's plan, to run on the Thames and other waters in this country. I had obtained from Mr. Fulton (through a mutual friend) a full description, and the drawings of his inventions and discoveries relating to steam navigation with the result of his labours in America. But I found it impossible to convince any of them that steamboats could be made to run with safety and profit in the English waters. . . ."

". . . Many of my personal friends urged me strongly not to waste my time and money on so hopeless a task as that of introducing steam navigation into England. Even the great and scientific engineer, John Rennie (father of the present eminent Sir John Rennie), urged me, with parental kindness, to drop all thoughts of bringing these boats into use—and this after having Fulton's plans before him, and fully admitting their success in America."

In the spring of 1814, Mr. Peter Ewart expressed to Dyer the opinion that "it did not appear likely that they (*i.e.* steamboats) could ever come into general use in the waters of England," and this in spite of the fact that he knew of Bell's success on the Clyde in 1812.

Dyer goes on to say:

"In that year (*i.e.* 1814) I lent Mr. Ewart Fulton's specifications and drawings, which were sent by him to Boulton and Watt, and returned to me about six months after. I

[1] *Mem. Lit. and Phil. Soc.*, Manchester, third Series, 1865, vol. ii. p. 292.

have reason to believe that that eminent house was led thereby to make further and more exact inquiries concerning the progress of steam navigation in America; for they, as well as several other engineers, commenced building steamboats in 1815 and 1816."

Even Bell's success with his vessel the *Comet*, the centenary of which has just been celebrated, must be attributed in some measure to Fulton. Bell's account of their intercourse is given in a letter [1] he wrote in 1824.

"He came at different times to this country, and stopped with me for some time. He published, soon afterwards, a Treatise on Canal Declining Railways. I have this Book at hand, but you may obtain it by applying to Mr. Taylor, bookseller, London, price 21*s*. Mr. Fulton published this work in England in 1804, and on his way to France called on me; and also when he returned. He was employed by the American Government to come to England, to take drawings of our cotton and other machinery, which quickened his desires after all the engineering branches; these he took up very quickly. He was also a good painter, and excelled in miniature likenesses. When I wrote to the American Government on the great importance of steam navigation they appointed Mr. Fulton to correspond with me. . . ."

Although, from what has gone before, we know that this is a garbled account, yet it is just what one might expect from a comparatively uneducated man like Bell. We shall not be far wrong in gathering from it that he and Fulton first met in 1804, because that date is corroborated by another account given by Bell in 1816. If so, it must have been at the time that Fulton went to see Symington's *Charlotte Dundas*. [2]

It was a letter of Fulton's, written after he had achieved success with the *Clermont*, that stirred up Bell. He says:

"This letter led me to think of the absurdity of writing

[1] Morris, *Life of Henry Bell*, 1844, p. 74.
[2] See p. 179.

my opinion to other countries and not putting it in practice in my own country; and from these considerations I was roused to set on foot a steamboat for which I made a number of different models before I was satisfied."

The story of the difficulties and trials that beset his path is a long one; suffice it to say that five years, almost to a day, elapsed before he succeeded, although on a much smaller scale, in repeating Fulton's achievement.

James Watt, junior, in 1816, engined an experimental boat, and tried her across the German Ocean and up the Rhine. Thereafter his firm engaged very extensively in the marine engine business.

It was not very many years later—to be exact, in 1819—that Mr. Rennie had quite changed his mind, and he constantly thereafter urged upon the Admiralty the value of steam-tugs in towing men-of-war. Thus were the tables completely turned.

It will not be difficult for the engineering reader—with the aid of the drawings attached to Fulton's patents—to trace the evolution of the side-lever engine from his first engine of 1804; and we can, therefore, with every confidence, attribute the germ of this design to him, and thus give the credit where it is deserved.

After England, Russia appears to have had an attraction for Fulton as a field for enterprise. He wrote, in November 1811, to John Quincy Adams, then American Ambassador in Russia, to ask him to obtain an exclusive right for twenty years for a steamboat-service between St. Petersburg and Cronstadt, to be established in three years after obtaining the grant.

A Russian gentleman, Chevalier Swinine, wrote to Fulton a very significant letter, offering his services. How he had got wind of the affair does not appear, but an extract from his letter[1] will be of interest:

"Doubtless, Sir, it is known to you that for several months past I have been taken up with your admirable

[1] Sutcliffe, *Robert Fulton and the "Clermont,"* p. 296.

invention of the *steam boat*, dedicating all my knowledge for its introduction in Russia. As you have received the Imperial permission for this introduction, I offer you, Sir, my services which I flatter myself may be of great utility. Certainly it will be necessary for you to have the plan of the River Neva and of the channel from St. Petersbourg to Cronstadt to have the clearest information of the value of materials necessary for the construction of the steamboat, the description of other communications by water in Russia."

His conditions were that he should have the title "Superintendent of the Steamboats of Russia"; and, of course, that he should have an annual salary.

The principal point to observe is that Fulton had received the Imperial permission to introduce steamboats. Naturally he wanted a good deal more than this, and on April 12, 1812, he wrote[1] to the Chevalier, saying, that he must wait for Mr. Adams's answer, for until then he could not decide what to do.

We know that a steamboat, the *Emperor of Russia*, was on the stocks at the time of Fulton's death, and it has been suggested that it was built for the service under consideration, but as there were no means of getting it to Russia, this could not have been the case; the name must have been given merely as a compliment, but it goes to show that there was something below the surface. As a matter of fact, the first experiments on the Neva were made in November 1815, by Charles Baird, Superintendent of the Mines, with a barge which had been rebuilt for the purpose, and fitted with an engine of the side-lever type and an externally fired boiler having a brick chimney. These experiments were successful, and in 1817 Baird built a vessel 60 feet long especially for steam propulsion and with her established a passenger service between St. Petersburg and Cronstadt. This engine was almost identical with that shown on Sheet 2 of Fulton's second specification[2] and if the design was not obtained from him

[1] *Loc. cit.*, p. 295.

[2] See p. 318.

then all that can be said is that the coincidence is very remarkable. The boiler, too, was just the kind that Fulton was in the habit of fitting. Some day the true relation to one another of these significant facts will be made plain. We *do* know that Baird had a monopoly of steam navigation on the Neva for twenty years and thereout drew no small return.

Then again India seems to have had a fascination for Fulton, attracted no doubt by the size of her rivers and the teeming population on their banks.

He entered into an agreement with a certain Thomas Law[1] to introduce steamboats on the Ganges. In a letter[2] to him dated April 16, 1812, Fulton says:

"I agree to make the Ganges enterprise a joint concern. You will please to send me a plan how you mean to proceed to secure a grant for 20 years and find funds to establish the first boat. This work is so honorable and important. It is so grand an Idea that Americans should establish steam vessels to work in India—that it requires vigor, activity, exertion, industry, attention, and that no time should be lost. My *Paragon* beats everything on the globe for made as you and I are, we cannot tell what is in the moon; this Day she came in from Albany 160 miles in 26 hours, wind ahead."

The letter finished with the words

"Keep the Ganges Secret."

Here again, sad to relate, some hitch occurred, whether due to Fulton's death or not we do not know, and no steamboat was seen in India till eight years later when it was introduced from England.

[1] Thomas Law (*b.* 1759, *d.* 1834), son of Edmund Law, Bishop of Carlisle, and brother of Edward Law, first Baron Ellenborough, was an official of the Honourable East India Company in Bengal, 1773–91, when he resigned owing to ill health. In 1793, imbued with admiration for President Washington and for American institutions he went to the United States where he laboured to establish a national currency.

[2] Thomas A. Emmet Colln. Lenox Library, N.Y.

CHAPTER XI

CONSTRUCTION OF FIRST STEAM MAN-OF-WAR—ILLNESS AND DEATH—CHARACTER—HUDSON-FULTON CELEBRATION

WE now come to Fulton's final achievement, that of the construction of the world's first steam-propelled war-vessel, anticipating by more than thirty years the adoption of steam, even as an auxiliary to sails, for the propulsion of such vessels in the navies of Europe. He had been led by his torpedo experiments to try the effect of discharging cannon under water at different depths and had met with some slight success when not more than a few feet away from a target. It was for this that in 1813 Fulton took out his last United States patent.[1]

These submarine guns were named by Fulton in compliment to Barlow "Columbiads," and in pursuing the subject Fulton was led at the latter end of 1813 to design for them a special vessel which was to be propelled by steam. In November Fulton exhibited his plan to the President of the United States.

Since the outbreak of the war with England, the citizens of New York had been aroused to a realisation of the exposed position of their harbour and of its unprotected state. A meeting was held in the beginning of 1814 to concert methods of defence, and a Coast and Harbour Defence Association was formed. Fulton sub-

[1] Entitled: "for several improvements in the art of maritime warfare and means of injuring and destroying ships and vessels of war by igniting gunpowder under water or by igniting gunpowder below a line horizontal to the surface of the water, or so igniting gunpowder that the explosion which causes injury to the vessel attacked shall be under water."

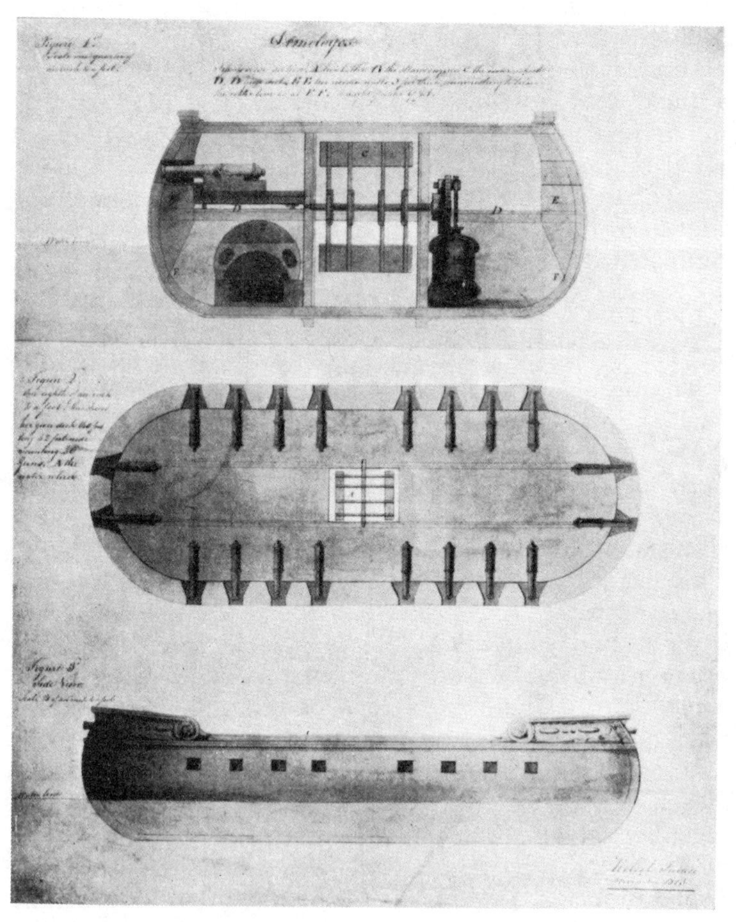

FULTON'S STEAM WAR SHIP "DEMOLOGOS," 1813

mitted to them a model, plans, and estimates of his proposed coast defence ship or floating battery. Favourable opinions were obtained from naval officers, and the committee memorialised Congress on the subject, offering to build the vessel at the estimated cost ($320,000) if after it was built and proved successful the Government would reimburse that sum to them. In March 1814 the National Legislature authorised one or more floating batteries to be built, equipped, and operated. The Association nominated a committee of five, who were recognised by the Government as their agents. Fulton, who entered body and soul into the enterprise, was appointed engineer.

The design of the vessel[1] was a total departure from previous practice in warship construction. Fulton's idea was to make his vessel invulnerable and so obtain the equivalent of a fleet at no greater cost than that of a frigate. The first necessity was to protect the propelling arrangements. This he did by having twin hulls as in his ferry-boats with the paddle-wheel in the space between the hulls and protected by an upper deck with bulwarks and stanchions. This deck also sheltered the engine, which was in one hull, and the boiler, which was in the other. These hulls had flat bottoms, bluff ends, and long parallel middle bodies, and were double ended so as to obviate the necessity for putting about. A rudder at each end or four in all were, of course, required. To make her invulnerable to the attack of any gun then known her main or gun deck was protected by a belt of solid timber 4′ 10″ thick. Incidentally the double hulls gave a steady gun platform for her armament which was to consist of thirty 32-pounders to fire red-hot shot. In addition to these she was to have hung over her bows

[1] Our account of this vessel and of the circumstances connected with its building is condensed from the "Report of H. Rutgers, S. L. Mitchel, and T. Morris, Commissioners superintending the construction of a steam vessel to Secretary of the Navy," dated New York, December 28, 1815.

two columbiads each capable of firing a 100 lb. projectile below the water line.

The keels were laid in the shipyard of Adam and Noah Browne on the East River, June 29, 1814. In spite of great hindrances due to the shortage of materials owing to the British blockade, to a scarcity of skilled labour, and to depreciation in the paper currency, little more than four months were occupied in building the vessel. On 29th October the *Demologos*—for so she was christened—was launched amid scenes of great popular enthusiasm.

An interesting description of the vessel from Fulton's own pen has been preserved in a letter[1] written to General Jonathan Williams of Philadelphia, the gentlemen of which city, emulating those of New York, were desirous of having a duplicate of the *Demologos* for the protection of the estuary of the Delaware.

NEW YORK,
November 23, 1814.

DEAR SIR,—Much occupied on monday (*i.e.* the 21st) in moving the steam vessel from the East into the north River, I did not receive your communication of 19 till yesterday *Tues*day.

Her length is on deck	167 feet
Breadth of beam	56 "
depth of hold	12 "
height of gun deck	8 "
Thickness of sides	5 "
power	120 horses

Commenced June 1st will be finished about 1 Janry.

Estimate for

Engine and hull about 150(000) $.

It will I believe cost Something more. Her Boilers of copper—which alone will do for salt water weigh

[1] In the New York Public Library, printed in *Bulletin*, vol. xiii. p. 580 and reproduced by their permission.

24 tons. All her valves and communications with salt water is Brass. She is pierced for 30 guns Long 32-pounders. She has 21 on Board with near 60 tons of material and now draws 9 feet 2 Inches of water with this weight. My two Steam boats the *Car of Neptune* and *Fulton* towed her through the water at the rate of 3½ miles an hour. There is now no room to doubt that when finished she will run from 4½ to 5 miles an hour in still water. The $150,000 estimate presented to the secretary of the navy was Independent of guns, coppering, *Sails, Anchors, cordage, Joiner's* work and Armament in general. All complete she may be estimated at 235 or 240,000 dollars.

How to construct one from under my eye and elsewhere than in this city I do not know. Here I have erected work shops, tools and machinery Suited to the construction of large engines and heavy works also, all the models of her castings and fixings, *which* alone is *a work* of some months, and has cost from 3 to 4000$. But the hull might be built at Phila.—and the principal part of the machinery be made here in the transport of which there will *only* be land carriage from Brunswick to Trenton which will cost less than to make the models. I must also remark that as this is a new Invention which *requires all my care* to render it as *complete and* useful as can reasonably be expected from my present experience, I *cannot trust the construction of the machinery or the fitting out of the* vessel to be directed by *anyone but myself* in which I will give every facility in my power to the Gentlemen of Phila.——

I am Sir Very respectfully
your most obedient,
ROBT. FULTON.

General JONATHAN WILLIAMS,
Phila.

It is pretty certain that the construction of this coast-defence ship for Philadelphia fell through rather because of the cessation of hostilities with Great Britain than on account of the death of Fulton. This sad event caused no serious delay in the construction of the New York vessel and the plans which he had matured so carefully were carried out without any serious hitch.

Further details of the *Demologos* are given in an Appendix,[1] and it is only necessary to note further that she was rigged with two masts having lateen yards and two bowsprits each spreading a jib.

By May 1815 her engines were on board and the machinery in such a forward state that it was possible to have a trial of her. On June 1, at 10 A.M., she left the wharf at the Brooklyn Ferry and proceeded under her own steam—no use being made of her sails—into the river with a stiff breeze ahead and against an ebb-tide. After four hours' trial she returned to Paulus Hook, some slight alterations dictated by experience were made, and she celebrated the Fourth of July by making a passage to the eastward of Sandy Hook and back, a total of 53 miles in $8\frac{1}{3}$ hours, *i.e.* at the rate of 6.4 miles per hour.

On September 11, with twenty-six of her guns, ammunition, and stores on board and drawing in consequence about 11 feet of water, she made another trip, realising on the average a speed of 5.5 miles per hour—*i.e.* much in excess of Fulton's guarantee. She put about by the double helm, reversed her course by the paddle-wheel alone, and manœuvred easily.

Owing to the termination of the war between Great Britain and the United States by the treaty of Ghent (December 24, 1814) the *Fulton*—for so she had been renamed in memory of her constructor—was never finally completed for service. She was laid up in the Navy Yard at Brooklyn, where she was used as a depot or receiving ship till June 4, 1829, when an explosion occurred accidentally, resulting in her complete destruction and the loss of twenty-five killed and nineteen wounded.

[1] P. 326.

She laid the foundation of the American Steam Navy, but was not followed by other vessels till after the lapse of many years.

That the *Demologos* or *Fulton* lost none of her terrors by rumour is apparent from a contemporary account of her published in Scotland.[1] The writer, after stating that he had been at much pains to procure full and accurate information about the "steam frigate" which "has been launched at New York," proceeds to give the following startling particulars:

"Length on deck 300 feet; breadth 200 feet; thickness of her sides 13 feet of alternative oak plank and cork wood; carries 44 guns, four of which are 100 pounders quarter deck and forecastle guns 42 pounders; and farther, to annoy an enemy attempting to board, can discharge 100 gallons of boiling water in a minute and, by mechanism, brandishes three hundred cutlasses with the utmost regularity over her gunwales, works also an equal number of heavy iron pikes of great length, darting them from her sides with prodigious force and withdrawing the same every quarter of a minute."

We can only echo the words of Dominie Sampson—"Pro-di-gi-ous."

It would be extremely interesting to know how the *Demologos* would have fared in action. That she would have precipitated the fundamental changes in the science of naval warfare which have been realised in our time is fairly certain. Indeed to show that the first steps in this direction were being taken we may mention the little known fact that the building of a steam sloop (H.M.S. *Congo*) was actually commenced in 1815 at Chatham, by the watchful British Admiralty. But the war with the United States was over, and she was altered before completion into a sailing-vessel, while her engines found a humble fate as a pump in Plymouth Dock, now Devonport Dockyard.

Fulton had also commenced before his death the con-

[1] *Edinburgh Evening Courant*, 31st August 1815.

struction of the submarine *Mute*, but she was never completed, and no particulars are available.

The calamity of Fulton's death, which deprived the United States of one of her most useful citizens, arose out of a cold which he had contracted about a fortnight before at Trenton, N.J., where he had appeared as a witness in the New Jersey ferry-boat case to which we have already alluded. In returning he and two friends were detained at Paulus Hook waiting for a boat because the Hudson was partly closed with ice. He occupied the time in visiting his works to examine the *Demologos* and the boats repairing for the ensuing season. In walking across the ice he got wet through and as a consequence was confined to his room for two or three days. Then, most imprudently, he ventured across to New Jersey to see the progress of the boats. This brought on inflammation of the lungs and other complications, to which he eventually succumbed early in the morning of February 23, 1815, in the fiftieth year of his age.

His death in the plenitude of his powers, while serving his country, was the occasion of mourning such as was customary only in the case of the greatest public men. The Legislature which was then in session passed a resolution that members of both houses should wear mourning for him. Resolutions expressing estimation of his worth and regret at his loss were passed by the Corporation of New York and the various learned societies of which he was a member. The funeral, which took place on the day following his death, was attended from his residence, No. 1 State Street, by officers of the National and State Governments, by the magistracy, the common council, members of learned societies, and a great concourse of citizens. Shops and business hours in New York were closed as a sign of respect. Minute guns were fired from the *Demologos* and the West Battery from the time the procession started till it reached Trinity Church in the heart of the city. The body, in a leaden coffin enclosed in mahogany with a plate engraved with his name and age, was deposited in the family vault of the Livingstons.

It seems to us that Robert Fulton ought to take a higher place than he has hitherto done in the roll of honour of the Anglo-Saxon race. As a thinker he saw clearly that free trade intercourse between nations, universal disarmament, the spread of education and of political liberty among all people, were necessary to the progress of the human race. But he saw more than this, for having imagination and a wide outlook he realised the needs of advancing civilisation and set himself with pluck and perseverance to supply them. As a worker he opened out new fields for human activity. He was a born engineer of the same type as James Watt and Thomas Telford, who had no greater amount than he of early training in the direction of their future careers. To mention as the offspring of Fulton's genius only the first workable submarine torpedo boat, the first commercially practicable steam vessel, and the first steam-propelled warship, is to entitle him to a place among the giants of the engineering profession. His early death and the fact that others entered into and benefited by his labours have tended to obscure the greatness of his achievements.

It cannot be denied that he ever neglected an opportunity of profiting pecuniarily by his inventions, but that can hardly be urged against him with society constituted as it was and is at present. He did not make any friends in England over his torpedo transaction with the Admiralty, as it was considered that he had been paid far more generously than he deserved. He had enemies too in America, for there is always prejudice against the owner of a monopoly, and the steamboat monopoly was felt to be an onerous one. It was, however, the money from the torpedo transaction and this monopoly that made the early development of the steamboat so rapid. Had it been left to Colonel Stevens it must have taken many years longer.

It is always interesting to have criticism of a man from a contemporary source and from a hostile quarter, so that we cannot refrain from quoting that of John Rennie, who, writing in 1817 to Sir John Barrow, Secretary to the Admiralty, says:[1]

"I send you Mr. Fulton's book on Canals, published in 1796 when he was in England and previous to his application of the steam engine to the working of wheels in boats. On the designs (*i.e.* as to bridges, &c.) contained in that book, his fame I believe principally rests, although he acknowledges that Earl Stanhope had previously proposed similar plans and that Mr. Reynolds of Coalbrookdale in Shropshire had actually carried them into execution; so that all the merit he has—if merit it can be called—is a proposal for extending the principle previously applied in this country. The first iron bridge was erected at Coalbrookdale in 1779 and between that and the publication of Fulton's book in 1796, many others were erected; so that in this department he has little to boast of. I consider Fulton, with whom I was personally acquainted, a man of very slender abilities though possessing much self confidence and consummate impudence."

This is quoted to show how completely a great man, even when in possession of the true facts, may misvalue the achievements of another. One is disinclined therefore to place any confidence in the value of his estimate as to any part whatever of Fulton's career.

Of Fulton's physical appearance, social gifts, and opinions we cannot do better than quote the description[2] given by his friend and biographer, Colden.

"Mr. Fulton was about six feet high. His person was slender, but well proportioned and well formed—Nature had made him a gentleman and bestowed upon him ease and gracefulness. He had too much good sense for the least affectation; and a modest confidence in his own worth

[1] Smiles, *Lives of the Engineers*, vol. ii., Smeaton and Rennie, p. 231.
[2] C. D. Colden, *Life of Robert Fulton*, pp. 257–8.

and talents gave him an unembarrassed deportment in all companies. His features were strong and of a manly beauty: he had large dark eyes, and a projecting brow, expressive of intelligence and thought: his temper was mild, and his disposition lively; he was fond of society which he always enlivened by cheerful, cordial manners and instructed or pleased by his sensible conversation. He expressed himself with energy, fluency, and correctness, and as he owed more to his own experience and reflections, than to books, his sentiments were often interesting from their originality.

In all his domestic and social relations he was zealous, kind, generous, liberal, and affectionate. He knew of no use for money but as it was subservient to charity, hospitality, and the sciences. But what was most conspicuous in his character was his calm constancy, his industry, and that indefatigable patience and perseverance which always enabled him to overcome difficulties.

He was decidedly a republican. The determination which he often avowed that he would never accept an office is an evidence of the disinterestedness of his politics; but his zeal for his opinions or party did not extinguish his kindness for the merits of his opponents."

A contemporary description[1] of Fulton's appearance and estimate of his character is:

"Among a thousand individuals you might readily point out Robert Fulton. He was conspicuous for his gentlemanly bearing and freedom from embarrassment, for his extreme activity, his height, somewhat over six feet —his slender yet energetic form and well accommodated dress, for his full and curly dark brown hair, carelessly scattered over his forehead and falling around his neck. His complexion was fair, his forehead high, his eyes dark and penetrating and revolving in a capacious orbit of cavernous depths; his brow was thick and evinced strength and determination; his nose was long and prominent, his

[1] *Robert Fulton and the "Clermont,"* p. 213.

mouth and lips were beautifully proportioned, giving the impress of eloquent utterance. Trifles were not calculated to impede him or damp his perseverance."

A good story is told of Fulton's quick mechanical intuition. A certain Redheffer announced that he had solved the problem of perpetual motion by a machine which he had invented and was exhibiting at a dollar a head in an isolated house in the suburbs of Philadelphia. Many were the ingenious theories brought forward to account for the phenomenon. Fulton so little believed in the discovery that he was with difficulty persuaded to visit the show. When he did so he noticed after a time, by the noise that the machine made, that the velocity varied during every revolution, leading him to suspect that it was driven by a crank. He roundly denounced the man as an impostor, and quickly showed that one of the innocent-looking wooden stays that supported the machine from the wall was in reality hollow, and accommodated a gut band. Following this clue, in a loft at the back of the house they found the motive power—a poor old wretch who while turning the handle with one hand was gnawing a crust with the other. The mob made short work of the machine, and Redheffer quickly made himself scarce.

Fulton had married on January 7, 1808, Harriet Livingston, a daughter of Walter Livingston of Tiviotdale and a second cousin of the Chancellor's—a union influenced without doubt by that fact. He had issue one son—named after his godfather—Robert Barlow Fulton (*b.* 1809, *d.* 1841 unmarried), and three daughters: Julia (*b.* 1810, *d.* 1848), married Charles Blight of Philadelphia, who had issue three children; Mary Livingston (*b.* 1811, *d.* 1860), married Robert Ludlow of Claverack, N.Y., who had issue one son; Cornelia Livingston (*b.* 1812, *d.* 1883), married Edward Charles Crary, who had issue five children and ten grandchildren.

By his will,[1] dated December 13, 1814, which is too long

[1] Given in full in Reigart's *Life of Fulton*, p. 206.

a document for insertion here, Fulton left out of the annual profits of the steamboats or from other property $9000 per annum and all his household effects to his wife during her lifetime, and $500 per annum for each of his children until they attained the age of twelve, and afterwards $1000 for each up to the age of twenty-one. He made bequests to his brother and sisters, relinquishing at the same time all sums of money that he had lent them at different times. The residue of his estate he left in trust for his children, each to receive his or her share with certain contingencies on attaining the age of twenty-one. In the case of the death of all his children before that of his wife, half of his estate was to go to the "promotion of an Academy of Fine Arts for historical and scientific paintings"; the other half was to be at his wife's absolute disposal. He further left to the widow of his friend Barlow all the copies of the latter's poem, the *Columbiad*, which had become Fulton's property. He further directed that the money owing to him from Barlow's estate was to be left to his widow's option as regards repayment during her lifetime. He appointed his wife and her brother-in-law, William Cutting, executors and trustees. The will was proved on February 27.

Fulton's widow, who had married meanwhile Charles Augustus Dale, came over to England in July 1817 and called on Boulton, Watt & Co. about the last engine ordered, which she seemed to think had not been delivered.

In 1825 Harriet Dale, James A. Hamilton, and others petitioned the New York Assembly[1] that they might be associated for banking purposes by an Act of Incorporation. Conditionally on their being granted this, they were willing to set aside the interest on the sum of $70,000 for the use and benefit of the heirs of Robert Fulton, who were stated to be "*utterly destitute of support*," no doubt owing to the action of the Court of Errors in the same year in declaring the monopoly invalid. This petition was de-

[1] *Journal of the Assembly*, 1825, pp. 440–2.

servedly unsuccessful. Philanthropy of this stamp is always to be viewed with suspicion.

Fulton's friends, however, were not at a loss and they petitioned the Senate and House of Representatives on behalf of his heirs claiming that he was in the service of the Government when he died and that certain sums of salary and out-of-pocket expenses were owing to his estate. On the 9th of April 1836 this petition was referred to the Secretary of the Navy to report thereon. After due examination on January 3, 1837, he found that $100,000 was due to the estate. A bill to grant this relief to Fulton's heirs did not, however, become law till July 1846, thirty-one years after his death, when the balance due to his estate was adjudged to be $76,300.

It can safely be said that till recently Fulton received scant honour even in his own country. As a consequence of his having been buried in the Livingston vault in Trinity Churchyard there was nothing to mark his resting-place even, and the spot was hardly known till in 1901 the American Society of Mechanical Engineers sought to atone for this neglect by the erection there of a column bearing on one side a bronze medallion portrait. Unfortunately, the portrait upon which the medallion is based, is to say the least of extremely doubtful attribution. On the occasion of the centenary of Fulton's successful introduction of steam navigation a number of gentlemen determined to erect in his honour a fitting monument in a prominent position on the shores of the Hudson overlooking the scene of his triumph. It was decided that the scheme should include a water-gate to New York City, with a landing basin, a building for the reception of distinguished visitors, and a maritime museum with Fulton's tomb as the central feature. A site 564 feet in length along Riverside Drive, on the west side of Manhattan Island, was chosen. After a limited competition among architects selected from a large number by preliminary open competition, the design of Mr. H. van Buren

ENGINES BEING TESTED

UNDER WAY.

P.S. "CLERMONT" AS REPRODUCED FOR THE HUDSON-FULTON CELEBRATION IN 1909

Magonigle was placed first. The design shows the water-gate flanked by colonnades on either side enclosing the basin, whence a flight of steps the full width of the basin leads up to an open peristyle. Fulton's tomb is to stand in the centre, with the museum building on the one hand and the reception building on the other. The peristyle is to be of white marble, while the rest of the buildings are to be of granite. It is somewhat mortifying to have to state that there is very little likelihood of the design being carried out, as all the money subscribed has been spent on the preliminary studies above mentioned and as public interest has waned.

A few words should perhaps be said about the Fulton centenary celebrations that were held to commemorate the beginnings of commercial steam navigation. These were delayed till 1909 so that they might be celebrated at the same time as the tercentenary of Henry Hudson's exploration of the river named after him. A full-size replica of the *Clermont* was built for the occasion by the Staten Island Shipbuilding Company, N.Y. The plans for this were drawn out by the well-known naval architects, Frank E. Kirby and J. W. Millard. To meet governmental requirements certain modifications had to be introduced in the engines, *e.g.* the valve gear and starting and stopping arrangements of the type used in modern walking-beam engines were substituted for the original tappet valve gear, &c., while the boiler was of steel instead of copper and worked at a pressure of 20 lbs. per square inch. The trial trip of this vessel took place on September 14, 1909.

The grand river pageant illustrating the history of the Hudson for 300 years took place on September 28, and was attended by representatives from most of the great Powers of Europe. Among other guests on board the *Clermont* were several descendants of Robert Fulton.

APPENDICES

APPENDIX A

PORTRAITS OF ROBERT FULTON

THE difficulty very often in the case of an inventor is to discover a portrait of any kind whatever, but as Fulton was himself an artist and cultivated the fine arts, portraits of him are numerous and the difficulty becomes rather that of discriminating amongst them, so great are the differences not only in merit but in the actual representation. Making every allowance for the fact that Fulton undoubtedly changed in appearance as the years went by, it is impossible to accept all the attributions. In the case of one of these reputed portraits, the artist is known to have never painted a portrait of Fulton, and in fact the individual portrayed is some one else altogether. Then, again, copies of these spurious portraits have been multiplied, so that further confusion has been created. Quite a number are attributed to Fulton's own brush, but as he was not a vain person it is difficult to believe that he would have painted himself very often. No one portrait has been generally accepted as the best, although if we judge by the number of times it has been reproduced West's portrait may be said to merit this distinction more than any other.

In attempting the following selection, consideration has been paid not only to the fame and distinction of the artist concerned but also to contemporary descriptions of Fulton's appearance, two of which have been already given.[1]

To descend to particulars and adhering to chronological order it is safe to accept a pencil drawing half-length by John Vanderlyn, in the possession of Judge Peter T. Barlow. It shows features much more softened than other likenesses, and was probably taken in Paris in 1798 at the age of thirty-three.

A marble bust by Jean Antoine Houdon, signed and dated An XII (*i.e.* when Fulton was in his thirty-ninth year and in Paris);

[1] pp. 268 and 269.

was exhibited in the French Salon of 1802, and is now in the Musée de Marine, the Louvre (see illustration). The virile face and the strongly marked yet pleasing features agree well with the descriptions, and suggest that this is the best likeness extant.

Till the mistake was pointed out by the author, the bust at the Louvre was thought to be merely a plaster cast of the original. We believe that the authorities there now contemplate withdrawing the bust from its present position in order to place it in the Salle Houdon along with the other works of that great sculptor.

The oil painting half-length attributed to Benjamin West, in the possession of Robert Fulton Ludlow, must have been painted in London at the age of forty or thereabouts. Although strong the face is heavy and the expression almost forbidding.

There is another portrait attributed to West in the possession of Robert Fulton Cutting. It is improbable that both are originals.

What looks very like a copy of the first of these, painted by Miss Emmet and engraved by W. R. Leney, is prefixed to Colden's *Life of Fulton*.

An oil painting half-length possibly by himself, in the possession of Dr. Gilbert L. Parker (see illustration), looks as if it had been painted about the age of forty when in London: nose and mouth seem too strongly marked, but otherwise the face is good. What St. Peter's at Rome is doing in the background we do not know.

The oil painting half-length by his friend Charles Willson Peale had been lost sight of for many years till a few months ago, when it was identified by Mr. Charles H. Hart in the Banquetting Hall of the Old State House of Pennsylvania, commonly called Independence Hall from its connection with the Declaration of American Independence. In this portrait, which is believed to date from 1808, and is now reproduced for the first time (see frontispiece), the hair is dark and curly; the eyes are light brown, having faded possibly from their originally darker hue; but on the whole it tallies well with the descriptions. Peale was not a great artist, but he preserved very real portraits of his sitters.

An oil painting half-length by John Wesley Jarvis, the celebrated portrait painter, is in the possession of the Misses Vinton. This must have been painted between 1808 and 1815. The virile face reminds one of Houdon's bust, and this portrait should be regarded as one of the best. The statue of Fulton at the Fulton Ferry House, Brooklyn, is based on this portrait.

A miniature half-length in the possession of C. Franklin Crary, by an unknown artist, but said to have been painted from life in Paris, was taken more probably in New York towards the end of Fulton's life, because the face is deeply lined and there is a far-off expression.

APPENDIX B

LIST OF PAINTINGS

By ROBERT FULTON

<table>
<tr><td>John Wilkes Kittera, miniature, c. 1786
Mary Kittera, miniature, c. 1786</td><td>Owned by the Historical Society of Pennsylvania.</td></tr>
</table>

Samuel Beach, miniature, *c.* 1786, owned by H. A. Boardman.

Joseph Bringhurst, oil, 1786, owned by Edward Bringhurst.

Benjamin Franklin, oil, *c.* 1786, claimed to be owned by the University of North Carolina, Chapel Hill, N.C.

Clementina Ross, miniature, *c.* 1786, owned by the Pennsylvania Academy of Fine Arts.

Margaret Ross, pastel, 1787, owned by Mrs. C. S. Bradford.

Ann Conyngham, miniature, owned by John Conyngham Stevens.

Colonel Michael McCurdy, miniature, owned by Mrs. George McHenry.

<table>
<tr><td>"Portrait of Young Gentleman," oil
"Portrait of Young Gentleman," oil</td><td>Exhibited at the Royal Academy, 1791; whereabouts unknown.</td></tr>
<tr><td>"Elisha raising the Widow's Son," oil
"Priscilla and Alladine from Spenser's Faerie Queene," oil
"Portrait of a Gentleman," oil
"Portrait of a Lady," oil</td><td>Exhibited at the Royal Society of British Artists, 1791; whereabouts unknown.</td></tr>
</table>

William Courtenay, ninth Earl of Devon, oil, 1791; whereabouts unknown.

<table>
<tr><td>"Mary Queen of Scotts under confinement," oil
"Lady Jane Grey the night before her execution," oil; whereabouts unknown</td><td>Both engraved in mezzotint[1] by William Ward, January 1793.</td></tr>
</table>

"Louis XVI in prison, taking leave of his family," oil; whereabouts unknown. Engraved by J. K. Sherwin, 1793.

[1] British Museum, 1878, 7, 13; 151 and 152.

"Portrait of a Lady" (Mrs. Murray), oil. Exhibited at the Royal Academy, 1793; whereabouts unknown.

Charles, third Earl Stanhope, oil, *c.* 1795; owned by Hermann Livingston.

Robert Fulton, oil, 1795 (attribution not certain); owned by Mrs. Robert Fulton Blight.

Rev. Edmund Cartwright, D.D., F.R.S., oil, *c.* 1796; whereabouts unknown. Engraved by T. O. Barlow, 1862.

Joel Barlow, oil, *c.* 1797; owned by Judge Peter T. Barlow. This is probably the best portrait painted by Fulton.

Ruth Barlow, oil, 1800; whereabouts unknown.

Joel Barlow, oil, *c.* 1800; owned by Robert Fulton Ludlow.

Fire of Moscow, panorama, oil, 1800.

Charlotte Villette, oil, 1802; whereabouts unknown.

Robert Fulton, oil, *c.* 1805 (attribution not certain); owned by Dr. Gilbert L. Parker of Philadelphia (see illustration).

Mrs. Walter Livingston, mother-in-law of Robert Fulton, oil, *c.* 1808; owned by Mrs. Hermann H. Cammann.

John Livingston, oil, *c.* 1810; owned by Robert Fulton Ludlow.

Abraham Baldwin, U.S. Senator, sketch, *c.* 1810; whereabouts unknown. Copied by E. G. Leutze and engraved by J. B. Forrest.

APPENDIX C

LIST OF WRITINGS

By ROBERT FULTON

"Small Canals." Signed article, *Star* newspaper, London, July 30, 1795.

A treatise on the improvement of Canal Navigation exhibiting the numerous advantages to be derived from Small Canals and boats of two to five feet wide, containing from two to five tons burthen. With a description of the machinery for facilitating Conveyance by Water through the most mountainous Countries independent of Locks and Aqueducts: including *Observations on the great Importance of Water Communications.* With thoughts on, and designs for, aqueducts and bridges of Iron and wood. Illustrated with seventeen plates.

London, 1796. 4to.

(The New York Historical Society possesses a unique copy containing the original drawings from which the engravings were made.)

Recherches sur les Moyens de Perfectionner les Canaux de Navigation, et sur les nombreux avantages de petits canaux, dont les bateaux auraient depuis deux jusqu' á cinq pieds de large et pourraient contenir une cargaison de deux à cinq tonneaux avec des dessins de construction nouvelles d'aqueducs et de ponts en bois et en fer. 7 plates.

Traduit par M. de Récicourt.

Paris, An 7 (1799).

Tratado do melhoramento da navegaçao por Cañaes . . . escrito na lingua Ingleza . . . e traduzido para a Portugueza . . . por A. C. Ribeiro de Andrade Machado da Silva.

Lisbon, 1800. 4to.

Report of the Secretary of the Treasury on the subject of Public roads and canals.
Contains letter by Robert Fulton dated December 8, 1807.
Washington, 1808. 8vo.

Torpedo War and Submarine Explosions.
New York, 1810. 4to.

De la machine infernale maritime oủ de la tactique offensive et defensive de la Torpille. Traduit de l'anglais par M. E. Minez de Taboada. 5 plates.
Paris, 1812. 8vo.

Letter to the Secretary of the Navy on the Practical use of the Torpedo.
Washington, 1811. 8vo.

Report on the Practicability of Navigating with Steamboats on the Southern Waters of the United States. New York, 1813.

Report of the Board of Commissioners of the Western Canal. Contains letter by Robert Fulton dated February 22, 1814.
Washington, 1814. 8vo.

Memorial of Robert Fulton and Edward Livingston in regard to Steamboats.
Albany, 1814.

Advantages of the Proposed Canal from Lake Erie to the Hudson River.
New York, 1814.

APPENDIX D

SIR EDWARD OWEN'S DESCRIPTION OF FULTON'S TORPEDO

Clyde in the Downes,
6th September 1807.

Sir,—When Mr. Robert Fulton was employed by the Government of this Country, I was ordered to make trial against the Enemy at Boulogne of the Machines invented by him for destroying Vessels by explosion under Water. My attention was therefore very particularly directed to the Weapon and the means of giving it effect, and I had in consequence a great deal of Conversation and of Correspondence with Mr. Fulton on the Subject and was by that means put in possession of most of his opinions on it.

I confess myself to have been of the Number who very much doubted its efficacy, and I believe in consequence of my doubts the experiment was made in Walmer Road of blowing up a brig with them, the result of which placed the power of the weapon beyond dispute and left the means and Policy of using it the only questions.

In the late Newspapers I observe an account of an experiment made by him at New York to prove their effect to the Magistrates of that Town, and as an Enemy's Coast at all times gives a great facility for using them against blockading ships I think it more than probable, that should the Negociations between this Country and America take an unfavorable turn, they may be used against our Naval Force upon that Station.

I take the Liberty therefore of enclosing you for the Information of My Lords Commissioners of the Admiralty, a Description of his Machine as latterly fitted with all the improvements which the experience of the Officers had suggested (and which left the Weapon very different from what was first proposed by him), to which I have added some suggestions as to the means of counteracting them, which shou'd Their Lordships think it necessary to communicate them to the Officers employed on the Coast of America may be improved by them when they understand the

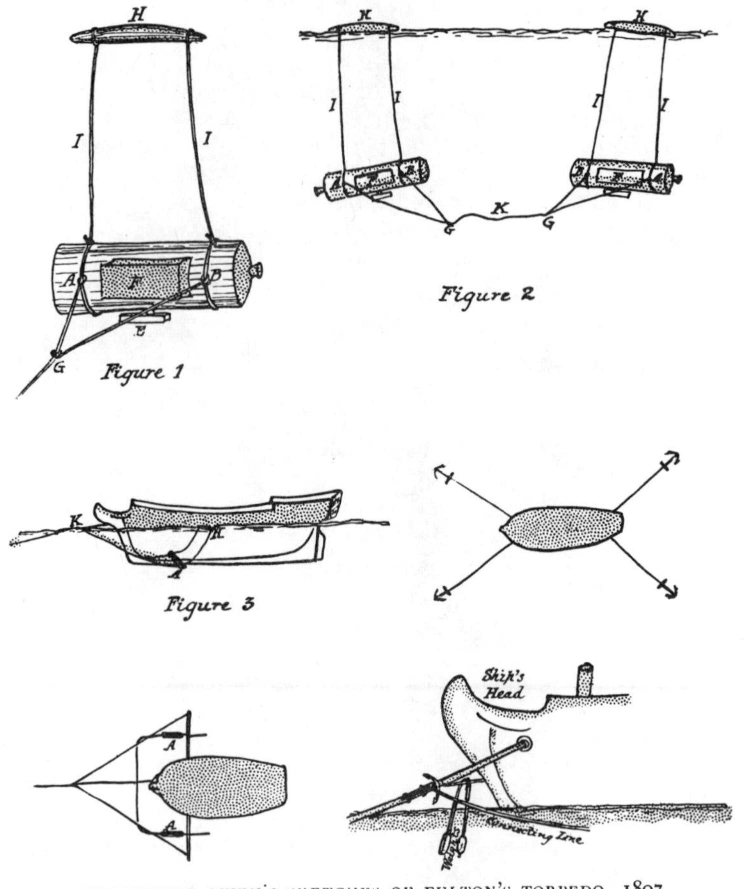

COMMODORE OWEN'S SKETCHES OF FULTON'S TORPEDO, 1807

nature of the Weapon they are threatened with. It is that their Lordships may if they think fit be enabled to convey to them this knowledge which very few officers had the means which presented themselves to me of acquiring, that I have written the enclosed description, which I have considered the more necessary as not only was the Weapon itself improved by Mr. Fulton from the knowledge that he gained by practise here, but he himself has gained a more material knowledge in the unreserved communications that he always had with Officers upon the Boulogne Station as to the proper times and means of using it especially the facility a Coast affords of choosing the Station most proper to send forth such an expedition according to the Tide and Wind.

I have the honour to remain,
Sir, your most obedient and
very humble Servant,
(Commodore) E. W. C. R. OWEN.

Hon. W. W. POLE,
&c. &c. &c.
minuted 7th Sepr.

Let copies of these papers be made in duplicate and sent to Adm. Berkeley for his information.

A DESCRIPTION OF THE MACHINE INVENTED BY MR. ROBERT FULTON FOR EXPLODING UNDER SHIPS' BOTTOMS AND BY HIM CALLED THE TORPEDO

FIGURE 1

A B The Copper Cylender made to contain about a Barrel of Gun Powder.

C The Neck of the Cylender by which the Powder is introduced it is afterwards bunged tight and covered over with White Lead and canvass to exclude the Wet.

D The Vent communicating with the Priming.

E The Lock screwed into the Vent and set to any given time but prevented from acting until the Machine is used by an Iron Pin, on withdrawing which the works are set in motion. Five minutes or even less is the time latterly adopted.

F A Box containing Cork which answers a double purpose. First if the Machine is laid obliquely across the Tide it presents to it a flat surface which makes it sheer under the Vessel's bottom, the box being on the side of the Machine from the Ship intended to be destroyed.

Secondly it takes from its specific Gravity leaving it when loaded but little heavier than its bulk of Water, so that when checked by a Line at the Water's edge it may incline upwards and float close to the Vessel's bottom.

G is a bridle by which it is attached to a Sweep rope to be laid across the Vessel's bow, and intended to give it an Oblique direction across the Tide and make it sheer under the Vessel's bottom.

H a Cushion of Cork attached to the Slings A B by the lines the length of which is calculated by the supposed Draft of Water of the Vessels to be attacked and serving to suspend the Machine at the proper depth from the Cushion which floats at the Surface of the Water.

FIGURE 2 represents two of these machines linked together for service where the several parts are represented by the same letters as in Figure 1. K a Line connecting the two Machines and meant to cross the Bows of the Vessel that is attacked and to hang upon her Cables whilst the tide sweeps the machines under her Bottom one on each side. The Moment the line from K to the bridle G comes taut the Machine takes a direction obliquely to the Tide which acting upon the flat Surface of the Box F sheers it directly under the Bottom whilst the buoyancy of the machine (being very little heavier than the Water it displaces) enables the Cushion H by the action of the Tide at the Surface to confine it close to the Vessel's bottom where it acts exactly as a Petard.

FIGURE 3 shews the Machine as intended to be placed. K is the bight of the Line which connects the two machines as hung upon the Cable. A is the Machine sheered under the bottom and buoyed up by the action of the Tide on the Cushion H which will perhaps be sunk a little by it.

The machines are fitted according to the side of the ship it is intended to place them so as always to keep the Box outside from the Ship and the Lock underneath so that its weight assisted by the lines which attach the Cushion may always keep the flat surface of this Box in a perpendicular direction to expose the greatest surface to the Tide.

A Fast rowing Boat is used for the attack, which having two of these machines properly fitted and connected, rows briskly across the Vessel's Bows between her and her Buoy, throwing the Machines overboard one on each side her Bows when the Rope which connects them hanging upon the Cable they are swept by the Tide into the position I have before described or where the Boat is too small to take two of the Machines, (as was the case with our Gigs when we tried them against the Enemy's Vessels at Boulogne) I have attached an empty Cask to the other end of the Line boring it full of holes to let it fill with Water when thrown overboard to act as a counterpoise to the Machine at the other end.

The efficacy of this machine it will be observed depends first on its being placed between the Ship and her Buoy, for if it was ahead of the Buoy the connecting line would hang upon the Buoy rope and be stopped by it. And

Secondly upon its being both under the Ship's bottom and close to it, for its greatest action must be upwards, and if any quantity of Water intervened that wou'd receive and destroy its force.

The Boats employed to use it can only act upon the Lee Tide (unless the Ship is moored) and it is only in a Tidesway that it can be used—the Nature of the Weapon too makes it wholly depend upon surprize, and it can in no instance scarce be used by force.

A good look out then and Guard Boats at the Buoys, will be the best security, but as an Enemy's Coast gives him always great facilities in using them against blockading Ships, the best look out may under special circumstances be unable to prevent it, it is however highly improbable that the Boat performing such a Service can escape unseen and therefore if every precaution has been taken, there may be time enough to destroy their effect (even if they have been placed) either by keeping them from under the bottom of the Ship, or by sinking them.

Mr. Fulton attributed our want of success at Boulogne entirely to their not getting fairly under the Vessel's bottom, and he in consequence since that time added the Box F to sheer them under; they were however (notwithstanding his experiment succeeded in Walmer Road and the Brig blew up) tried with that addition against the Enemy and with no more success, which I attribute to their not riding by their Cable but by springs which prevented them from getting under the bottom—to explain what I mean it is necessary to say that the births of the Flotilla I believe are in the center of four small Anchors with Hawsers wound with Chain which always remain and are slipped by the Vessels when they return to Port, but they do not ride by those Hawsers in bad Weather; they always drop an Anchor in this birth and appear to steady themselves in fine Weather only by the Hawsers and slip them when it blows. I have however no exact information on this subject, what I state is from my own observation.

If this has been the occasion of their failure at Boulogne perhaps a similar effect might be produced by keeping the Lower Studding Sail Booms out at night in the same manner as for Guest Warps and having a Rope thro' a Block at the end of each Boom bent to the Cable about 20 fathoms or more from the Bows which wou'd keep the Machines clear of the Bows as represented by A A in the above Figure. This may be attended with inconvenience particularly on Weather Tides when it may be necessary to overhaul these Ropes and keep them stepped to the Cable near the Hawse out of the Way—and [as] its effect might not be certain the following precaution may therefore be taken for sinking them.

Let a Fire Grapnel be kept lashed to the Cable outside the Cutwater upon Lee Tides with the Shank down and Flukes upwards so that if the connecting Line of the Machines sweeps the Cable it may catch upon the Hook of the Fluke, a stout Rope shou'd be passed round the Cutwater under the Cable and each end bent to a Weight (a Pig or two of Iron Ballast) at the Cat Heads—under the Charge of the look out men to be cut away at a Moment's notice. Axes shou'd also be kept at all times by the Cable ready to cut it.

By this plan supposing the sweep Rope K Figure 3 to be across the Cable it must as the Machines draw it taut hook upon the Fluke of the Grapnel and the Weights let go from the Catheads wou'd overlay the connecting line—in this situation the Cutting the Cable wou'd sink the whole together, and the Ship shooting into a clear birth to Seaward may of course bring up again.

The sending a man on the Cable to cut the connecting Line wou'd seem the readiest and most effective plan, but I had much Conversation with Mr. Fulton on that subject and it was intended to substitute a chain buoyed with Cork.

On the other side[1] I have endeavoured to shew the supposed positions of the Cable, Grapnel and Weights when let go.

The Cable shou'd not be cut without some such precaution for the Machines wou'd drift of course with the Ship, and as she gathered headway the Line wou'd hang across her Stern and the machines be placed as well or better than before.

[1] *i.e.* of the paper.

APPENDIX E

FULTON'S U.S. PATENT SPECIFICATION OF 1809

WRITTEN DESCRIPTION OF THE STEAM BOAT[1]

Kalorama, District of Columbia, January first, Eighteen hundred and nine.

I Robert Fulton, native of Pennsylvania, citizen of the United States of America and now living at Kalorama in the district of Columbia, give the following written description of my discoveries, inventions and improvements on Steam Boats.

To obtain the power for driving the boat, I make use of Messrs. Boulton and Watt's Steam Engine, but instead of a beam above the Cylinder, I have a triangular cast iron beam on each side of it, and near the bottom of the boat; the base of the Triangle is seven feet long, in the centre of the base a perpendicular is raised, three feet six inches high, which is the Vertex of the triangle, the two triangles are fixed on one strong iron shaft, so that they play together. On the top of the piston rod, there is a Tee piece, or strong iron bar, which moves in guides at each side of the Cylinder, from each end of the Tee piece, and passing down by the sides of the Cylinder is a strong bar of forged iron, called a shackle, which is connected by a shackle pin to the end of the beam, thus the end of the beam moves through a curve in a perpendicular direction, and its vertex moves through a curve in a horizontal direction; the other end of the triangle is cast with a weight of iron sufficient to balance the weight of the piston and all the weight on the opposite idea of the fulcrum or centre of the base line. From the vertex of each triangle a shackle from six to eight feet long, is connected with a crank which is fixed on each shaft of the propeller wheels; close to each crank is a cast iron wheel about 4 feet 6 inches diameter, each driving a pinion 2 feet 3 inches diameter, these two

[1] The text of this and of the succeeding specification is taken from a MS. copy in the possession of the Patent Office Library. It appears to have been obtained from Mr. Joseph C. Dyer by Mr. Bennett Woodcroft, F.R.S., when the latter was preparing his work on "the Rise and Progress of Steam Navigation," 1848. Woodcroft was subsequently appointed Clerk to the Commissioners of Patents and gave this MS. to the Library. A better copy exists at Birmingham among the Boulton & Watt MSS. in the possession of Mr. George Tangye; this was made in 1816, without doubt from the same original. The two copies have been collated for the present work.

pinions are on one shaft, in the centre of which is a fly-wheel 10 feet diameter. The movement for the air pump is taken from the base line of the beam, and 21 inches from the fulcrum. The condensing-water comes through the sides or bottom of the boat by a pipe which enters the condenser, and is regulated by a cock or valve. The Hot well, the forcing pump to replenish the boiler, the steam gage, the safety valve, the float in the boiler to regulate the quantity of water, the plug tree and hand gear &c. &c. are so familiar to all persons acquainted with the steam engine and may be arranged in such a variety of ways as not to require a description—I prefer a propelling wheel or wheels, to take the purchase on the water, they may be from 8 to 20 feet diameter, and divided into any number of equal parts from 3 to 20, each wheel may have from 3 to 20 propellers, but a wheel or wheels from 12 to 15 feet diameter, each with from 8 to 12 propellers will be found to apply the power of the engine to great advantage.

Hitherto I have placed a propelling wheel on each side of the boat, with a wheel guard or frame outside of each of them for protection; a propelling wheel or wheels may however be placed behind the boat, or in the centre between two connected boats. To give room for the machinery, passengers, or Merchandize, I build my boats five or more times as long as their extreme breadth at the Water line. The extreme breadth may be one third from her bow or in the middle, in which case the water line will form two equal segments of a circle united at the ends.

To diminish the plus and minus pressure, I make the bow and stern sharp to angles of at least 60 degrees, and that the boat may draw as little water as possible, I build it flat or nearly so on the bottom. Having mentioned the essential component parts of a steam boat, and its mechanism, its successful construction and velocity will depend—First, on an accurate knowledge of her total resistance while running 1, 2, 3, 4, 5 or 6 miles an hour in still water. Second, on a knowledge of the diameter of the Cylinder, strength of the steam and velocity of the piston to overcome the resistance of a given boat while running 1, 2, 3, 4, 5 or 6 miles an hour in still water.

Third, on a knowledge of the square feet or inches which each propeller should have and the velocity it should run to drive a given boat 1, 2, 3, 4, 5 or 6 miles an hour through still water.

It is a knowledge of these proportions and velocities which is the most important part of my discovery on the improvement of Steam Boats. The following definitions, Tables and calculations will lead to a clear idea of them :

DEFINITIONS[1]

By head pressure is meant the total pressure against the bow when the boat is at rest.

By stern pressure is meant the total pressure against the stern when the boat is at rest.

Plus pressure is the additional pressure against the bow while the boat moves forward; it is occasioned by the fluid being displaced, and is in addition to head pressure.

Minus pressure is a diminution of stern pressure occasioned by the fluid not pressing so strongly against the stern when the boat moves forward as when at rest.

Friction arises either from the adhesion of the particles of the fluid to the surface of the body, or from the roughness of the body, or from both these causes united.

Bow resistance is plus pressure, and the friction of the water against the bow united.

Stern resistance is minus pressure, and the friction of the water against the stern united.

TABLE OF FRICTION, OF PLUS & MINUS PRESSURE AND OF THE RESISTANCE OF ONE SQUARE FOOT OF PROPELLER

Nautical Miles an Hour	1	2	3	4	5	6
When a boat is smooth and clean the friction on every 50 square feet will be	.70	2.36	4.74	7.75	11.32	15.43
The plus & minus pressure on each foot of bow of 60, the stern being also 60 degrees . . .	.88	3.31	7.15	12.37	18.93	26.78
The plus & minus pressure on each foot of bow of 20 deg: the Stern being also 20 degrees . .	.61	2.29	4.97	8.64	13.30	18.90
The resistance of one square foot of propellers is	3.25	13.09	29.36	51.95	80.76	115.71

[1] These definitions appear in the "Report" of the experiments made by Beaufoy published about 1800. They were copied by Charnock in his valuable *History of Naval Architecture*, 1802, vol. iii. p. 387. Fulton, therefore, had plenty of sources of information open to him. He seems to have taken the definitions verbatim.

By this table the total resistance of all lengths, widths and drafts of Water of all boats with bows and sterns on angles of 20 or 60 degrees may be calculated.

The resistance of one square foot of propeller is also shewn; hence when any particular sized boat has been determined on, and the number of miles which she is to run in still water has been decided: First find her total resistance for that velocity, then by the table also find the number of square feet or inches of a propeller, which while running a velocity equal to the boat, will make a resistance equal to the boat. It will consequently follow that the resistance of the boat and propellers being equal, they will pass through equal spaces in equal times, and while the boat advances one mile the propellers will strike through the water one mile backwards; therefore, if the boat is to run 1, 2, 3, 4, 5 or 6 miles an hour the speed of the propellers in the water must be 2, 4, 6, 8, 10 or 12 miles an hour, one half of each of these velocities is spent in striking water back to create a resistance, equal to the resistance of the boat, the other half is to overtake as she advances. For example, when a boat moves one mile an hour, the water runs along her sides with a speed of one mile an hour; were the propellers to run only one mile an hour, they would not touch the water which was running from them with any force, but if they run two miles an hour, they would strike the water with the force of one mile and create a resistance equal to the resistance of the boat. The following is the method of finding the total resistance of a boat and of calculating the power and proportions of the machinery to the speed which she is to run. For these calculations say boat 154 feet long, 18 feet wide, drawing 2 feet of water. Bow and Stern on angles of 60 degrees, Steam engine making a 4 foot stroke and 15 double strokes a minute, equal two feet a second, the boat to run four miles an hour.

	lb.
Plus and minus pressure on one foot 12.37 lb. multiplied by 36 feet the boat's bow	445.32
Friction on 848 feet of bow and stern at 7.75 lb. for every 50 square feet	131.75
Friction on 2200 square feet of the body of the boat .	341.
Total resistance of the boat .	918.07
A like power for the propellers	918.07
Total power .	1836.14

to be felt at the end of the propellers running 4 Miles an hour, or 6 feet a second, this is three times as fast as the piston moves, hence 1836.14 must be multiplied by 3 equal 5508.42 lb. or the power of the engine. A cylinder 27 inches diameter equal 729 round inches and 8 pounds to the inch, gives 5832 lb.; the periphery of the propeller wheel must run 8 miles an hour or 12 feet a second equal 720 feet a minute, wheels 14 feet diameter, 44 round and 16 revolutions a minute will give 704 feet a minute which is sufficiently near. The total resistance of the boat is 918.07 lb. The resistance of one square foot of propeller running 4 miles an hour is 51.95 lb. 17½ square feet give resistance 909.12 this is 8¾ feet in each propeller; by this example all necessary calculations may be made.

I make use of sails and take advantage of the wind to aid the engine, or when the wind is sufficient I stop the engine, throw the wheels out of gear and move by the power of the wind only.

To prevent the boat making lee way, she has lee boards, or boards which are let down into the water while she is sailing; hitherto there have been two lee boards on each side of the boat, one on each side near the bow, and one on each side near the stern. That the helmsman may steer to advantage, I place the wheel for steering, and lead the tiller ropes so near the middle of the boat as to enable him to have an uninterrupted view forward. In any case where a current against the boat is superior to the power of the engine to pass it, I propose to cast anchor in such waters, or obtain any other fastening which will enable me to warp the boat by the power of the engine from station to station until the rapid be past.

Such Steam boats as are for Passengers, I build with births, good Sophas and beds, Kitchen, bar, and Ice magazine, with every convenience for giving breakfasts, dinners, tea and suppers either in the cabins or under an awning or awnings on deck.

(Signed) ROBERT FULTON.

Witness.

JOHN R. LIVINGSTON.
MATURIN LIVINGSTON.

1st Jany. 1809 A.D.

Kalorama, district of Columbia, January 1st, Eighteen hundred and nine, I Robert Fulton native of Pennsylvania, Citizen of the United States of America, and now residing at Kalorama in the district of Columbia, give the following description of my inventions or discovery for constructing boats or vessels which are to be navigated by the power of steam engines, believing myself to be the original inventor or discoverer of the following combinations and the first who has laid down rules that will secure success in building such boats or vessels; no patent or publication having hitherto appeared, in which exact and mathematical principles are explained to guide Artizans to success in works of this kind.

I do not consider the successful construction of a steam boat to depend on any new form of steam engine or boiler; such combination will relate to the engine only, and cannot be an improvement of importance unless they produce a greater power with less fuel than is produced by those which are made on the principles of Messrs. Boulton & Watt's Steam engine; which principle of Steam engine I prefer to all others for obtaining the necessary power to drive the boat, and I assert that to give the greatest velocity to a boat with given power of Steam engine, she must be built on the following principles:

First.—The boat must be so constructed that for any determined weight she is destined to carry, she should present the least possible resistance. For this purpose her Bow and Stern should be sharp to angles of at least 60 degrees and as much sharper as consistent with strength.

Secondly.—She may be made of a length that her friction will equal her plus and minus pressure (*here follow a repetition of the Definitions already given on page* 291). After such length has been established should it be desired to have a more powerful engine and a boat to carry a greater cargo, it will be optional to make her longer, and thereby increase her friction or load her to draw so much water that her plus and minus pressure will equal the friction of the intended additional length; in both cases the total resistance will be equal while the boat moves in a right line in still water, but loading will be preferable to increasing her length as the demonstrations on this principle will hereafter exhibit.

Thirdly.—I give the preference to a water wheel or wheels with propelling boards, to gain a purchase on the water, which wheel may have any number of arms and propelling boards from three to twenty; eight arms and propelling boards to each wheel will be found to apply the power of the engine to great advantage. Each wheel may be from six to twenty feet diameter; that will depend on the speed which the boat is to run, as will be seen hereafter. From 12 to 15 feet will usually be the best diameter. Previously to adopting wheels, I made experiments on paddles which formed nearly an eliptical movement as delineated in drawing first figure

DRAWING No. I ATTACHED TO FULTON'S U.S. PATENT SPECIFICATION, 1809

first, on endless chains with propelling boards as indicated in figure second, on flyers like those of a smoke jack figure third, none of which are so simple and effectual as wheels, and I mention this to shew that I have not adopted wheels until convinced of their superior advantages which the calculations hereafter will demonstrate.

Fourth.—When the speed which the boat is to run in still water has been determined, whether 1, 2, 3, 4, 5 or 6 miles an hour, and the power to drive her the intended velocity has been calculated, the diameter of the cylinder of the steam engine, the length of the stroke of the piston, the strength of the steam to be used, and the number of strokes which the piston will strike in a minute, must be calculated to give the power required.

That any determined power of steam engine shall drive a given boat, with the greatest speed which such engine can effect will depend on certain exact proportions which shall hereafter be explained, between the shape of the bow and stern of the boat, her length, draft of water, velocity and total resistance; and the diameter of her wheels, the velocity of their periphery, and the square feet of their propelling boards which continually act against the water; a boat may be moved by the power of a steam engine although exact proportions are not observed, but to drive her with the greatest speed, with a given power, the proportions must be adhered to. It consequently follows, that they who attempt to construct steam boats without knowing the proportions and velocities, proceed without any certain guide, and cannot give rules to secure success in building and navigating steam boats of various dimensions and velocities, so as to apply the power of the engine to the greatest advantage. Be it therefore known that I found my claim to exclusive right for my invention or discovery, not only to my particular mode of combining boats and machinery, but also to the necessary form of the boat or boats, to the size of the propelling boards, and the velocity they should run, proportioned to the shape of the bow and stern of the boat, her draft of water, velocity, friction and total resistance, and to the calculations on the power of the steam engine to give the whole the necessary velocity.

The successful construction of steam boats depends on these parts being well proportioned, whether wheels or any other propellers be used; with the right proportion of the parts above mentioned, steam boats may be navigated by the propelling power of wheels, endless chains, or paddles, but without the proportions which shall hereafter be explained, they cannot be successfully navigated, with either wheels, endless chains, paddles or any other mode of taking the purchase on the water; it therefore follows that an exact description of the form of the boat and of the proportions and velocities of the machinery are the most important parts of this invention or discovery, in addition to which I have given modes of combining the boat and Mechanism so as to secure success in building Steam boats for Passengers or Merchandize.

THE DEMONSTRATIONS ARE AS FOLLOWS:

Drawing second is a table of the resistance of bodies under water at the depth of 6 feet. In these calculations let it be understood that the weight or moving power runs thro' the same space in the same time as the body which is drawn through the water. Figure first is a plank one foot square one inch thick. It required 3.25 lb. moving one mile an hour to draw it one mile an hour. Figure 2nd is a Cube one foot square, 3.05 lb. is necessary to draw it one mile an hour, the Cube has less resistance than the plank; the reason is that the water not having time to close in behind the plank increases the minus pressure more in this case, than the other, but it has time to run along the sides of the cube, filling in behind and not increasing the minus pressure in so great a degree.

Figure third is a parallelopiped one foot square 10 feet long, it requires 3.39 lb. to draw it one mile an hour, here the resistance is increased one ninth more than in the cube; this arises from the length of the body and the friction of the water on its sides. Figure fourth is ten feet long, one foot square with a bow and stern sharpened to angles of 60 degrees, and it requires 1.63 lb. to draw it one mile an hour. This is not half the resistance of figure third, and proves that a bow and stern on angles of 60 degrees may be estimated at less than half the resistance of flat ends; as half the power is saved by a bow and stern on angles of 60 degrees, it may be lead to the hope that an advantage of importance may be obtained by a more acute angle, but figure 5th which is 20 degrees requires 1.48 lb. to draw it one mile an hour, this is an economy of not quite one eighth of the power which was necessary to draw figure 4th and not of sufficient importance in most cases to risk so sharp and weak a bow or diminish the space in the boat. Figure 6th is a friction plank 21 feet 3 inches long 1 foot broad, 3 inches thick, it required 1.40 lb. to draw it one mile an hour. Figure 7th is a short friction plank 1 foot 3 inches long,

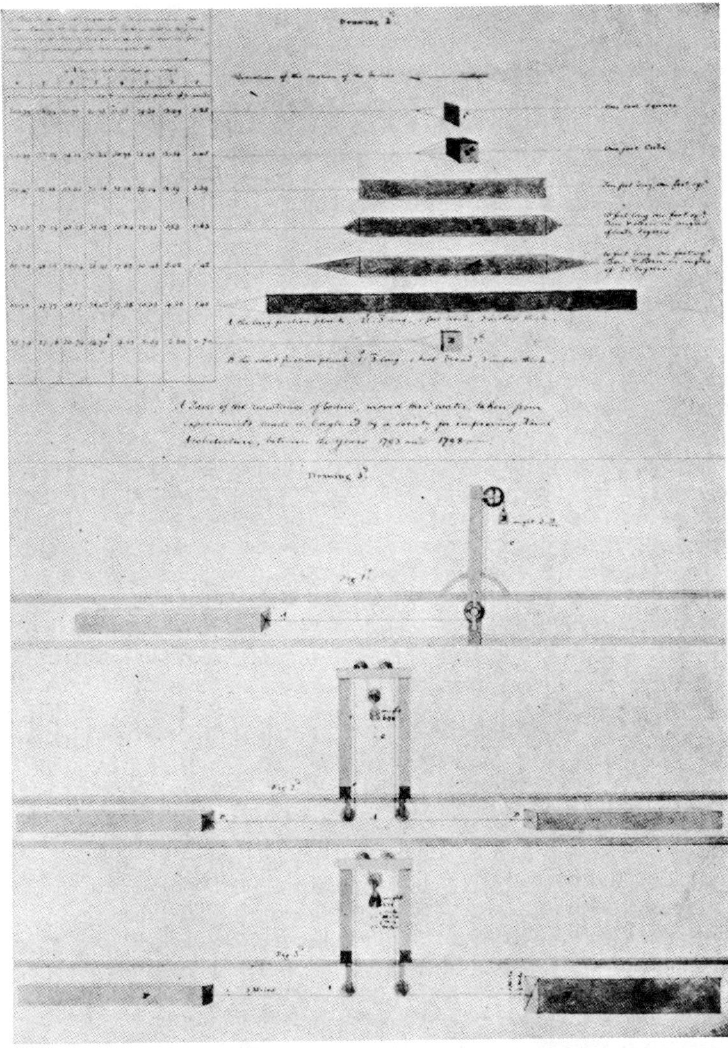

DRAWINGS 2 & 3 ATTACHED TO FULTON'S U.S. PATENT SPECIFICATION, 1809

1 foot broad 3 inches thick, it required 0.70 lb. to draw it one mile an hour; the two ends of these bodies their breadth and thickness are exactly alike; but the long plank contains exactly 50 square feet of surface for friction more than the short friction plank—therefore subtract the resistance of the short plank from the long one, and the remainder will be the friction on 50 square feet running 1, 2, 3, 4, 5 or 6 miles an hour it will stand thus:

Miles an hour	1	2	3	4	5	6
Long friction plank . . .	1.40	4.96	10.33	17.38	26.02	36.17
Short do. plank . . .	0.70	2.60	5.59	9.63	14.70	20.74
Friction of 50 Square feet	0.70	2.36	4.74	7.73	11.32	15.43

ANALYSIS OF THE TOTAL RESISTANCE OF FIGURES 4 & 5

FIGURE 4TH BOW & STERN 60 DEGREES

Miles an hour	1	2	3	4	5	6
From total resistance . . .	1.63	5.83	12.21	20.64	31.02	43.25
Deduct friction on top surface .	0.17	0.58	1.16	1.89	2.76	3.76
Remains resistance as a boat .	1.46	5.25	11.05	18.75	28.26	39.49
Then deduct friction on sides & bottom	0.58	1.94	3.90	6.38	9.33	12.71
Remains plus & minus pressure .	0.88	3.31	7.15	12.37	18.93	26.78

FIGURE 5TH BOW & STERN 20 DEGREES

Miles an hour	1	2	3	4	5	6
From total resistance . . .	1.42	5.02	10.46	17.62	26.41	36.74
Deduct friction on top surface .	0.18	0.61	1.23	2.01	2.93	4.00
Remains resistance as a boat .	1.24	4.41	9.23	15.61	23.48	32.74
Then deduct friction on sides & bottom	0.63	2.12	4.26	6.97	10.18	13.84
Remains plus & minus pressure .	0.61	2.29	4.97	8.64	13.30	18.90

By this Analysis the plus and minus pressure is discovered. The friction on fifty square feet is also known from which it will be necessary to ascertain the total resistance on any length of boat or width or draft of water. On the comparative resistance of friction and plus and minus pressure, to ascertain the length of boats which will carry the most weight with the least resistance.

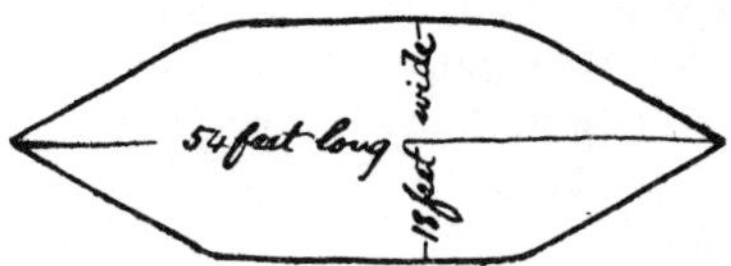

This figure represents the bow and stern of a long boat; on this the plus and minus pressure, the square feet of friction and tonnage will be ascertained. I have made it 18 feet wide, 54 feet long drawing 2 feet of water; Bow and Stern on angles of 60 degrees; should a boat be constructed wider, longer, or to draw more water, her plus and minus pressure and friction will increase in proportion, or diminish if she be narrower, shorter, or draw less water. While drawing 2 feet of water this figure represents a bow of 36 feet which multiplied by 12.37 lb. the plus and minus pressure of one foot running

	lb.
four miles an hour, gives plus and minus pressure . .	445.32
her sides which are under water and bottom equal 848 square feet on which the friction is	131.75
Total resistance while running 4 miles an hour	577.07

	tons
She displaces 1232 Cubic feet of water equal to . .	38.5
Add 50 feet to her length this will displace 1800 Cubic feet, or	56.25
Total	94.75

	lb.
Friction on this 50 feet additional length	170.5
Total resistance	747.57

	tons
The Steam engine and machinery will weigh	30
The boat will weigh	60
Total	90

This leaves only 4.75 tons for Cargo. As her two feet draft gives 94.75 tons, one foot more draft will give 47 tons 750 lb. and to this amount additional cargo may be carried. It is now to be seen which mode will cause the least resistance whether loading the boat 47 tons 750 lbs. and make her draw one foot more water or add such a length to her as to carry the 47 tons 750 lb. without drawing more than two feet water. If she be loaded to draw one foot more it will give

	lbs.
In plus and minus pressure	222.66
In friction along one additional foot of the sides . .	31.00
Total resistance for 47 tons 750 lbs.	253.66

If the boat should be made longer to carry the additional cargo there will also be the weight of the additional length of boat to carry,

	lbs.
Every lineal foot of the body of the boat will displace 36 cubic feet of water or	2232
Every lineal foot of the boat will weigh about . . .	1232

Thus every lineal foot of the boat will carry 1000 lbs. or half a ton. The boat must therefore be made 95 feet longer to carry the 47 tons 750 lb. which additional length gives 2900 square feet of friction, equal 325.50

The plus and minus pressure and friction of the one additional foot of draft is only 253.66

The economy of power by draft of water is . . . 71.84

Added to this economy of power the shorter boat will be less expence in building and be navigated with greater ease and security than the long one.

If width be added to carry the 47 tons 750 lbs. the additional plus and minus pressure and friction will amount to as much resistance as the additional draft of water to carry a like cargo; hence when sufficient length and width have been estimated to carry the machinery with the intended cargo and give stability to the boat, the greatest economy of power will be to let her draw her water; when her draft of water is ascertained, let the calculations of her total resistance be made on her draft of water, form of bow and stern and friction as before stated.

Drawing third shows the proportions, which the surface of the propelling boards which continually act against the water, should bear to the plus and minus pressure, the friction and total resistance of the boat; figure first represents a parallelopiped 10 feet long one foot square to run one mile an hour.

Its plus and minus pressure is 2.83
Its friction 56
Total resistance 3.39

It therefore requires 3.39 lb. falling one mile an hour to draw it one mile an hour or while it moves to A the weight B would descend to C. Figure second shews 2 parallelopipeds each ten feet long, one foot square, placed at equal distances from the centre A. B is a weight of 6.78 lb. which descending to C will draw each parallelopiped to its respective D D,[1] the two bodies having equal resistance pass through equal spaces in equal times with equal powers, this proves that whatever may be the total resistance of a boat if the propelling boards, which continually act against the water, are calculated in square feet to make a resistance equal to the boat they will repel the water one mile an hour while the boat advances one mile an hour, total two miles. The propellers must therefore run through the space of two miles that the boat may run one mile; one mile of which the water yields from the propellers; the other mile is to overtake the boat, in this case the resistance being equal, the power consumed by the boat and propellers will be equal. For example, a boat ten feet long, one foot square, running one mile an hour requires 3.39
The propellers in repelling the water 3.39
Total 6.78

With this equal resistance of boat and propellers, half the total power is consumed on the boat and half on the propellers. It is now to be considered if there is any better application of the total power and what rules can be given to economise from the propellers and give to the boat, or at least to avoid consuming more than half the power in the propellers. Figure third exhibits two parallelopipeds each ten feet long, E is two feet square, presenting 4 feet to the water. I will in this case call it the propeller, and F

[1] In this and the following demonstrations the weight hangs to a free pulley, consequently while it descends one foot it draws the cord one foot, on each side of the pulley, total two spaces equal the spaces D D run through by the parallelopipeds.

the boat, which being one foot square, presents one foot to the water and will require 3.39 to draw it one mile an hour E having four times as much bow, Stern and friction as F it has four times the resistance, and with 3.39 will move only half a mile an hour; the weight G will descend equal one mile and a half in an hour; had the bow and stern of E presented only one square foot like F, it would have moved one mile an hour, while F moved one mile, and the weight G would have descended equal two miles as power is a compound of weight and velocity; the additional half mile, which the weight would move through in the same time would be a loss of one fourth of the power; hence could the combinations of a steam boat be so made, that the square feet of the propellers, which continually act against the water, should have four times the resistance of the total resistance of the boat, one fourth of the total power would be expended on the propellers and three fourths on the boat. The total resistance of the boat before calculated is 747.57 lbs.

The resistance of one square foot running 4 miles an hour is 51.95 the resistance of 14⅓ feet 744.60 thus the resistance of propellers 14⅓ nearly equal the resistance of the boat. Such propellers and boat would pass through equal spaces in equal times, with equal powers, but that the propellers may move through half the space of the boat, they must equal 4 times 14⅓ or 57⅓ feet which is 28 feet and 96 square inches to each propeller, equal 9 long by 3 feet one inch wide. This shews the advantage which might be gained by large propellers if they are not too unwieldy to be conveniently applied; in reducing them to a convenient size, care must be taken that they should not be too small. To prove this let E be the boat and F the propeller; in this case the boat has 4 times the resistance of the propeller and will move only one mile, while the propeller moves two, total three miles. The weight G will descend equal 3 times; in these proportions two thirds of the total power will be consumed on the propellers and one third on the boat.

If the boat or parallelopiped presented 16 feet of bow, and the propeller only one foot the propeller must repel . . . an hour, in this proportion four fifths of the total power would be consumed in the propellers and 1/5 on the boat. This shews the errors which have been committed by all those who have attempted to navigate steam boats with small paddles, which should have a great velocity. Having shewn the advantage to be gained by propellers, whose numbers of square feet should be such as to make a resistance equal to the total resistance of the boat, they repelling with the same velocity which the boat advances.

I will now assign my reason for preferring a water wheel or wheels to take the purchase on the water. As the resistance of the boat in advancing is constant, the propelling power should be constant also, it is therefore important to have a propeller which shall be constant, of sufficient size and velocity with the least complication and friction. For the boat on which these calculations are made, the propellers should equal 14⅓ feet, a propeller on each side of the boat, 2 feet 4 inches wide, 3 feet long will give the square feet required if the boat be calculated to run 4 miles an hour, the propellers must run 8 miles an hour through the water, which is 12 feet a second or 720 feet a minute. A wheel 14 feet diameter making 16 revolutions in a minute, will give the desired velocity and an engine of sufficient power to make 16 double strokes in a minute will keep up the perpetuity of motion. Were a crank movement and paddles of any kind used, each paddle must be 2 feet 4 inches wide and 3 feet long or to that amount in square feet if placed on the side of the boat as in drawing first figure 4th—there must be two such paddles on each side that two may enter the water the moment the other two come out, thus keep up the continued propelling power. The two paddles must also be placed side by side, and not one behind the other as in figure first, for if placed one behind the other, the fore paddle having struck the water back with the velocity of 4 miles an hour the boat running forward say 4 miles an hour, the water would pass her sides under her hindmost paddle with the rapidity of 8 miles an hour. The hindmost paddle having a velocity of only 8 miles an hour would not run faster than the water consequently could produce no good effect; for this reason, endless chains and every kind of propeller which is arranged in a line behind each other for taking the purchase on the water, are erroneous combinations, it is the foremost paddle acting in water which has not been put in motion, that does the execution and no other. As paddles must stand side by side and if placed on the side of the boat must have two on each side, it would make an inconvenient projection of 7 feet from each side; if placed behind the boat as in figure 5th two paddles will do, each should equal 14⅓ square feet.

That the boat may run 4 miles an hour the paddles must run through the water at the speed of 12 feet a second, or 720 feet a minute; suppose each paddle to strike 8 feet in the water, each must make 90 strokes in a minute the piston of the engine making

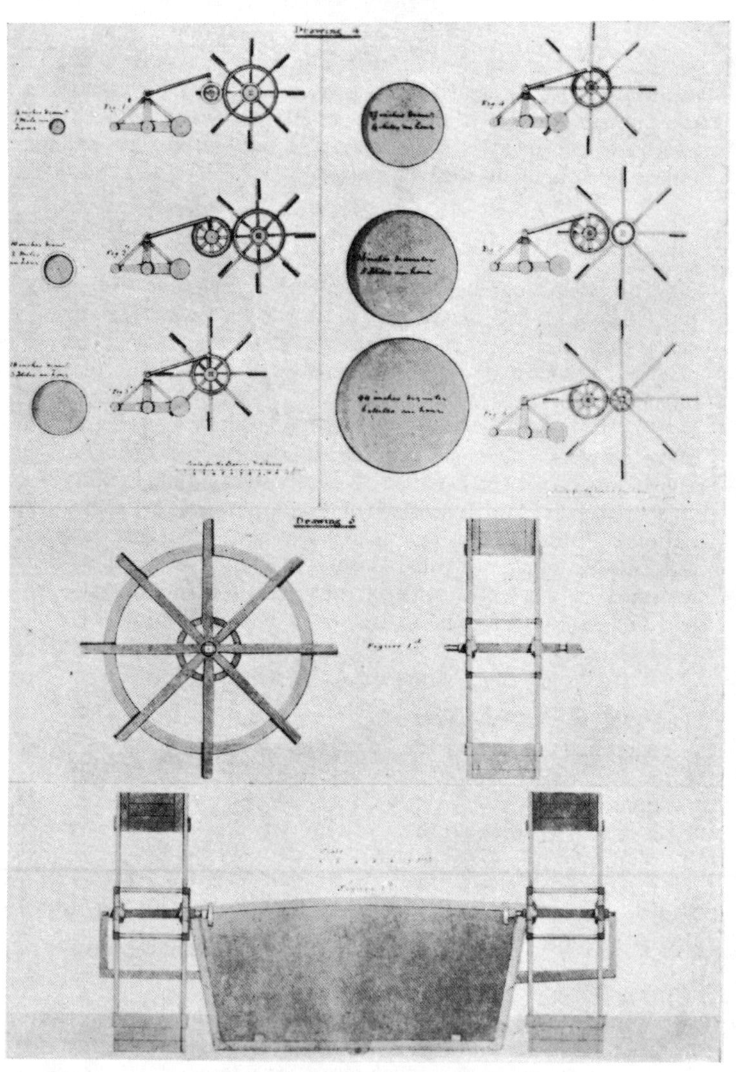

DRAWING 4 & 5 ATTACHED TO FULTON'S U.S. PATENT SPECIFICATION, 1809

15 double strokes in a minute will require a wheel and pinion multiplied 6 to 1: that is the first wheel from the engine 12 feet, the pinions to move the paddle cranks two feet, by such arrangement and proportions a boat may be navigated with paddles but not so effectually as with wheels.

OF THE PROPORTIONS AND VELOCITIES

The following is the method of calculating the power and proportions of the machinery to the speed which the boat is to run giving the power of the steam engine, diameter of the wheels, size and velocity of the propellers, to drive a boat from 1 to 6 miles an hour, these calculations will be made on a boat 154 feet long 18 feet wide drawing 2 feet of water, bow and stern on angles of 60 degrees, the steam engine double power, the steam acting above and below the piston alternately, the piston making a 4 foot stroke, and 15 double strokes in a minute equal 2 feet a second; although these dimensions may be varied the same principles of calculations must be adhered to. (See the Analysis of the total resistance of Figures 4 and 5 p. 297, also the friction table, p. 291, and Drawing 2nd for the resistance of one square foot.)

ONE MILE AN HOUR

The plus and minus pressure of one foot 0.88 lbs. which multiplied by 36 feet the boat's bow is . . .	31.68
Friction on 848 feet of bow and stern, at 0.70 for 50 square feet is	11.90
Friction on 2200 square feet of the body is . . .	30.80
Total resistance of the boat .	74.38
A like power for the propellers	74.38
Total power	148.76

This power must be felt at propellers, repelling water one mile an hour or 1½ foot a second, which is one fourth slower than the motion of the piston, consequently one fourth may be deducted from 148.76 leaving 111.57 the power of the engine, a cylinder 4 inches diameter equal 16 round inches and 8 pounds to the inch gives 128 lb. which is sufficient power. The periphery of the propeller wheels must run two miles an hour or 3 feet a second equal 180 feet a minute. If 11½ feet diameter, 34½ feet round

5 revolutions and a quarter in a minute gives 181 feet, the engine strikes 15 double strokes a minute, the wheels make $5\frac{1}{4}$ revolutions in a minute, this is a proportion of near three to one, hence the first mover or pinion from the engine may be 2 feet diameter, the wheel on the water wheel shaft 6 feet diameter as in drawing 4th figure 1st the total resistance of the boat is 74.38 lbs. one square foot of propeller, running one mile an hour is 3.25 resistance 23 feet will give 74.75 this $11\frac{1}{2}$ feet in each propeller.

TWO MILES AN HOUR

	lbs.
The plus and minus pressure of one foot multiplied by	3.31
36 feet the bow of the boat is	119.16
Friction on 848 square feet of bow and stern at 2.36 for 50 ft.	40.12
Friction on 2200 square feet of the body of the boat .	103.84
Total resistance of the boat .	263.12
A like power for the propellers	263.12
Total power	526.24
to be felt at the propellers running 2 miles an hour or 3 feet a second, this is 1/3 faster than the piston moves, hence 1/3 must be added to	526.24
	175.41
Power of the Engine	901.65

A cylinder 10 inches diameter equal 100 round inches and 8 pounds to the inch gives 800.00.

The periphery of the wheels must run 4 miles an hour or 6 feet a second equal 360 feet a minute if 12 feet diameter $37\frac{1}{2}$ round 10 revolutions will give 375 feet a minute which is sufficiently near. The total resistance of the boat is 263.12, one square foot of propeller moving 2 miles an hour is 13.09 lb. 20 square feet will give resistance 261.80 lb. this is 10 square feet to each propeller. The wheels making 10 revolutions and the piston striking 15 double strokes is a difference of one third. The first mover from the engine may be 4 feet diameter, and the wheel on the propeller wheel shaft 6 feet diameter as in drawing 4th figure 2nd.

THREE MILES AN HOUR

The plus and minus pressure of one foot is 7.15 multiplied by 36 feet of the bow of the boat is	257.40
Friction on 848 square feet of bow and stern at 4.74 for 50 feet is	80.58
Friction on 2200 square feet of the body of the boat is .	208.56
Total resistance, of the boat .	546.54
A like power for the propellers	546.54
Total power	1093.08
to be felt at the propellers running three miles an hour or $4\frac{1}{2}$ feet a second, this is twice and a quarter faster than the piston moves therefore $\frac{1}{4}$= . . .	1093
must be doubled	2186.16
and a quarter added	273.27
Power of the Engine	2459.43

A cylinder 18 inches diameter equal 324 round inches and 8 lb. to the inch gives 2592 lb. purchase. The periphery of the propeller wheels must run 6 miles an hour, or 9 feet a second equal 540 feet a minute if 12 feet diameter, $37\frac{1}{2}$ round from 14 to 15 revolutions will give the desired velocity, the piston striking from 14 to 15 double strokes; in this case the first mover from the engine may be direct on the crank of the propeller wheel as seen in drawing 4th figure 3rd.

FOUR MILES AN HOUR

Plus & minus resistance of one foot 12.37 lb. multiplied by 36 feet the bow of the boat is	445.32
Friction on 848 feet of bow & stern at 775 for 50 square feet	131.75
Friction on 2200 square ft. of the body of the boat .	341.00
Total resistance of the boat .	918.07
A like power for the propellers	918.07
Total power to be felt at the propellers	1836.14
running 4 miles an hour or 6 feet a second; this is three times faster than the piston moves hence 1836.14 must be multiplied by 3.	
Power of engine	5508.42

U

A cylinder 27 inches diameter equal 729 round inches, 8 pounds to the inch gives 5832.00 purchase. The periphery of the propeller wheels must run 8 miles an hour, or 12 feet a second, equal 720 feet a minute. If 14 feet diameter, 44 feet round, 16 revolutions in a minute will give 704 feet a minute.

In this case the Engine must make 16 strokes a minute and act direct on the propeller wheel shaft as in drawing 4th figure 4th. The total resistance of the boat is 918.07. The resistance of one square foot running 4 miles an hour is 51.95 lbs. or 17½ square feet will give 909.12 resistance this is 8¾ feet in each propeller.

FIVE MILES AN HOUR

Plus & minus pressure of one foot 18.93 multiplied by 36 the boat's bow is	681.48
Friction on 848 square feet of bow & stern at 11.32 for 50 feet is	192.44
Friction on 2200 square feet of the body of the boat is .	498.08
Total resistance of the boat .	1372.00
Equal resistance of the propellers	1372.00
Total power	2744.00
to be felt at the propellers running 5 miles an hour or 7½ feet a second: this is three times and 3/4 faster than the piston multiplied by	3
	8232.00
Add 3/4 of 2744	2058
Power of the Engine	10290.00

A cylinder 36 inches diameter equal 1296 round inches and 8 lb. to the inch gives 10,368 pounds. The periphery of the propeller wheels must run 10 miles an hour or 15 feet a second, equal 900 feet a minute.

If 14 feet diameter, 44 round, 20½ revolutions will give 902 feet a minute. In this case the wheels running 20½ revolutions, the engine striking 15 double strokes, the multiplication of wheel and pinion is one fourth, the first mover from the engine may be 4 feet diameter, the pinion on the propeller wheel shaft 3 feet diameter, as in drawing 4th figure 5th.

The total resistance of the boat is	1372.00
The resistance of 1 sq. ft. running 5 miles an hour is 80.16—16½ feet gives	1332.54

This is 8¼ feet to each propeller. As 5 miles an hour requires a cylinder of 36 inches diameter, it will now be necessary to see if the weight of the boat, engine & machinery, will not make her draw more than two feet of water and cause a greater resistance than the engine could drive 5 miles an hour,

	tons
her bow and stern displace	38.5
her body 100 feet long will displace 3600 cubic feet equal to	112.5
Total	151.0

	tons
Every lineal foot of the boat will weigh 1200 lb. . .	94.0
Machinery	40.0
	134.0

This leaves 17 tons for Cargo, it is therefore practicable to drive such a boat 5 miles an hour.

SIX MILES AN HOUR

Plus & minus pressure of one foot 18.90 lbs. multiplied by 36 feet the boat's bow is	680.40
Friction on 848 square feet of bow & stern at 15.43 for 50 ft. is	262.31
Friction on 2200 square feet of her body is . .	678.92
Total resistance of the boat .	1621.63
Equal power for the propellers	1621.63
Total power	3245.26
to be felt at the end of the propellers running 6 miles an hour or 9 feet a second, this is 4½ times faster than the piston, hence multiply by	4
	12973.04
Add half of 3243.26	1621.63
Power of the engine	14594.67

A cylinder 44 inches diameter equal 1936 round inches & 8 lb. to the inch will give 15472 pounds purchase. The wheels must run 12 miles an hour or 18 feet a second, equal 1080 feet a minute. If 17 feet diameter 53 feet round, 20 revolutions will give 1060; in this case the wheels making 1/4 revolutions more than the piston strikes; the first mover from the engine may be 4 feet diameter, the pinion on the propeller wheel shaft 3 feet diameter, as in drawing 4th figure 6th.

The total resistance of the boat is 1621.63. The resistance of one square foot of propeller running 6 miles an hour is 115.71—14 square feet gives 1619.981 resistance this is 7 feet for each propeller. The engine & machinery here estimated would not weigh 17 tons more than the engine calculated for the boat which was to run 5 miles an hour, it therefore appears that the boat might carry an engine of a power to drive her 6 miles an hour, but she would then be so loaded as not to admit of cargo or additional weight without making her draw more water and create a resistance which the engine could not drive 6 miles an hour. These demonstrations show the little refinement of combination & calculation which is necessary to construct a steam boat to run 1, 2 or 3 miles an hour; 4 miles an hour requires exact proportions & good execution; 5 miles an hour is difficult to effect with the most accurate proportions and perfect workmanship.

As to six miles an hour, were it attempted and to succeed, I should consider it more a work of curiosity than utility, as I do not believe it possible to build a steam boat with any engine which is now known, to run 6 miles an hour in still water and carry either passengers or Cargo to pay the expences.

I prefer making my calculations to run from 4 to 4½ miles an hour in still water; whatever may be the tide or current in her favour must be added to her velocity in still water; whatever the tide or current may be against her must be deducted from her speed in still water.

DESCRIPTION OF THE MACHINERY

Drawing 5th figure 1st shews the manner of constructing the wheels—figure 2nd exhibits a section of the boat and the manner of suspending the wheels. A A are knees which project beyond the wheels to support the wheel guards at B B, see the ground plan of them in drawing 8th, C is a hollow Keel to collect the water from her flat bottom and conduct it to the pump.

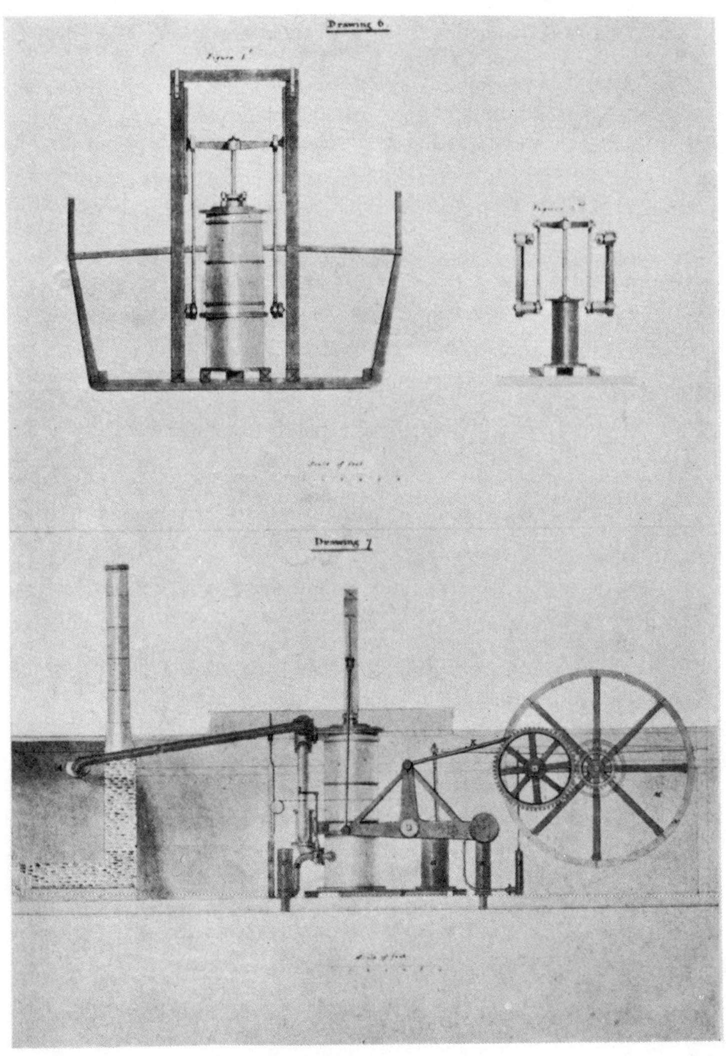

DRAWINGS 6 & 7 ATTACHED TO FULTON'S. U.S PATENT SPECIFICATION, 1809

DRAWINGS 8 & 9 ATTACHED TO FULTON'S U.S. PATENT SPECIFICATION, 1809

Drawing 6th figure 1st is the mode of placing the cylinder in the boat, A the cylinder B the condenser, C a passage in a cast iron bed to conduct the water and air from the condenser to the air pump D D the shackles, E E the ends of the beam.

Figure 2nd is the air pump, C the passage in the cast iron bed, D D a section of the Beam E E cast to the beam that the shackles F F may be so constructed as to give space for the shackles G G to move past them.

Drawing 7th A the boiler, B the steam pipe, C a cylinder to receive condensing water through the bottom of the boat, D a condensing tube, E the condensing cock, F cast iron bed with a tube in it to communicate from the condenser to the air pump, G the air pump H a tube to let off the waste water when discharged from the air pump, I the forcing pump to supply the boiler from the hot well. The movement for the air pump is taken from the beam at J. K is the shackle from the beam communicating from the crank of the wheel L on the shaft of which is the propeller wheel M. N is the fly wheel.

Drawing 8th is a ground plan of the machinery. By aid of the preceding drawings every Mechanician can understand this combination. A A the propeller wheel guards. B B sliding box to put the propeller wheels in or out of gear.

Drawing 9th a perspective view of the machinery. A the tube from the forcing pump to supply the boiler, B a valve and weight to let off the surplus water when the float in the boiler has raised so as to shut the cock C, the weight must be more on each round inch of its valve than the pressure of the steam at its highest temperature on each round inch of the boiler.

Drawing 10th is a ferry boat composed of two boats each of which is the segment of a circle. They are separated 10 feet and have a platform built over the wheels and machinery being in the centre, the carriages and passengers enter or land from each end, passing to the right or left of the machinery. There are two rudders at each end, the tillers of the two at either end are united by a bar, so that they act by one movement. As the boat is not designed to put about, either end may run foremost, in which case the end that acts as bow has the rudder pinned. By figures 1st 2nd and 3rd every mechanician, who has previously examined the preceding drawings, will understand the combination of the boat and machinery.

Drawing 11th is another mode of constructing a ferry boat, the boiler is placed on one side of the boat, the cylinder and principal movements on the opposite side the fly wheel in the bottom and running horizontally, the carriages drive through the centre of the boat. She is not intended to put about, but having two rudders either end acts as bow, the end acting as bow has the rudder pinned. A, figure 4th, is a stage, one end of which floats on the water, rising and falling with the tide so as always to be even with the platform of the boat and give a commodious mode of entering or landing.

Drawing 12th[1] represents a boat to carry merchandize. I will estimate her the same length and width as the boat on which the calculations of proportions and velocities are made, that boat while drawing 2 feet of water displaced 151 tons, the boat and machinery weighs 134 tons, which leaves 17 tons for merchandize; let her draw 2 feet more of water total 4 feet she will then carry 151 & 17 equal 168 tons.

TO RUN 4 MILES AN HOUR

Plus & minus resistance of one foot 12.37 multiplied by 72 feet the boat's bow	890.64
Friction on 1048 square ft. of bow & stern at 7.75 for 50 square feet	155.00
Friction on 2600 sq. ft. of the body of the boat . .	403.00
Total resistance of the boat .	1448.64
A like power for the propellers	1448.64
	2897.28
running 4 miles an hour or 6 feet a second this is 3 times as fast as the movement of the piston, hence multiply by	3
Power of the Engine	8691.84
A cylinder 33 inches diameter equal 1199 round inches and 8 pounds to the inch gives	9592.00

this is the power required to run 4 miles an hour by the action of the propellers; but it may happen that the current opposed to the boat will in some places run 4 miles an hour; if so the boat would stand still. As such rapids will rarely be of great length,

[1] This drawing is missing, both from the Patent Office Library and from the Boulton & Watt MSS., unless, as seems likely, it is that shown on the plate facing p. 294.

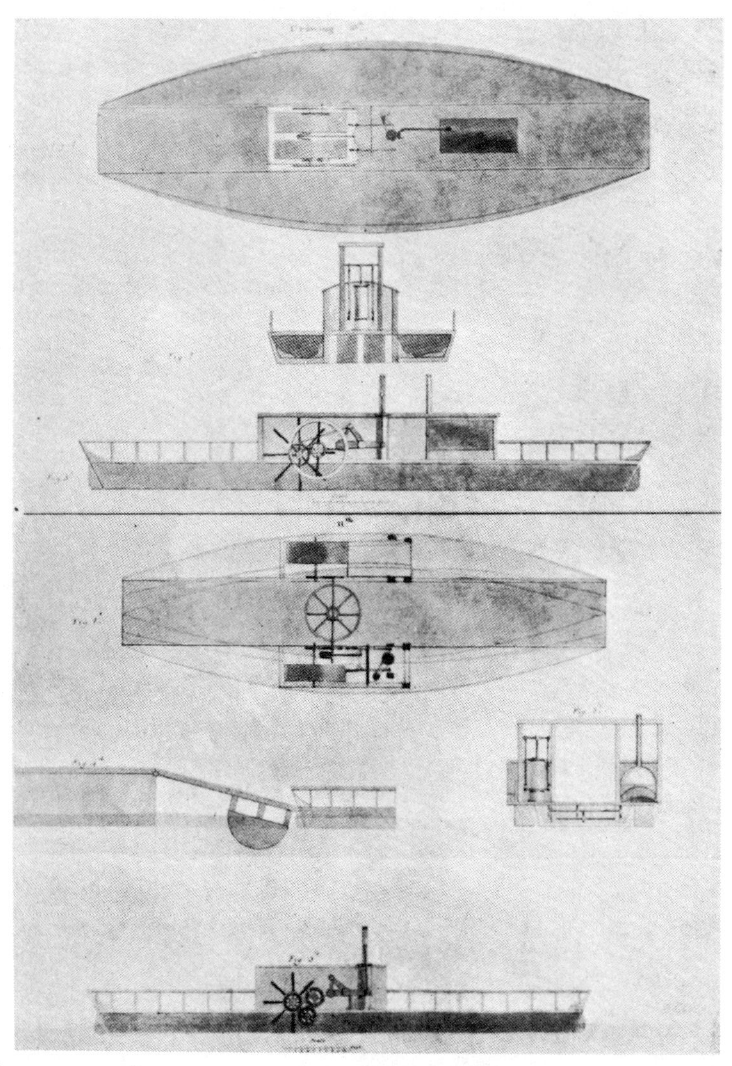

DRAWINGS 10 & 11 ATTACHED TO FULTON'S U.S. PATENT SPECIFICATION, 1809

I propose to pass them by sending a good row boat ahead with an anchor and a rope 500 or 1000 yards long; the anchor being cast the other end of the rope must have two or three coils round a windlass or capstan which is worked by the engine, this having the point of purchase on ground, the calculations on wheel and pinion may be such as to draw the boat against the current of 6 miles or more an hour, as indicated in the drawing, when the boat shall be drawn home to the anchor. She must be anchored or made stationary till the row boat runs ahead with the anchor and rope to another station, and so on till the rapid be passed; when opportunity offers the towing rope may be made fast on shore to posts, rocks, trees or any other body of strength.

RECAPITULATION of the COMBINATIONS and DISCOVERIES which I have made and consider as essential to the successful CONSTRUCTION and NAVIGATION of STEAM BOATS.

First, the method of ascertaining the total resistance of the boat when running from one to six miles an hour. Second, the demonstrations on the superior advantage of a propelling wheel or wheels for taking the purchase on the water. Third, the demonstrations on the proportions which the propelling boards should bear to the total resistance of the boat, and the velocity which they should run compared with the intended velocity of the boat. Fourth, the method of calculating the power of the engine to supply the loss of power on the propellers and overcome the total resistance of the boat while running from one to six miles an hour.

The developement of these principles is indispensable to the most perfect construction of Steam Boats; it is owing to a want of an accurate knowledge of these principles that the essays on Steam Boats which have been made in different countries for 30 years past have hitherto failed. It consequently follows, that those who are not possessed of this knowledge cannot make a steam boat to run four miles an hour unless by chance nor can they give rules to secure success in building steam boats of various dimensions and velocities. In the developement of the principles, the proportions, velocities, and power being ascertained, the remainder is nothing more than mechanical combination, which may be varied in a variety of methods, but which cannot be considered an improvement unless a greater speed be obtained with less fuel than by the methods I have described.

Having been the first to discover and describe the exact principles and proportions on which steam boats should be built, and having given a mechanical combination, the utility of which is proved by practice, I shall consider every attempt to construct such vessels on those principles as an infringement on my rights.

As to the Mechanism I have thought it sufficient to give only one mode of combining Steam Boats for Passengers, for Merchandize and for Ferries, in each of which sails are used as an aid to the engine.

(Signed) ROBERT FULTON.

Witnessed by
JOHN R. LIVINGSTON.
MATURIN LIVINGSTON.

Note in Bennet Woodcroft's handwriting: [The Patent of which this is the specification bears date Feby. 11th, 1809.]

APPENDIX F

FULTON'S U.S. PATENT SPECIFICATION OF 1810

DESCRIPTION IN WORDS OF INVENTIONS TO MOVE BOATS OR VESSELS BY THE POWER OF STEAM ENGINES.

October 2nd 1810. I, ROBERT FULTON native of Pennsylvania and citizen of the United States of America, now residing in the City of New York, give the following description of my inventions and discoveries, for constructing boats or vessels which are to be navigated by the power of Steam Engines, believing myself to be the original inventor and discoverer of the following combinations: To obtain the power for driving the boat I make use of Watt and Boulton's Steam Engine, or any other steam engine of equal power, my claim to invention not extending to the steam engine, but to the proportioning combining and applying it in such a manner to a boat or vessel of such dimensions as to drive her to a certainty more than four miles an hour in still water.

After having determined the length, width and draft of water of the boat, the details of my Patent dated February 11th 1809 will shew the mode for ascertaining her total resistance while running 1, 2, 3, 4, 5 or 6 miles an hour in still water, also the mode for proportioning the power of the Engine, the velocity of the Piston, and diameter of the water wheels with the velocity of their periphery and the size of each of their propellers to overcome any given resistance of boat while running 1, 2, 3, 4, 5 or 6 miles an hour in still water. Having been the first to demonstrate the superior advantage of a water wheel or wheels, I claim as my exclusive right the use of two wheels one over each side of the boat to take the purchase on the water; To turn such wheels forwards or backwards, I claim as my combinations and exclusive right the following modes for communicating the power from the piston rod of the steam engine, to them. First, by two triangular beams which are described in the details of my Patent dated 11th Feby. 1809 and only mentioned here to bring together my several combinations. Second, by wheels without a beam; in this case a crank or crank wheel is on each side of the cylinder, to which shackle bars descend from the cross bar on the top of the piston rod, which turning the cranks the water wheels being connected with their axis, turn also these two crank wheels drive two wheels of equal diameter, from which a movement may be taken to work the air pump, which two wheels drive two pinions on the shaft of which is the fly wheel or wheels. Third, by means of a cast or wrought iron beam on each side of the cylinder near the bottom of the boat; from a cross bar on the top of the piston rod, a shackle bar descends on each [side] of the cylinders and connects with the ends of the beams, a shackle bar rises from the other end of each beam to a cross bar, from which cross bar shackle bars descend to turn two cranks or crank wheels, to the axles of which the water wheels are connected, the two crank wheels drive two pinions on the shaft of which the fly wheels are fixed. Fourth, by means of a cast or wrought iron beam above the cylinder, which receives motion from the piston rod; from the other end of the beam a strong shackle bar gives motion to a crank, on the axle of which, or connected with it are the two water wheels. From the crank shaft a movement may be taken to turn the fly-wheels or by using sun and planet wheels the shaft of the sun will act as fly and drive the water-wheels by means of a pinion on the sun wheel shaft and a wheel on the water wheel shaft, thus if required reducing the revolutions of the water wheels to half the number of revolutions of the fly or if the water wheels are put on the shaft of the sun wheels, and weighted with iron they will act without any other fly, but not to such advantage as with a fly and water wheel because a rapid moving and small propeller is a loss of power—I use coupling boxes or any other means to throw the propelling wheels in or out of gear, or to throw one wheel out and work the other as may be required. This convenience in combining the machinery of Steam boats I claim as my discovery and exclusive right whatever may be the mode by which it may be executed. I also claim as my invention and exclusive right the guards which are round the outside of the propelling wheels, which guards may support the outside gudgeons of said propelling wheels and give the convenience of a deposit for fuel, bins or lockers for various materials, water closets for the convenience of Passengers, and steps to enter from or go into the row boats, which guards protect the wheels from injury by wharves, vessels &c. &c. I claim as my invention to project from the side or sides of the steam boat beams or timbers or spars or fenders of wood or Iron of any kind, to guard or protect, the water wheels from injury by wharves, vessels &c. &c. I also claim the exclusive right to cover the water wheels whether by boards, netting or grating canvass or leather or in whatever manner it may be done to prevent them throwing water on deck or entangling in ropes. I claim as my invention to place the tiller and steering wheel and pilot and steersman further forwards in steam boats than is usual in other vessels, the necessity of which is, that the boat being long and the deck covered with passengers the pilot could not see forward unless near the middle of the deck; hence any one who moves a steersman further forward in a steam boat than is usual in other vessels shall be considered as using this part of my invention in the convenient arrangement of steam boats. I claim as my invention the strait and diagonal braces which I have placed in the sides of my steam boats to give them strength to support the weight of the Engine, Boiler and machinery and which braces extend from a line behind the boiler to a line forward of the machinery. I claim as my invention to set the engine and machinery in a frame which is laid on the bottom of the boat which frame must be of a length, breadth and strength to bear the weight of the machinery and working of the engine and divide it over so great a surface of the boat as to do her no injury. I also claim as my invention to accommodate a steam engine to a boat, my mode of setting the air pump and machinery behind the cylinder, that is, on the side opposite the hand gear and which is the reverse of the mode in which Engines are put up on Land. I claim as my invention and exclusive right the combination of sails with a steam engine to drive a boat, I being the first who have done so and proved by practice the utility of the union of the two powers of Wind and Steam. Hence as a boat may be rigged a variety of ways, my invention is not, for any particular mode of rigging, but for the discovery and proof by practice of the importance of using sails with a steam engine to drive a boat.

I claim as my invention my particular mode of proportioning and placing a propelling wheel or wheels in the Stern of a boat, which wheel or wheels are in a chamber formed by the two sides of the boat extending aft one or more feet further than the extreme diameter of the propelling wheel, to each of which side projections there is a rudder, which two rudders connected by a cross bar working on pivots cause them to move together and parallel to each other, from this cross bar or from the rudders the ropes or chains for steering lead on to the pilot.

To put a propelling wheel or wheels in motion at the stern of a steam boat a movement may be carried from the Engine to it or them by bevel wheels and shafts to opposite the centre of the axle of the propelling wheel and between two wheels or by bevel wheels and a shaft on one side of one propelling wheel, or by a triangular beam at the engine and long shackle bars moving in guides on rollers, and which communication may be performed by shackle bars leading along the center of the boat turning a crank between two wheels or by a shackle bar on each side of the propelling wheel, each acting on a crank on each end of the shaft of the propelling wheel. (Signed) ROBERT FULTON.

Witness
(Signed) JOHN NICHELSON
(Signed) GEO. LYON.

New York. October 2nd 1810. I, ROBERT FULTON native of Pennsylvania and citizen of the United States of America, give the following description of my inventions and discoveries for constructing boats or vessels which are to be navigated by the power of Steam engines believing myself to be the original Inventor of the following combinations to produce the desired effects; To Obtain a power to drive the boat I make use of Messrs. Boulton & Watt's steam engine or any other Engine of equal power (my claim to invention not extending to the Steam Engine, but to the proportioning combining and applying it in such a manner, to a boat of such dimensions, as to drive her with certainty more than four miles an hour in still water).

In constructing a steam boat either for Passengers or Merchandize, the first consideration is the number of Passengers or tons to be carried, on which the length, width, and draft of water of the boat must be determined. Then by referring to the details of my Patent dated Feby. 11th, 1809, the mode to ascertain her total resistance while running 1, 2, 3, 4, 5 or 6 miles an hour in still water will be seen, also the mode of proportioning the power of the Engine, the velocity of the piston, and the diameter of the Water wheels with the velocity of their periphery and the size of each of their propellers to overcome the resistance of any given boat while running 1, 2, 3, 4, 5 or 6 miles an hour in still water. It is a knowledge of these proportions and velocities detailed in my said Patent which is an important part of my discovery for the

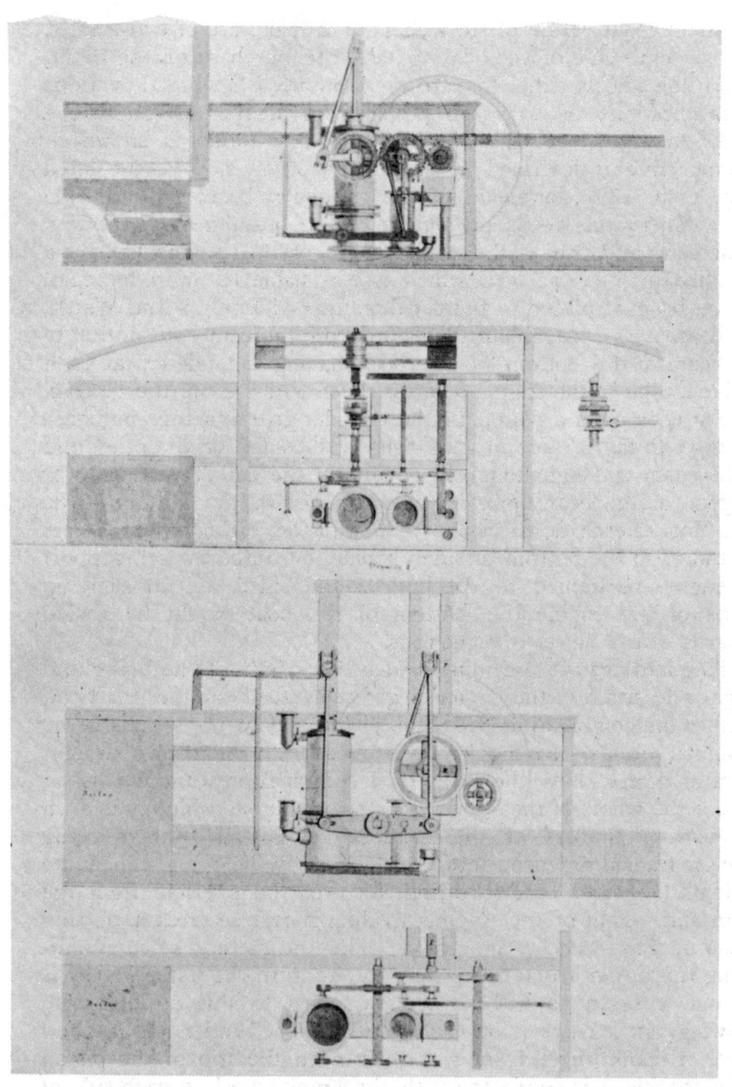

DRAWINGS 1 & 2 ATTACHED TO FULTON'S U.S. PATENT SPECIFICATION, 1811

successful construction of steam boats. I make use of two wheels, one over each side of the boat to take the purchase on the water, to turn the wheels either forward or backward I have made various communications to carry the power from the piston rod to the cranks or shafts of the wheels. The first mode is shewn in drawing 7th and described in the details of my said Patent dated Feby. 11th, 1809, by means of two triangular beams and shackle rods. This mode keeps the weight of the beam near the bottom of the boat and causes the whole strain of the Engine to have a horizontal pull in the boat, which is less liable to injure her than when a beam is placed in the usual manner of Boulton and Watt's, which causes a perpendicular pressure from the centre of motion of the beam to the bottom of the boat, having a tendency at each double stroke of the engine to press down and raise up the bottom.

For example if a piston in the cylinder give four tons purchase moving two feet a second, four tons will be felt on the other end of the beam and eight tons will be felt on the center of motion or gudgeon of the beam, pressing from thence to the bottom of the boat, thus at each down stroke of the piston, eight tons will press downward to the bottom or sides, should the timbers which support the engine be framed to the bottom and sides, and at each up stroke of the engine the bottom of the boat would be pulled upwards with a power of eight tons.

To guard against the injury which the weight of the boiler and weight and strain of the engine might cause to the hull of the boat, whether the combinations from the piston rod to the wheels be by triangular beams, or straight beams below the deck, or a straight beam or beams above the deck, or a combination without a beam, I place the whole of the Works in a strong frame, which is laid on the bottom timbers of the boat, which bottom timbers being strongly framed or kneed into the sides of the boat, and the frame having a long and broad bearing, receives the pressure from the beam and weight of the Engine dividing it over so great a portion of the boat as to do her no injury. The 2nd method of communicating the power from the piston rod to turn the water wheels is without a beam as will be seen annexed to this specification, Drawing 1st. There is on each side of the Cylinder a crank and wheel or crank wheel, from a cross bar on the top of the piston rod a shackle A is connected with the crank wheel on each side of the cylinder, thus while the engine is in motion the two cranks are turned round, and the water wheels indicated by the circle B connected with the shafts of said cranks are turned also. The crank wheels give motion to two wheels of equal diameter C from which a movement is taken for the air pump by a shackle descending from D, to the lever E from which rises a shackle F, on each side of the air pump, which shackle connects with a cross bar on the top of the bucket and piston rod of the air pump gives the necessary movement for pumping.

The levers E at the end G work the plug tree H. I shews one pinion of the fly wheel shaft, the fly may be put on the outside of the boat as shewn in the ground plan. To work the forcing pump, to supply the boiler and a pump to clear the boat of water, a movement may be taken K & L, *m m m m* are weights put into the wheels to balance the weight of the piston, its rods, cross bar and shackles. In working a steam boat it is important to provide a means to throw the water wheels out of gear, to try the movements of the engine or to work one wheel at a time when necessary; N in the ground plan shews the mode of casting off the movement of the engine from the water wheel shafts by a *tee*-piece O on the shafts of the water wheels, and a sliding coupling box P on the shafts of the cranks; various other modes of throwing the wheels out of gear may be contrived, such as by a square or angular coupling box or sliding the water wheel inwards and outwards or by a bayonet as delineated Q in drawing 1st or by two wheels throwing the teeth in and out of gear. The mode here described has been successful in practice. Therefore being the first to discover the utility and practice of throwing water wheels when applied to steam boats in and out of gear, I claim it as a part of my combination and exclusive right, whatever may be the method by which it shall be executed.

The third manner of communicating the power from the piston rod to the water wheels is in drawing 2nd by means of a cast or wrought iron beam on each side of the cylinder, near the bottom of the boat as at A, the two beams are fixed on a strong iron shaft as will be seen by the ground plan. On each side of the cylinder a shackle rod B connects the cross bar on the top of the piston rod to the ends of the beams as at D and from the other end of each beam as at E a shackle rod C rises to the cross bar F from whence two shackles G descend to the crank wheels H to the shafts of which the water wheels are connected as indicated by the circle I. J is the pinion of the fly wheel (see the ground plan) K the fly wheel, a movement for the air pump is taken from the beams at L by two shackles which rise to the cross bar on the top of the piston or bucket rod of the air pump. M is a lever re-

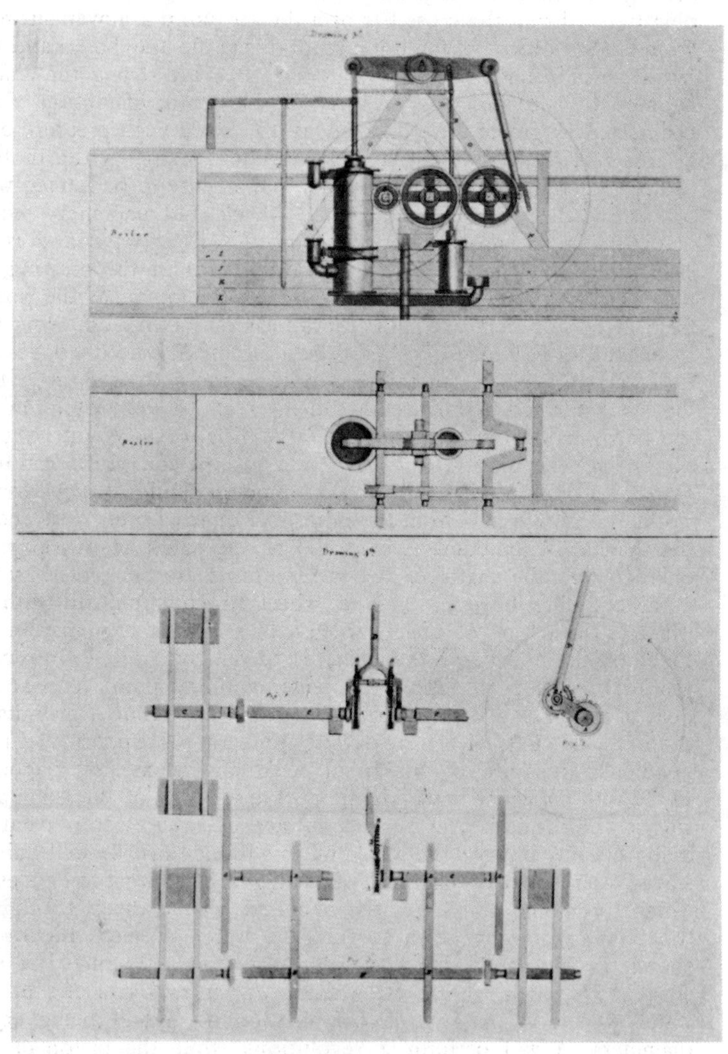

DRAWINGS 3 & 4 ATTACHED TO FULTON'S U.S. PATENT SPECIFICATION, 1811

ceiving motion from the piston rod to work the plug tree, N is the plug tree. From the cross bar over the air pump a movement may be taken to work the forcing pump to supply the boiler and the pump for clearing the boat of water; O P Q are strong timbers to support the perpendicular pressure of the centre of motion of the beam, and weight of the works, so as to divide such pressure over a large surface of the boat, and prevent her racking by the motion of the engine, in these timbers, other timbers are to be framed with braces and diagonals to support the wheels and machinery, which combination of timbers may be arranged various ways, and is so easy conceived that I have not shewn them in the drawing, to prevent confusion. The fourth mode to communicate the power from the piston rod to the water wheels is shewn in drawing 3rd by means of a wrought or cast iron beam A placed above the Cylinder, this beam which need not be more than 8 or 9 feet long is connected by links, and the lever B, to the piston rod in the usual manner of Boulton & Watt's Engine thereby producing a perpendicular motion for the piston rod, or the piston rod may work by a cross piece on its top running in guides. The lever B works the plug tree C from the other end of the beam by means of the shackle D, the crank E is turned to the shafts of which crank on each side, the shafts of the water wheels are connected by the usual coupling boxes. F is a wheel to communicate with G which is the pinion of the fly wheels, they in this combination are to be on the outside of the boat, H is the rod of the air pump, the forcing pump to supply the boiler and the pump to clear the boat of water may receive movement from the beam A or links of the rod. H, I, J, K, L are strong timbers to support the perpendicular pressure of the beam A from whence rise diagonals M, N with sufficient braces to support the action of the beam and works, and divide it over such a surface of boat as to prevent its doing her any injury; the whole of this frame must be well bolted, stayed and buckled together. Drawing 4th shews two modes in which I combine and apply the sun and planet wheels to convey the power from the beam to turn the water wheels. Figure 1st shews the sun and planet wheels A, B and AB united by one shackle D which wheels BB driving AA turn the shafts of the water wheels CC. In this combination A and B being equal diameters, A will perform 2 revolutions while the piston of the engine makes one stroke down and one up. In such case the water wheels performing two revolutions for each double stroke of the engine, no other fly wheels than the water wheels will be required, they must be made heavy with iron. This has been proved by an experiment which was made on the North River steam boat in 1808, having lost both her wheels near Esopus, propelling boards were put on the fly wheels which then were over the outside of the boat. The fly wheels had twice the velocity of the water wheels, that is, the fly wheels performed two revolutions while the engine made one double stroke, in this manner the boat worked well from Esopus to New York, not so well however as with her water wheels which made only one revolution, while the piston made one double stroke because it is an error to have a small and rapid moving propeller, as shewn in the details of my Patent dated Feby. 11th, 1809. Figure 2nd shews the side view of the sun and planet movement, D the shackle to connect with the engine beam. Figure 3rd shews a mode to combine the sun and planet movement so as to give the water wheel only one revolution while the piston makes one double stroke, the wheel A and shaft C performing two revolutions for one double stroke of the engine, let D a tooth wheel on the shaft C be half the diameter of E a tooth wheel on the water wheel shaft F and then the water wheels will perform only one revolution for each double stroke of the engine, by this mode of combining or with wheel and pinion the water wheels may be given any required velocity for boats moving under four miles an hour, or more than five miles an hour. Thus the fly wheel or wheels will perform two revolutions for each double stroke of the engine. These modes of combining in a compact manner and adapting the beam and Sun and planet movement to convey the power from the piston of the engine to turn water or propelling wheels when applied to steam boats I claim as my invention.

In all these combinations to accommodate the engine conveniently to the boat I have placed the air pump, beam and movements behind the cylinder, that is on the side opposite to the hand gear, Whereas Messrs. Boulton & Watt place the beam, and air pump on the same side of the cylinder with the hand gear and work the air pump from the lower end of the plug tree, which mode of combining would be very inconvenient for a boat, hence for Steam boats I claim it as my particular arrangement and combination to set the air pump beam or beams and movements for the wheels behind the cylinder. See Drawing 5th figure 4th, instead of a vat round the condenser and air pump I have a tube as at A descending through the bottom of the boat, in this the water from the river rises and passes through the cock B into

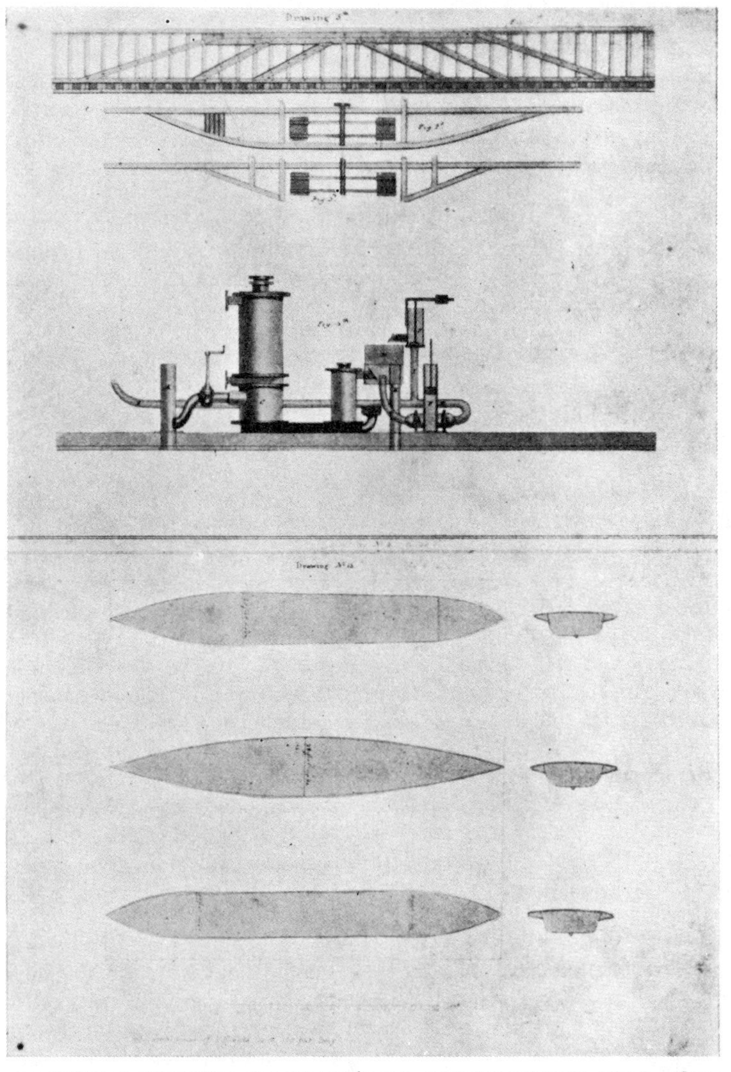

DRAWING 5 ATTACHED TO FULTON'S U.S. PATENT SPECIFICATION, 1811 (DRAWING 6 IS MISSING ; SEE NOTE ON P. 325)

the condenser C, from the reservoir of hot water at the discharging valve of the air pump at D a tube for the waste water E descends through the bottom of the boat. F is a forcing pump receiving hot water through the tube G and forcing it into the boiler by the tube H when the boiler is supplied, the waste water rises by the pipe I through the valve J and escapes by the pipe K into D; the valve J is held down by means of a sufficient weight at L to balance the elasticity of the steam in the boiler, this mode of nourishing the boiler is very convenient for a steam boat and much superior to the usual mode of placing engines on land, with a hot well over the boiler, and from 8 to 10 feet higher than the water in the boiler. To give the sides of the boat strength and prevent her bending with the weight of the machinery I put in her on each side and extending from behind the boiler to forward of the Machinery in total length 60 or 80 feet more or less, parallel and diagonal braces as shewn Figure 1st drawing 5th which braces should be of Oak let into the side timbers and well bolted the whole well secured to the bottom timbers of the boat, this invention of side bracing to strengthen steam boats I claim as my invention and exclusive right.

I also claim as my invention and exclusive right the frame work or guards round the outside of the water wheels as shewn Figure 2nd Drawing 5th the outer side of which guards support the outer ends of the shafts of the water wheels which guards may be one plain band of timber curved or angular or formed to give the convenience of a deposit for wood or coals inside chambers for fish, provisions or other purposes stairs on the sides to make an easy descent into the boats and necessaries or water closets for the convenience of passengers as in my boats on the Hudson River; all which conveniences resulting from the wheel guards—together with every kind of covering to the wheels to prevent them throwing water on deck or entangling ropes, I claim as my invention and exclusive right; I also claim as my invention the simple projection of beams or timber or braces of iron or wood of any kind as indicated figure 3rd Drawing 4th with or without diagonals, *the object of which is to guard the wheels from injury by wharves vessels &c.*

I also claim as my invention (it making part of the convenience of my combinations) my manner of placing the steering wheel further forward than is usual in vessels steering with a wheel and so near the center of the boat that the pilot can see forward without interruption and from his position give orders to the Engineers how to work the engine, this mode of placing the steering wheel is very convenient in long steam boats particularly when the Deck is covered with passengers; to the wheel or wheel and pinion or any other instrument to communicate motion from the Pilot to the rudder the tiller or rudder ropes or chains may lead to he inside or outside of the boat. I shall consider the moving the steering wheel or the pilot or the Steersman while steering to a position in steam boats further forward than is usual in other vessels, as an infringement of this part of my invention for convenience and safety. I also claim as my exclusive right my combination of sails with a steam engine to drive a boat, I being the first who have done so and proved by practice the utility of the union of the two powers of wind and steam on a boat. Drawing 6th shews the manner in which I now rig my boats, but be it understood that as a boat may be rigged an infinity of ways, I consider the proof of the utility and practicability of uniting sails with a steam engine to drive a boat as my invention and discovery and my exclusive right whatever may be the manner in which the mast and sails or masts, bowsprit and sails are placed or worked.

I claim as my invention the four modes which are shown in drawing 7th and 8th for conveying the power from the piston rod of the steam engine to turn a wheel in the stern of a boat; figures 1st and 2nd shew a crank or crank wheel on each side of the cylinder as at A which turn the wheels B on the axis of which is a bevel wheel C driving another bevel wheel, D conveying the power by the shaft E to the bevel wheels F, G which turn the water wheel H, the bow of this boat is made sharp like my steam boats already described, but her stern as at I is of a width to admit the wheel H and turns up like the stern of a scow. The sides J, J extend aft one or more feet further than the extreme diameter of the water wheel and are united by timbers K and a neat finish on the stern, this forms a chamber for the wheel and guards it against ice, timbers &c. &c. On the stern projections J, J are the two rudders L, L united by a box M which plays on pins or bolts at N, N causing the rudders to move together and parallel to each other. O, O the steering ropes to lead to the wheel on deck. The fly wheels are over the sides P, P and may have guards round their outsides, they are put in motion by the pinions Q, Q. R is a lever to work the plug tree, S the plug tree, the air pump may be worked by an oval round the shaft B, B or it and the other pumps may be worked by such movements as are already described in my other combinations. In Drawing 8th figure 1st is a combination at the Cylinder and fly wheel air

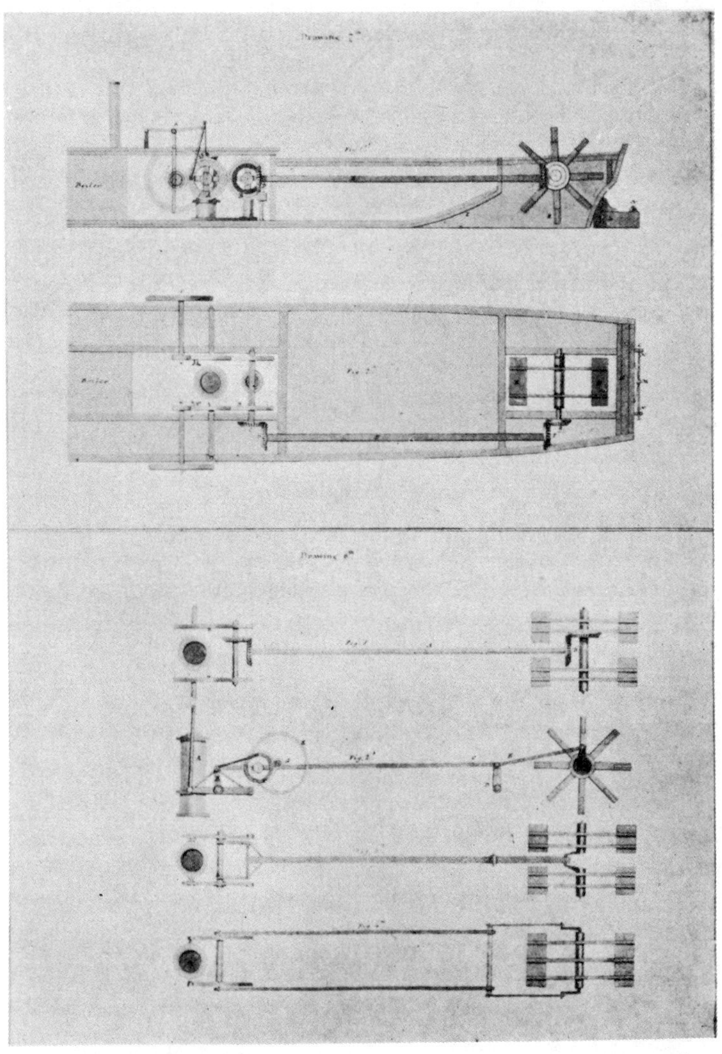

DRAWINGS 7 & 8 ATTACHED TO FULTON'S U.S. PATENT SPECIFICATION, 1811

pump &c. like that in the last drawing, but here the shaft A instead of being on one side of the water wheel works in the middle of it as at B. Figure 2nd, in this combination the shackle rods A give motion to the triangular beams B which communicate to the long and strong bar C which is connected to another beam D communicating by the shackle rod E the power from the engine to the crank of the water wheel. Figures 3rd and 4th are ground plans of this combination, Figure 3rd working by one rod in the center of the water wheel and Figure 4th by a rod on each side of the water wheel. In this combination figure 2nd the fly wheels may be over the sides of the boat and put in motion by shackles from the triangular beam B turning the wheels F driving the pinions G of the fly wheel or wheels H. In this mode of combining with a wheel behind the boat it must be observed that its diameter, velocity of its periphery and surface of each propeller must be proportioned to the intended velocity and resistance of the boat to be driven as will be seen in the details (dated Feby. 11th, 1809) of my Patent for Steam boats. As to the fly wheel or wheels to steam boats on the Seine at Paris in 1803 proves that a Steam boat may be made to act without a fly or that the water wheels may be made to serve for fly wheels also. This I prove by throwing the flies out of gear and working without them, the reason is when the engine has put the boat in motion her action forward has a power to pull the propellers of the water wheels round by drawing them against the water and thus making the crank pass the point where it would be in a right line with the shackles. Having been the first who made this discovery it is my intention to construct a pair of water wheels to act as *flies*, should they succeed, I claim this discovery as my exclusive right. I also claim as an important discovery in the construction of Steam boats, and one on which their success greatly depends that to drive a boat by the power of a steam engine 4 or 4½ miles an hour in still water she must be of a size to displace more than 50 tons of water. The reason is that the resistance of a boat displacing only 50 tons of water is much greater in proportion to her capacity to carry passengers or merchandize, than the resistance of a boat displacing 110 or more tons of water is in proportion to her capacity to carry passengers or freight, and the weight of the engine and machinery is much greater in proportion to the volume of the small boat, than it will be in proportion to the volume of the large boat. For example, 1st Boat 90 feet long 10 feet wide drawing 2 feet of water bow and stern on angles of 60 degrees she will displace 1600 cubic feet of water or about

50 tons being 2 feet in the water she will present 20 feet to the water the plus and minus resistance of one foot to 4 miles an hour

	lbs.
is 12 lb. 37/100 multiplied by 20 the bow of the boat .	247
Friction on 1220 superficial feet of bottom and sides at 7.50 for 50 superficial feet	165
Total resistance of the boat running 4 miles an hour	412
a like power for the propellers	412
Total power felt at the propellers	824
The boat running 4 miles an hour is 6 feet a second, this is 3 times faster than the piston runs hence multiply by	3
Necessary power of the Engine the piston running 2 feet a second	2472

This will require a 17 inch cylinder allowing 9 lbs. clear purchase to the round inch. This engine will occupy at least 33 feet by 6 in the boat and with water in the boiler weight of machinery &c. would weigh 20 tons, the boat built strong to support such an engine would weigh 25 tons or more hence if 12 tons of Passengers or merchandize were put in her it would press her down 6 inches or more in the water increasing her resistance and hence the same engine could not drive her 4 miles an hour nor could she carry an engine to run 4½ miles an hour.

Example 2nd. My first steam boat on the Hudson's River was 150 feet long 13 [feet] wide drawing 2 feet of water bow and stern 60 degrees; she displaced 3640 cubic feet, equal 100 tons of water; her bow presented 26 [square] feet to the water;

	lbs.
Plus and minus resistance of 1 foot running 4 miles an hour, 12.37 lb. multiplied by 26 the boat's bow . . .	321
Friction on 2380 superficial feet of bottom and sides at 7.5 lb. for 50 superficial feet	352
Total resistance of the boat running 4 miles an hour	673
A like power for the propellers	673
Total power felt at the propellers	1346
The boat running 4 miles an hour is 6 feet a second; this is 3 times faster than the piston hence multiplied by .	3
Necessary power of the engine, the piston running 2 feet a second	4038

This will require a 22 inch cylinder allowing 9 lb. purchase to the round inch: this engine would not occupy in the boat more space than in the small one and it would not weigh two tons more than the 17 inch cylinder; hence say weight of engine 22 tons, weight of boat 40 tons, total 62 tons, this leaves 38 tons for passengers or merchandize with ample space before it could bring her down to 2 feet in the water, but drawing not more than 18 inches before cargo or passengers were in and her resistance being diminished near 1/3, the above power would drive her 4½ miles an hour.

The two preceding examples exhibit in a clear point of view the advantage to be gained in building a large boat to carry a large and powerful engine; all persons who have tried experiments on steam boats before me, seeing the weight which loaded the boat and great space which was occupied when Watt & Boulton's engine was adopted, attempted to construct engines powerful, lighter and more compact than those of Watt and Boulton and thus they endeavoured to accomodate the engine to a small vessel hoping by that means to drive her 4 miles or more an hour or if they did not endeavour to compress and lighten the engine they always built their boats and engines on too small a scale and thereby made it impossible to gain a velocity of 4 or 4½ miles an hour in consequence of working on erroneous principles. I discovered this error and not attempting to accomodate an engine to a small boat, I constructed a large boat and accomodated its dimensions to a large and powerful engine.

The success of my boats on the Hudson River has proved the truth of these principles and the importance of my discovery that to construct useful and convenient steam boats which shall run more than 4 or 4½ miles an hour in still water they must be of a size to displace more than 50 tons of water and this discovery, making an essential part of my invention and combination, I claim the exclusive right to construct steam boats of a size exceeding a displacement of 50 tons of water by which means I am enabled to accomodate the boat to the engine and produce a velocity from 4 to 5 or 6 miles an hour. (Signed) ROBERT FULTON.

NOTE.—Drawing 6th, belonging to the above specification, is missing from its place on the plate facing p. 320, and instead there is a "Drawing No. 13" representing "the water-lines of 3 boats each 150 feet long," but what they refer to one can only conjecture.

APPE

TABLE OF DIMENSIONS OF STEAMBOAT

Name of Vessel.	Date.	Length, Ft.	Breadth, Ft.	Depth, Ft.	Draught, Ft.	Tonnage.	Name of Builder.	Boilers. Length, Ft.	Boilers. Width, Ft.	He I
North River . }	1807	133	13	7	2	100	Charles Browne	20	7	
†*Clermont* . . }	1808	149	17.9	7	2	182½	Do.	...	...	.
Rariton . . .	1808	...	...	...	...	120	Do.	...	...	.
†*Car of Neptune* .	1808	175	24	8	2.5	295	Do.	18	9	
†*Paragon* . . .	1811	167	26.9	7.75	...	331	Do.	21	9	I
New Orleans . .	1811	138	...	...	...	...	N. J. Roosevelt	...	...	.
Firefly	1812	81	14	4.5	...	...	Charles Browne	14	8	
Jersey	1812	78	32	7	...	118	Do.	20	9	
York	1813	78	32	7	...	118	Do.	20	9	
†*Richmond* . . .	1813	154	28.9	10	...	370	Do.	21	9	I
Washington . .	1813	135	25	9	...	275	Do.	20	8	
Fulton	1813	133	29	9	4	327	{ Adam and Noah Browne }	20	9	
Nassau. . . .	1813	78.5	33	7	...	...	Charles Browne	20	10	
Demologos. . .	1814	167	56	20	10	247.5	{ Adam and Noah Browne }	22	12	
Olive Branch. .	1816	124	30	8	...	...	Noah Browne	...	...	..
Connecticut . .	1816	140	33	...	...	...	...	...	...	..
†*Chancellor Livingston* . .	1816	157	33.5	10	7.25	526	Llew. Eckford	26	12	I
†*Emperor of Russia*	1816	134	30	9.5	...	330	Adam Browne	...	Three	..

Camden, ferry-boat (1812), *Vesuvius* (1813), *Aetna*, *Natchez*, *Enterprise*, and submarine M

† These dimensions are from the I

X G

IGNED OR BUILT BY ROBERT FULTON

Engines.			Paddle-wheels.				Speed, miles per hour.	Route or Service for which used.
Type.	Cylinder.		Diam., Ft.	Floats.				
	Diam., In.	Stroke, In.		No.	Length In.	Breadth, In.		
Bell crank 20-h.p.	24	48	15	8	48	24	4.6	Hudson River New York to Albany
...	...	...	...	...	...	...	...	Rariton River
...	33	52	14	...	48	28	7.6	Hudson River
...	32	48	16	8	52	30	...	Hudson River
...	34	...	...	...	...	...	...	Mississippi River
...	20	45	12.5	...	42	24	...	New York to Newburgh
...	20	48	12	one wheel	48	24	...	Ferry, New York and Jersey City
...	20	48	12	one wheel	48	24	...	Ferry, New York and Jersey City
...	33	52	15	8	57	30	...	Hudson River
Bell crank 30-h.p.	28	48	14	8	48	27	...	Potomac River
...	36	48	15	8	58	28	...	Long Island Sound
...	20	52	12	one wheel	48	24	...	Ferry, New York and Brooklyn
120-h.p.	48	60	16	one wheel	14	48	5.5	New York harbour guardship
...	36	48	16.33	10	57	30	...	New York and New Brunswick
...	40	54	17	10	57	30	...	Long Island Sound
Square Cross head, 60-h.p.	40	60	18	8	70	36	6.5	Hudson River
...	36	60	16	...	58	30	...	

(1815) are mentioned by different writers without, however, giving particulars.
York Custom House records.

INDEX

THE END